The Observation Protocol for Academic Literacies

BILINGUAL EDUCATION & BILINGUALISM

Series Editors: **Nancy H. Hornberger** *(University of Pennsylvania, USA)* and **Wayne E. Wright** *(Purdue University, USA)*

Bilingual Education and Bilingualism is an international, multidisciplinary series publishing research on the philosophy, politics, policy, provision and practice of language planning, Indigenous and minority language education, multilingualism, multiculturalism, biliteracy, bilingualism and bilingual education. The series aims to mirror current debates and discussions. New proposals for single-authored, multiple-authored or edited books in the series are warmly welcomed, in any of the following categories or others authors may propose: overview or introductory texts; course readers or general reference texts; focus books on particular multilingual education program types; school-based case studies; national case studies; collected cases with a clear programmatic or conceptual theme; and professional education manuals.

All books in this series are externally peer-reviewed.

Full details of all the books in this series and of all our other publications can be found on http://www.multilingual-matters.com, or by writing to Multilingual Matters, St Nicholas House, 31-34 High Street, Bristol, BS1 2AW, UK.

BILINGUAL EDUCATION & BILINGUALISM: 139

The Observation Protocol for Academic Literacies

A Tool for Building Expertise for Teachers of English Learners

Magaly Lavadenz and Elvira G. Armas

MULTILINGUAL MATTERS
Bristol • Jackson

DOI https://doi.org/10.21832/LAVADE9018
Library of Congress Cataloging in Publication Data
A catalog record for this book is available from the Library of Congress.
Names: Lavadenz, Magaly C., author. | Armas, Elvira G., author.
Title: The Observation Protocol for Academic Literacies: A Tool for Building
    Expertise for Teachers of English Learners/Magaly Lavadenz and Elvira G.
    Armas.
Description: Bristol; Jackson: Multilingual Matters, 2024. | Series: Bilingual
    Education & Bilingualism: 139 | Includes bibliographical references and index.
    | Summary: "This book presents a validated observation instrument to support
    and develop the pedagogic expertise of teachers of English Learners in US
    schools. With real examples of classroom observations, it offers teachers,
    researchers and policymakers a tool for professional development, classroom
    research and program improvement"—Provided by publisher.
Identifiers: LCCN 2023032850 (print) | LCCN 2023032851 (ebook) |
    ISBN 9781800419001 (paperback) | ISBN 9781800419018 (hardback) |
    ISBN 9781800419032 (epub) | ISBN 9781800419025 (pdf)
Subjects: LCSH: English language—Study and teaching. | English teachers—
    Training of. | Observation (Educational method)
Classification: LCC PE1128.A2 L353 2024 (print) | LCC PE1128.A2 (ebook) |
    DDC 428.0071/073—dc23/eng/20230831
LC record available at https://lccn.loc.gov/2023032850
LC ebook record available at https://lccn.loc.gov/2023032851

British Library Cataloguing in Publication Data
A catalogue entry for this book is available from the British Library.

ISBN-13: 978-1-80041-901-8 (hbk)
ISBN-13: 978-1-80041-900-1 (pbk)

Multilingual Matters
UK: St Nicholas House, 31-34 High Street, Bristol, BS1 2AW, UK.
USA: Ingram, Jackson, TN, USA.

Website: www.multilingual-matters.com
Twitter: Multi_Ling_Mat
Facebook: https://www.facebook.com/multilingualmatters
Blog: www.channelviewpublications.wordpress.com

Copyright © 2024 Magaly Lavadenz and Elvira G. Armas.

All rights reserved. No part of this work may be reproduced in any form or by any means without permission in writing from the publisher.

The policy of Multilingual Matters/Channel View Publications is to use papers that are natural, renewable and recyclable products, made from wood grown in sustainable forests. In the manufacturing process of our books, and to further support our policy, preference is given to printers that have FSC and PEFC Chain of Custody certification. The FSC and/or PEFC logos will appear on those books where full certification has been granted to the printer concerned.

Typeset by Deanta Global Publishing Services, Chennai, India.

Contents

	Acknowledgments	vii
1	Building Expertise for Teachers of English Learners: Introduction to the Observation Protocol for Academic Literacies (OPAL) Instrument	1
2	Seeing What's There: Sharpening Our Observation Skills	18
3	OPAL Domain 3: Comprehensibility	38
4	OPAL Domain 4: Interactions	60
5	OPAL Domain 1: Rigorous and Relevant Curriculum	80
6	OPAL Domain 2: Connections	110
7	Using the OPAL for Professional Learning, Research and Evaluation Purposes	125
	Appendix A	142
	Appendix B	153
	Appendix C	157
	Appendix D	165
	Appendix E	167
	Appendix F	168
	Appendix G	171
	References	176
	Index	186

Acknowledgments

We first wish to thank the many educators who allowed us to make their experiences and teaching practices for their English Learner students visible through the vignettes, observations and examples captured in this book.

Many colleagues and experts supported the development of the OPAL instrument, the Institute and this book. Our appreciation is extended to Robert Rueda, PhD; Hyo Jin Lim, PhD; Kristen Anguiano, PhD; Elizabeth Jiménez; Gisela O'Brien, PhD; Deborah Lennon; Nidia Hernández; Carmen Valles; and many graduate assistants over the years.

Additionally, we gratefully acknowledge the partnership support from the PROMISE (Pursuing Regional Opportunities for Mentoring, Innovation, and Success for English Learners) Initiative as well as 23 participating schools in the Southern California region.

Finally, we extend our deepest appreciation to our families for their enduring patience, love, encouragement, understanding and support throughout this OPAL journey.

1 Building Expertise for Teachers of English Learners: Introduction to the Observation Protocol for Academic Literacies (OPAL) Instrument

In this chapter, we introduce the OPAL as a classroom observation instrument intended to be used to observe and support teachers of English Learners. Derived from research-based practices and theoretical principles, the OPAL consists of 18 indicators categorized into 4 domains. We provide an overview of research and theoretically based practices for English Learners and describe the rationale for the development of the OPAL. We also discuss the process through which we created the OPAL, along with guidance provided to readers about how we present a broad range of levels of implementation – high to low – across the vignettes and snapshots. It is important to keep in mind that the OPAL is not intended to be used as an evaluative tool. Our intent has always been that it be used to support and develop teacher expertise for English Learners by using classroom evidence collected through the OPAL tool to enhance the instructional dialogue that occurs in schools.

Introduction

Even prior to the devastating effects of the COVID-19 pandemic, English Learners' (ELs) educational access and outcomes suffered from inequitable schooling opportunities and divides as compared to their native-speaking English peers.[1] During and after the pandemic, ELs and their families faced even greater educational and technological divides than all other student groups (Star *et al.*, 2022), while emerging research documents the disproportionately negative and ongoing academic, linguistic and mental health effects of the pandemic (Hartshorn & McMurry, 2020; Lavadenz *et al.*, 2021). Support for teachers of ELs is more greatly needed, more than ever, as it is fundamental to the success of this diverse student population (Sugarman & Lazarin, 2020). It is with the intent of providing support to teachers of English Learners through structured, research-based observations that we developed the Observational Protocol for Academic Literacies (OPAL). This book is a result of over 15 years of development and training provided to over 500 educators; it has been written to provide users with the necessary background information, practice and guidance to use the OPAL effectively with pre-K–12th grade teachers of English Learners to support and enhance instruction using research-based practices and to elevate professional dialogues in schools.

The OPAL is an 18-item Likert scale classroom observational instrument developed around a 4-construct theoretical model – (1) rigorous and relevant curriculum, (2) connections, (3) comprehensibility and (4) interactions – and is intended for use in preschool through 12th grade second language and content area classrooms for professional development, coaching and/or research and evaluation. As this book is intended primarily for teachers' use, the emphasis is on a reader-friendly approach. We provide 19 classroom examples from teachers of English Learners to set the stage for how these 4 domains within OPAL 'come alive', thus bridging theory-to-practice for teaching English Learners. We begin by describing the theories and research that an inter-disciplinary team of researchers, statisticians and content experts used to develop the OPAL. In this chapter, we describe the theoretical frameworks – sociocultural theory and language acquisition research – that were used for teaching English Learners across a variety of content areas and that undergird the OPAL as a research-based observation instrument.

Classroom observations are prearranged and range from 20 to 30 minutes in duration. Prior to each observation, a purpose and/or focus for that observation is determined and agreed upon by the teacher and observer. When the OPAL is used as a basis for coaching, these agreements are foundational to establish neutrality, as well as to develop a non-judgmental supportive role for the observer. The observer uses the OPAL observation form to provide feedback for the classroom teacher as notes based on evidence gathered during the observation, as well as a rubric score (if the teacher and the observer have agreed in advance that a numerical score will be given). Regardless of whether Likert scale scores are used or not, the descriptive notes provide objective statements about classroom practices, interactions, resources and student engagement. These notes will be used as part of the follow-up conversations between the observer and the teacher and guided by the reflection questions that are provided in the chapters on each of the OPAL domains (Chapters 3 to 6 of this book).

An essential aspect of the process of using the OPAL is in regard to the stance in which the OPAL can be used to support district-wide, school-wide or collaborative teacher professional development efforts when observation results are to inform priorities in English Learner professional development. We provide examples of how teachers, school leaders, teacher educators and researchers use the OPAL based on agreements between and among users; these processes and agreements are described in Chapter 7.

The context

More than 5.4 million US public school students are identified as English Learners; of these, 4.4 million are Spanish speaking. Consistently, California accounts for approximately 20% of the nation's overall English Learner population (Ruiz Soto *et al.*, 2015). The OPAL was originally developed for teachers of English Learners in California, with the subsequent goal of responding to the nation's growing migrations of English Learners and their families to states that have traditionally enrolled fewer English Learners.

As the English Learner population grows, they will require assets-based language, academic and social-emotional supports to be successful in school, career and life (de Jong, 2022). The mounting achievement deficit faced by English Learners marks them as among the largest group of underserved students in schools in the United States. Demographic data indicate that the population of English Learners in K–12 schools has increased by more than 1 million students since 2000, with ELs representing 10.4% of the total student enrollment (U.S. Department of Education, Office of English Language Acquisition, 2022) while study after study reveals racial, language and socioeconomic achievement gaps. The National Assessment of Educational Progress (NAEP) data reveal significantly enduring and widening gaps between English-proficient students and English Learners, with only a small percentage of eighth-grade English Learners achieving proficient levels in reading (4%) and math (6%); non-English Learners, by contrast, score at 36% proficient in reading and 35% in math. Seventy-one percent of English Learners score *below* 'basic' on eighth-grade NAEP reading and 69% in math (National Center for Education Statistics, 2015), and their graduation rates are depressed as well (Center on Education Policy, 2005). Given the persistent national achievement gaps between English Learners and their native English-speaking peers, educators continue to engage in 'courageous conversations' (Rosa, 2019; Singleton, 2021) that focus on developing and implementing internal policies and practices to improve the education of English Learners.

The English Learner achievement gap also signals a corresponding *instructional support gap*, in which educators have limited opportunities to receive comprehensive and sustained professional development based on their own actual practice. This type of professional development for teachers of English Learners facilitates their own learning about their practice so that they can better analyze, reflect and improve on research-based practices for English Learners (Heritage *et al.*, 2015; Saunders & Goldenberg, 2010; Solano-Flores & Trumbull, 2003; Teemant, 2014; Teemant *et al.*, 2022; Villegas & Lucas, 2002). However, such professional development requires valid and reliable observation tools if teachers are to feel confident that when they open the doors of their classrooms, those who observe are fair, knowledgeable and able to support them in refining their key practices with and for their English Learners. Currently, there are few classroom observational measures designed explicitly to support teachers of English Learners across multiple grade levels and content areas (August & Blackburn, 2019; Echevarria & Short, 2004; Goldenberg *et al.*, 2013; Teemant, 2014; Teemant *et al.*, 2022; Waxman *et al.*, 2009). The chapters in this book respond to this need, presenting a valid and reliable classroom observation instrument for pre-K–12 teachers of English Learners. This book will prepare observers of teachers of English Learners with tools and processes that they can use to collect evidence on effective teaching practices for English Learners. Further, observers might include teacher-peers, coaches, school leaders and researchers in the use of this instrument as a means to understand and support effective practices for teachers of English Learners.

An important caveat: neither the OPAL nor this book is intended to be used to evaluate teachers, nor to be part of a system of teacher evaluation. Instead, the OPAL is designed to support teacher reflection, dialogue and inquiry about their instructional practices. This approach to teacher learning is based on the same frameworks of sociocultural theory that we use in the OPAL tool (Bruner, 1978; Rogoff, 2003; Teemant *et al.*, 2022; Tharp, 2018; Tharp & Gallimore, 1988). Sociocultural theory posits that schools and classrooms can serve as social contexts for learning. For the adults involved, the application of sociocultural theory has the possibility of creating a community of practice wherein teachers and others are engaged in dialogue about what they see in their own classrooms and, in turn, build upon their expertise (Lave & Wenger, 1991; Wenger, 1998; Wenger-Trayner & Wenger-Trayner, 2020). The theory, for both adults and children, also takes an assets-based approach to learning – in other words, it holds that humans possess strengths, knowledge and skills that act as the starting points for new learning. Viewed through this lens, the classroom evidence collected with the OPAL tool can serve as an opportunity for teachers and observers to refine and deepen their understanding of their own current practice, to learn about what the evidence gathered during the observation reveals about their strengths and to engage in dialogue about where they want to go next.

Thus, for the users of the OPAL, the conclusion of the observation visit is not the end; rather it is just the beginning of an opportunity to facilitate teacher learning in at least three ways: (1) to provide coaching support for individual teachers; (2) to identify and agree upon areas of targeted professional development based on observations across grade levels, content areas, school or district; and (3) to identify trends, shifts and changes in teacher practices over time. We further discuss these uses of the OPAL in Chapter 7.

In the next section, we answer the following questions: *(1) What theories about teaching English Learners were used in the development of the OPAL?; (2) Does the OPAL measure teaching practices for English Learners (is the OPAL valid)?; and (3) Can experienced OPAL observers yield consistent results across multiple observations (is the OPAL reliable)?*

OPAL's Theoretical and Empirical Frameworks: Conceptualizing Teacher Expertise with English Learners

The conceptual underpinnings of the OPAL are grounded in research-based teaching practices for English Learners, as well as in sociocultural theory and second language acquisition theory (Kibler *et al.*, 2015; MacSwan, 2020; Walqui & Van Lier, 2010). Combined, these frameworks provided us with key insights that were distilled into a set of key teaching practices that eventually informed the OPAL indicators and the OPAL domains. This section briefly highlights each of the frameworks.

Research-based teaching practices

To begin, we frame teacher expertise in Table 1.1, using Fillmore and Snow's (2018) synthesis of the five domains of teacher knowledge, skills and attitudes required for effective second language educators. The OPAL enacts these concepts through a proactive positioning of the teacher as a knowledgeable professional who is accomplished in curriculum, linguistics and cross-cultural understanding, as well as acting as assessor and student advocate for English learners.

Walqui's (2001) model of teacher expertise depicts accomplished teachers as those whose pedagogic practices are informed by deep reflection about themselves, their students and the communities in which they live. This reflection further affects the curriculum and their practice. The research on the development of expertise for teachers of English Learners, informed by a synthesis of the literature on second language acquisition and a theoretical stance informed by constructivist and sociocultural perspectives, led us to develop and validate a classroom observation protocol that allows for teacher reflection and improvement of practice.

Sociocultural theory and second language acquisition

Teaching and learning English are complex processes not explained by language theories or methods alone (Walqui & Van Lier, 2010). The relationship between language majority and minority groups, language

Table 1.1 Conceptualizing teaching expertise with English Learners

Role/Functions	Definition	Application in second language classrooms
Teacher as communicator	Strives for understanding of students' cultural ways of talking and of his or her own language output.	Understands cultural discourse patterns that are different from his or her own to avoid misunderstanding and instructional disruption.
Teacher as educator	Plans instruction based on knowledge of the target language and of the content, as informed by the students' backgrounds and needs.	Assesses, designs curriculum and instructs students in linguistically and academically appropriate ways.
Teacher as evaluator	Determines students' levels of language and academic proficiency in order to guide planning.	Designs for flexible groupings that consider specific student performance abilities. Utilizes objective learning criteria that consider diverse family socialization and linguistic patterns.
Teacher as an educated human being	Is knowledgeable of basic English linguistics and of sociopolitical factors that influence academic achievement for diverse learners.	Skillfully incorporates knowledge of the structure of English while considering regional, dialectical and attitudinal differences between him or herself and the students.
Teacher as agent of socialization	Is aware of the cultural and linguistic 'funds of knowledge' that students bring with them to school and uses this knowledge to build understanding of the culture, language and traditions in the United States.	Facilitates transition from home to school without decreasing expectations for student learning. Incorporates an additive approach to L2 learning.

Source: Fillmore, L.W. and Snow, C. (2018) What teachers need to know about language. In C. Adger, C. Snow and D. Christian (eds) *What Teachers Need to Know About Language* (2nd edn, pp. 8–51). Multilingual Matters/Center for Applied Linguistics.

status, immigration, economics and language policies add complexity to learning a second language (Cummins, 2000; de Jong, 2011; Skutnabb-Kangas, 2000; Wright, 2019). Notions such as additive bilingualism (in which the new language augments the first language) and subtractive bilingualism (in which the first language is eliminated) shape the sociocultural context for learning English. Cummins (2000) provided educators with a framework for understanding the complex relationship between the development of the primary language and the second language from the standpoint of language status. Cummins's work explains the language minority status of immigrant students, but also status more generally, as embedded in interactions between teachers and students, and between students. Effective instruction for English Learners is not only a matter of quality instruction, teacher expertise and appropriate instructional programs; it must also address the micro-level contacts that English Learners have with others in schools (Collier & Thomas, 2002). Sociocultural and second language acquisition theory and research

(Goldenberg, 2012; Lightbown & Spada, 2013) also indicate that English Learners require access to comprehensible, rigorous and relevant content instruction *and* opportunities to link content with prior knowledge through active classroom participation that maximizes engagement. We reframe this research on teacher expertise and effective instruction for English Learners through four essential areas of practice: (1) rigorous and relevant curriculum; (2) connections with students' backgrounds, interests and experiences; (3) comprehensible input; and (4) interactions between teachers and students and between students and peers. These four essential areas make up the four domains of the OPAL.

The OPAL's Four Domains

This section provides an overview of each of the four OPAL domains (see Tables 1.2–1.5), along with examples of key practices that are grounded in the sociocultural and second language research and theoretical frameworks. All domains, and the subsequent 18 indicators of practice, are interconnected conceptually to reflect instructional coherence (Walqui, 2001).

Invitation to journey in multilingual classrooms: Experiencing the OPAL domains

Later, in Chapters 3–5, each of the OPAL's key practice indicators will be brought to life through our partnership with 16 teachers whose commitments to creating opportunities for transparent, objective and reflective examination of classroom practices for English Learner students make these 19 classroom scenarios possible. We use pseudonyms throughout our book and are grateful to them for opening their doors and sharing their expertise. We highlight *8* vignettes (written descriptions of actual classroom lessons from our observations) and *11* snapshots (shorter, more concise versions of an observation); these were developed based on actual classroom observations. The context for each set of vignettes is provided to give the reader an overall picture of factors that may have influenced decision-making processes, delivery of instruction and classroom practices. These include content area, grade level, English Learner language proficiency level(s) and focus on content standards. Because these classroom observations occurred in California, content standards are specific to those adopted by the California State Board of Education: (1) Common Core State Standards (CCSS) for English Language Arts and Literacy in History/Social Studies, Science and Technical Subjects and Mathematics (CDE, 2010/2013); (2) Next Generation Science Standards (CDE, 2013); (3) History Social Science Content Standards (CDE, 1998/2000); and (4) English Language Development (ELD) Standards (CDE, 2012). Nationally, each state determines the standards that are taught in schools. Several states across the nation have adopted the same or similar Common Core standards for English and math while others have revised, edited or created other versions to respond to their state context. As such, we expect that readers will (1) recognize similarities in the content *and* language standards connections presented for each vignette and (2) engage in the proposed 'reading and scoring' steps to examine practices for English Learners using the OPAL indicators.

Across the United States educational entities are required to meet federal and civil rights requirements for English Learner students by providing programs and services that enable them 'to attain both English proficiency and parity of participation in the standard instructional program within a reasonable amount of time' (U.S. Department of Education, Office of English Language Acquisition, 2017: 1). For our purposes we focus on three main types of language programming for ELs which include: (1) bilingual; (2) dual language; or (3) Structured English Immersion (SEI). The first two programs use primary language instruction to develop literacy skills and content knowledge in the student's primary language, while simultaneously leveraging English Learners' primary language skills and knowledge to accelerate English language development and academic achievement. The difference between these two bilingual models is that transitional bilingual programs focus on transitioning students to an all-English setting, whereas dual language programs focus on primary language (L1) maintenance and bilingual/biliteracy development. In contrast, SEI programs provide instruction overwhelmingly in English and do not develop or maintain English Learners' primary language.

Preview of key practices in the OPAL instrument

Our descriptions of practice in the OPAL domains reflect the ways teachers can build on students' language, culture and content learning in interrelated and integrated ways. As readers journey through classrooms, they will have opportunities to reflect on classroom practice and score each of the OPAL's 18 indicators using the OPAL instrument (Appendix D) and the OPAL Descriptor Rubric (Appendix C).

Implementing a rigorous and relevant curriculum

Table 1.2 provides a definition of the OPAL's rigorous and relevant curriculum domain, along with a list of key practices. Readers will briefly 'journey into classrooms' such as a tenth-grade biology SEI setting where Mr Pierce conducts an end-of-unit biology lesson and English Learner students are asked to write an explanatory/informational text synthesizing the key elements/processes of protein synthesis, or a fifth-grade classroom where students are working in groups to complete a Public Service Announcement (PSA) as part of their urban ecology unit of study.

Table 1.2 OPAL Domain 1: Rigorous and Relevant Curriculum

What is it?	Key practices
A *rigorous and relevant curriculum* is cognitively complex, relevant and challenging. It allows educators to value and capitalize on students' linguistic and cultural backgrounds.	• Establish high expectations based on content *and* English Language Development (ELD) Standards that address students' linguistic and academic needs. • Engage students in problem solving and critical thinking. • Present lessons and units of study to promote cross-curricular understanding based on cognitive *and* language proficiency levels. • Identify learning objectives that address language and content standards. • Use curricular materials that represent cultural perspectives. • Provide access to materials *and* content in student's primary language. • Provide opportunities for students to transfer what they know from their first language to English.

The key practices in the *rigorous and relevant curriculum* domain of the OPAL actualize sociocultural theory and second language acquisition by emphasizing high expectations based on students' linguistic and academic needs. The practices ensure that teachers are aware of the need to provide access to 21st-century materials and resources that encourage their students to think and engage critically. Encouraging English Learners to use their first languages, while often (mis)perceived by educators as a hindrance to learning English, helps counter the negative and deficit orientations regarding English Learners that stem from focusing on what they do not know and are not able to do based on standardized test results (Abedi, 2008; Lucas & Beresford, 2010). One of the aspects of differentiated instruction for English Learners is that teachers should encourage students to actively transfer skills between their primary language and English. This can be as simple as pointing out cognates in both languages to explicitly teaching differences in the phonologies (sound systems) and/or grammatical differences between the first or second language. To do this, teachers need to have basic background knowledge of the features of their students' primary languages. For example, knowing that there are no consonant blends in Vietnamese can help teachers address this in oral language or writing instruction (Tang, 2007).

English Learners' academic success depends on their being supported in acquiring and using the academic language required for success in school. Schleppegrell (2012) describes 'academic language' as the discourse used in academic, professional and technical contexts, characterized by its high-level, discipline-specific vocabulary and rhetorical styles. The OPAL addresses specific aspects of content area instruction with the types of interactions/tasks (processes) that can yield maximum results for English Learners across language proficiency levels (beginning to advanced) and across the four language domains of listening, speaking, reading and writing.

Bridging connections

We explore how educational settings can value and cultivate the educational and personal experiences English Learners bring to the classroom, rather than ignoring or trying to replace these experiences, thus enabling students to make meaningful connections and apply or extend new learning to their community, history or social reality. Readers can 'visit' Mrs Garcia's dual language kindergarten classroom where she presents a lesson on community workers and culminates with a walking tour of the school to visit the workers in the office, the library, the cafeteria and the busses. Readers will also reflect on examples of classroom practice that engage English Learners in conducting research/inquiry in one's community with a focus on action. Table 1.3 provides a definition of the OPAL's connections domain, along with a list of key practices.

Instruction that values and cultivates the personal experiences English Learners bring to the classroom, rather than ignoring or trying to replace these experiences, enables students to make *meaningful connections* with what is being taught and what they already know (Cummins, 2000; King & Lanza, 2019; Morita-Mullaney, 2018). Making connections to students' cultures and life experiences by moving beyond core curricular materials, which often do not reflect students' lives, is another example of differentiating instruction. English Learners benefit from teachers' explanations and modeling of thinking strategies and processes to solve complex tasks (Chamot & O'Malley, 1994; Gersten & Baker, 2000). Think-aloud protocols are excellent examples of metacognitive strategies that encourage students to speak out loud what they are thinking. For English Learners, think-alouds can occur in their strongest language and for beginning English Learners this may be their first language (Lavadenz, 2003).

Table 1.3 OPAL Domain 2: Connections

What is it?	Key practices
Bridging connections with students' prior knowledge is the ability to link content to students' lives, histories and realities.	• Plan for opportunities to value and link students' personal experiences to classroom learning. • Present supplemental materials that represent students' cultural backgrounds and interests. • Ask and model explicit questions that guide students' thinking.

Table 1.4 OPAL Domain 3: Comprehensibility

What is it?	Key practices
Comprehensibility is the attainment of maximum student understanding in order to provide access to content for all students.	• Check frequently for understanding within each lesson. • Informally assess students' understanding during a lesson and adjust the lesson based on this assessment. • Plan for instruction that scaffolds the task by using visuals, graphic organizers and gestures to clarify concepts. • Target key academic vocabulary and provide multiple opportunities for students to 'own the words'. • Provide linguistically appropriate instruction by questioning and identifying tasks appropriate to each student's level of language proficiency.

Teaching for maximum comprehensibility

Readers are invited to explore key indicators of comprehensibility for English Learners (see Table 1.4). They'll meet Mr Hidalgo who over the course of the first semester of instruction introduced and developed Reciprocal Teaching to help his seventh-grade English Learner students interpret and discuss text while leveraging the use of their primary language to access and comprehend grade-level content, or second grade teacher Ms Gomez who consistently uses interactive writing strategies to record and model the structure of informative/explanatory texts in order to explain learned concepts.

Some aspects of comprehensible instruction for English Learners have long been a part of sheltered instruction, including access to a rigorous, standards-aligned curriculum through cycles of input, clarifications and questioning, as well as support for primary language development (August & Shanahan, 2006; de Oliveira *et al.*, 2018; Echevarria & Short, 2004; Goldenberg, 2012; Hopkins *et al.*, 2015). Additive approaches to learning content and language are essential characteristics of equitable and differentiated instruction for English Learners. Practices such as visuals, graphic organizers and manipulatives increase access to the content areas for English Learners across language proficiency levels. Teachers should identify key vocabulary for content and language development. It is critical to provide multiple opportunities for students to use and internalize academic vocabulary as well as language structures. This maximizes comprehensibility during directed instruction and scaffolds comprehension during independent reading (Carlo *et al.*, 2004; Gibbons, 2015, 2018).

Another strategy that promotes comprehensibility is the 'preview-review' method. In this method, at the completion of a lesson or unit, a review of what was learned is conducted using the student's primary language. This review can be either teacher-directed or student-led. Students' primary languages may also be used to preview or introduce new concepts at the beginning of a unit or lesson. The preview-review method increases English Learners' comprehension of content presented during the lesson delivered in English (Gibbons, 2018; Mercuri, 2015; National Academies of Sciences, Engineering and Medicine, 2017; Ovando *et al.*, 2003). It is more effective than translating concepts or content during lesson delivery because it helps students become familiar with the content prior to the presentation of the lesson. Consequently, it allows students to concentrate on understanding the lesson and results in increased comprehensibility and language learning.

Multiple opportunities for interaction

Table 1.5 highlights the definition and key practices essential in creating meaningful interactions for English Learners. Readers can extend their learning through a 'visit' into Mr Rico's classroom who has established routines to promote autonomy and accountability for collaborative group work differentiated based on students' individual academic, developmental and linguistic levels, or Mr Triggs who uses the STAR (Substitute, Take things out, Add things and Rearrange) Writing Strategy to conduct peer editing sessions.

Cooperative learning is a key instructional strategy for English Learners because it enhances interactions among students, promotes the development of positive academic and social support systems for English Learners, prepares students for increasingly interactive environments and allows teachers to manage large classes of students with diverse needs (Holt, 1993). Flexible student grouping and collaborative routines engage students in talking about content in relevant, meaningful and structured ways. These routines are scaffolds that promote student autonomy. From simple processes such as structured turn-taking, to individual roles/jobs or responsibilities in small group work, to varying partners with 'bilingual buddies', students who actively participate in classroom discussions with others are more engaged in learning the content.

Bruner (1978), like Vygotsky (1962, 1978), focused on the social and cultural aspects of learning. He suggested that people understand better

Table 1.5 OPAL Domain 4: Interactions

What is it?	Key practices
Interactions are varied participation structures that facilitate access to the curriculum through maximum engagement and leadership opportunities.	• Assess students' linguistic, academic and social abilities in order to create flexible groupings. • Modify classroom structures and procedures to include accountability as part of collaborative work. • Create classroom routines that promote student autonomy and build self-monitoring skills. • Model and provide time for students to participate in academic discourse across the content areas.

when the material has personal significance, not just through attention to facts. Knowledge and memory are constructed through meaningful interactions with peers and adults in their environments. Learning must be a process of discovery where learners build their own knowledge, through conversations and dialogue with teachers and peers. Swain (1986) maintained that interactions are part of developing communicative competence in students – this means that students need to be able to talk, question and use the discourse of various genres to gain competency in both English and the content area. Teachers guide interactions to provide opportunities for students to gain competency in English by explicitly modeling the type of language required for specific genres and provide structures that allow students to practice these orally and in writing.

The OPAL's development was guided by conceptual frameworks that encapsulate essential elements of professional development with the intent of building teacher knowledge and supporting effective practices with students whose first language is not English. This observational protocol focuses on much more than the implementation of a single lesson in a given content area. The OPAL purports to measure overall teacher instructional practices that impact content and language development, as well as classroom environment and interactions.

The next section provides the summary of the classroom observation study we conducted to ensure that the constructs, domains and indicators that we drew from the research and practice are technically valid and reliable. Because of the results of the validation study, we can have the confidence that the OPAL is both a reliable and powerful tool for describing teachers' capacities in working with English Learners.

Results of the OPAL Classroom Observation Validation Study

The OPAL was developed and validated between 2006 and 2008 in 22 schools and more than 300 pre-K through 12th grade classrooms in Southern California. To ensure rigorous technical validity for the instrument, we used a three-stage process to define and test the model. Figure 1.1 illustrates the three phases, which include the development of the 18 indicators through the research literature on teachers of English Learners practices (phase one: Content Validation); the statistical process of sorting these indicators into the corresponding OPAL domains (phase two: Exploratory Factor Analysis [EFA]); and the further statistical testing of the 'fit' between the indicators and the domains (phase three: Confirmatory Factor Analysis [CFA]). These three phases ensure the technical validity of the instrument – that is, that the OPAL measures what it purports to measure. Additionally, to test for internal consistency, Cronbach's alpha results (0.77) indicate that the items are adequately generalizable across second language classrooms. Appendix A includes the full results of the OPAL Technical Report.

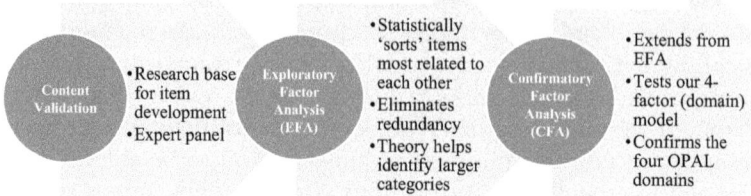

Figure 1.1 OPAL's three-phase validation process

The three-phase technical validation process for the OPAL demonstrated with a high degree of confidence that the OPAL effectively measures teacher practices, classroom interactions and educational contexts from sociocultural and language acquisition perspectives. In other words, the OPAL is a valid and reliable instrument, a research-based observation tool that, when used appropriately, can serve to support teachers of English Learners.

The OPAL observation protocol utilizes a six-point Likert-type scale (one to six, low to high) to rate instruction for academic literacies. Academic literacies are defined as a set of 21st-century skills, abilities and dispositions developed through the affirmation of and in response to students' identities, experiences and backgrounds (see Appendix D for the OPAL instrument form). Part of the development and validation of the instrument included a review of the overall research on classroom observations (Byrne & Schneider, 1986; Echevarria *et al.*, 2010; Hyson *et al.*, 1990; Micceri *et al.*, 1990; Pianta & Hamre, 2009; Roberson, 1998), as well as research focusing on classroom observations for English Learners. We found few behavioral observation instruments that measure classroom practices and teacher-student interactions, and even fewer that have been developed *exclusively* to examine teacher practices for English learners (Coady *et al.*, 2019; Echevarria & Short, 2004; Goldenberg *et al.*, 2013). Of the few classroom observation studies we found, the Sheltered Instruction Observation Protocol (SIOP) (Echevarria & Short, 2004), based largely on the second language acquisition theories of Krashen (1985), is used to plan and observe entire lessons. Another instrument, the Classroom Qualities for English Language Learners or CQELL (Goldenberg *et al.*, 2013) in Language Arts Instruction, is an observation protocol for only one content area, English language arts (ELA), and was developed for the elementary school level only. Coady *et al.* (2019) adapted only two of the four domains for ELs in Danielson's Group Framework for Teaching. The OPAL, by contrast, serves as a 'wide-lens' classroom observation protocol for grades pre-K through 12 and is applicable across all subject matters as indicated in our validation study. The observation period can be completed in 20–30 minutes.

Overview of the Chapters

In this book, we lead readers through the process of learning how to use the OPAL instrument with confidence and reliability. We modeled the exercises after our OPAL Institutes, which comprised three full-day 'train-the-trainer' professional development sessions. These Institutes were conducted in person with no more than 25 participants and 2 lead trainers and used a combination of video selections and written vignettes to build inter-rater reliability within the groups. Inter-rater reliability is the statistical process that measures the degree of agreement among raters when rating a given observation. Raters are said to be in 'consensus' rating when they score the same level of evidence at approximately 70%, usually using the statistic known as Cohen's kappa coefficient (Cohen, 1960).

The Institutes provided opportunities for OPAL participants to apply the science of observation through the process of viewing and reading evidence with the OPAL instrument, then scoring and writing the evidence observed. This book provides readers with opportunities to use the principles and practices we have developed for the OPAL instrument in a written format but does not preclude readers from continuing to practice these principles and practices with other materials, including the many classroom videos available online.

Ultimately, the OPAL was created, validated and operationalized with the goal of generating conversations about teaching and how to teach English Learners more effectively – the instrument responds to educators' sense of urgency and desire to reduce the 'instructional gap'. Implementation scores on the OPAL's six-point Likert scale and the complementary anecdotal notes are intended to provide teachers and other users with 'conversation starters' about their own and each other's practices, allowing them to reflect and refine those practices so that English Learners are more engaged, more interactive and more successful. Use of the OPAL is not, however, a panacea for other problems and issues that our schools, students and their families face. Nonetheless, we remain optimistic that open and professional dialogue among educators will enliven and improve the school experience for students and their teachers. To that end, the remainder of the book is organized as follows:

Chapter 2: Seeing What's There: Sharpening Our Observation Skills

Chapter 2 discusses classroom observation techniques, using ethnographic note-taking as the primary mechanism for observing. The chapter also provides general guidelines for observer etiquette and planning for observations.

Chapter 3: OPAL Domain 3: Comprehensibility

This chapter introduces actual classroom vignettes and a variety of snapshots to support readers in beginning to establish inter-rater reliability. We begin with Domain 3 (Comprehensibility) because comprehensibility has been emphasized the most in teacher preparation programs, site- and district-level training sessions and resource materials for teachers of English Learners. We guide readers through the process of referencing evidence by using vignettes – written descriptions of actual classroom lessons from our observations. We also use classroom 'snapshots', which are shorter, more concise versions of an observation. Vignettes and snapshots are used by observers/readers to determine a score for each of the indicators in this domain based on the six-point Likert scale used in the OPAL. These scores are cross-referenced with the video scoring guide that was established by the Calibration Committee in the original OPAL Institute.

Chapter 4: OPAL Domain 4: Interactions

Chapter 4 replicates and applies the same process for establishing inter-rater reliability to another OPAL domain. This chapter uses another set of classroom vignettes and snapshots from a variety of grade levels and content areas to illustrate classroom practices that promote interactions that maximize engagement, leadership opportunities and access to the curriculum.

Chapter 5: OPAL Domain 1: Rigorous and Relevant Curriculum

Chapter 5 applies the same process for establishing inter-rater reliability to OPAL Domain 1 (Rigorous and Relevant Curriculum). This chapter uses different classroom vignettes and snapshots from different grade levels and content areas to focus on curriculum that is cognitively complex, relevant, challenging and appropriate for linguistically diverse populations.

Chapter 6: OPAL Domain 2: Connections

Chapter 6 applies the same process to the final OPAL domain of Connections, using different classroom vignettes and snapshots from different grade levels and content areas for this domain.

Chapter 7: Using the OPAL for Professional Learning, Research and Evaluation Purposes

This chapter describes the various uses of the OPAL. We use the results from survey data we collected from 'graduates' of the OPAL Institutes between 2010 and 2016 to provide examples of how the OPAL has been used to create professional development for other teachers as well as how graduates have taught others how to use the tool. Additionally, we provide examples of how the OPAL is currently being used across a variety of research/evaluation projects to assess changes in teachers' practices over time. We also consider how schools have used OPAL results to prioritize the types of professional development teachers receive by identifying levels of implementation of research-based practices.

Conclusion

Framing effective, differentiated instruction for English Learners in the context of complex social, political and educational conditions is a challenging task. The four domains identified in this chapter are central to differentiating instruction for English Learners. Supporting the development of teachers' expertise with English Learners by using students' linguistic and cultural resources in differentiated ways will allow us to develop students' academic competencies in English and other languages to positively affect their overall success and achievement.

Note

(1) The term 'English Learners' is used to refer to students who speak a language other than English who receive specialized instruction in English and, if enrolled in a bilingual/dual language program, also receive instruction in their primary language. The authors acknowledge and encourage the use of the term 'Emergent Bilingual Learners' given its focus on the potential to leverage bilingualism as a resource, both cognitively and socially (García, 2009; Martinez, 2018). At present, 'English Learners' remains the term used in federal policy, legislation and court cases and is used throughout this book for consistency with federal terminology.

2 Seeing What's There: Sharpening Our Observation Skills

> *I felt as if my lens was out of focus. I could see things that I had never noticed before. I saw inequity in the system that I possibly was aware of, but hadn't realized ... With this PD, I suddenly realized that these are different techniques ... if you use them in the right way. You can move students very quickly so that the playing field is leveled.*
> – OPAL Institute Participant (Teacher Leader)

This chapter shows readers how to collect evidence using a written vignette, a description of a lesson from an actual classroom from our observations. Undergirded by the conceptual and practical approach in creating a 'community of practice' for supporting teachers of English Learners from Chapter 1, we situate professional collaboration with the following: (1) a disposition for 'making learning visible' by opening the doors of the classrooms to colleagues and peers; (2) professional learning that includes learning how to observe non-judgmentally in classrooms; and (3) engaging in reflection and dialogue based on the evidence from classroom practice. This chapter provides background knowledge in 'ethnographic notetaking' and activities that prepare the reader to begin noting evidence with clear focus and skill. It also includes a practice activity applying concepts from one of the OPAL domains so that readers can learn how to take anecdotal notes (without scores) from a written vignette. The vignettes included represent a range of grade levels, content areas and school contexts with teachers who have agreed to have us capture their practices with English Learners. Most vignettes in this book have been transcribed from videotaped sessions and/or summative observation notes. The vignettes were created to describe instances of learning and teaching that serve to anchor the readers' observation of teacher experiences and they have clear purposes in this book. The vignettes:

- Illustrate practices of real teachers with actual students in today's classrooms from which readers can learn to seek evidence in order to score using the OPAL instrument.

- Provide opportunities to score using the OPAL's six-point Likert scale to determine varying levels of implementation of research-based practices for English Learners.
- Encourage discussion and reflection with OPAL users about the situatedness of teaching and learning to teach more effectively with English Learners.

The vignettes include background information describing the context in which they were developed, including the type of school community, grade level, English language proficiency levels of the students, the grade level or content area and the topic/focus of the lesson observed. We use vignettes and snapshots (shorter, more concise versions of the vignettes) to develop OPAL users' facility with using anecdotal evidence to support the scoring of the OPAL's 18 indicators of research-based practice (see the complete OPAL instrument in Appendix D). Additionally, we engage in conversation with participants to encourage documentation of judgement-neutral statements (anecdotal notes) about 'seeing/reading what is there' in the vignettes (evidence), rather than expressing their opinions about what *should be* there or about *what is missing* in their lesson. The key questions considered in this chapter are:

FOCUS QUESTIONS:

1. What does it mean to collect evidence of teaching English Learners in classrooms?
2. How can we enhance our observation skills? What tools and processes can we use?

Before we turn to learning how to score a vignette, it is important to reiterate that the OPAL was created with the intent of supporting teachers of English Learners. It should not be used to individually evaluate teachers for hiring, retention or salary purposes.

The Purpose of the OPAL

Our overarching purpose in developing the OPAL over 15 years ago was to provide teachers of English Learners with evidence of practices used in English Learner classrooms. With this evidence, teachers could then engage in collaborative and supportive dialogue and build on demonstrated practices. As we describe in the next sections, effective practices for teachers of English Learners are enhanced when observation is guided; non-judgmental conversations about observed practices require that the observer (and the teacher) agree to withhold critiques that are negative or hypercritical and instead focus on 'what's there' rather than 'what's not there' or what could have or should have taken place. Using the OPAL as a tool for professional learning requires that teaching professionals engage in collaborative conversations as a part of a robust program of professional learning (August & Blackburn, 2019). In this chapter, we frame the OPAL as both *a tool* and *a process* for professional learning, and we argue that both these aspects are of equal value. Learning to observe with the OPAL is the process of making learning visible by adopting key ideas from the 'science' of evidence-gathering outlined in the discipline of ethnographic research (Douglas, 2009).

Visible learning for teachers of English learners

Teaching is often an isolated act, and it is sometimes difficult to follow up on the professional development that teachers receive to determine its impact on student learning. Researcher John Hattie (2012) conducted a meta-analysis of the relationship between professional development practices on student learning as measured by standardized test scores. His book, *Visible Learning for Teachers: Maximizing Impact on Learning*, is a collection of evidence-based research that examines the impacts of professional development on student learning. Written for pre-service and in-service teachers, as well as administrators, *Visible Learning* draws on a meta-analysis of over 800 studies; it explains how to apply the 'what works' to any classroom by extrapolating what expert teachers do to improve student learning. Making learning visible according to Hattie (2012) is both a process and a result – it is the recognition of the impact of expert teachers on their students' learning enacted through the belief in their students' capacities for learning. Expert teachers, according to Hattie, help create learning climates in classrooms in which students feel safe in taking risks about their own learning, and where learning occurs with and from their peers. By 'seeing' their teaching through their students' eyes, expert teachers can represent the subjects they teach in multiple ways, monitor and adjust their instruction based on their students' understanding, and seek and use feedback about their teaching (Hattie, 2012; Hattie & Clarke, 2018). As the teacher quoted at the outset of this chapter indicated, teachers of English Learners need to be supported to focus on the needs of their students.

Tools such as the OPAL are only one part of the process of building teacher expertise. To build expertise, teachers also need to observe others' teaching practices from an objective and non-judgmental stance – a skill that will also help make teaching 'visible' for teachers of English Learners (Hattie, 2012). Visible teaching for teachers of English Learners can be possible if teachers can learn to 'see what's there', learning how to look for and take notes about the evidence in a teaching session that can be connected to levels of implementation in the OPAL tool. As introduced in Chapter 1, the OPAL's four domains describe research-based practices that are essential for effectively supporting and differentiating instruction for English Learners. Yet we recognize that observing teaching practices will yield the greatest results when the observations serve to support and enhance teacher reflection, both individually and as collaborative professional development. In other words, the evidence that is gathered from the instrument can be most effective when it is part of an integrated professional development program.

The National Standards for Professional Learning (Learning Forward, 2011/2022) assert that in order to increase educator effectiveness and improve results for all students, schools should use a variety of sources and types of student, educator and system data to plan, assess and determine levels of learning. To increase individual and collective teacher performance, programs of professional development need to foster a culture of collaborative inquiry and learning (Learning Forward, 2011/2022). Such programs begin with the affirmation that all teaching professionals engage with one another to access or construct knowledge and skills and with the disposition and receptivity to learning that is meaningful and useful (Learning Forward, 2011/2022).

Teacher reflection and actions to support English learners' language and academic development

We apply Walqui and Van Lier's (2010) definition of reflection as sociocognitive processes and open perspectives that involve a deliberate pause to examine beliefs, goals or practices in order to gain new or deeper understanding leading to actions improving the learning of students. Thus, reflection with action serves as one of the core principles behind the OPAL. The top portion of Figure 2.1 represents the strength of teacher reflection in our efforts to continually learn and refine our practice through these main components:

- Reflective practice: from awareness to action.
- Builds on the strength and wisdom of teaching colleagues.
- Provides opportunities to discuss new strategies before, during and after implementation.
- Supports critical thinking.
- Encourages innovation.
- Enhances learning for *all* students.

We can enhance our practice and our knowledge by creating non-threatening professional communities of practice (Lave & Wenger, 1991; Wenger, 1998; Wenger-Trayner & Wenger-Trayner, 2020) that build on the strength and wisdom of teaching our teacher colleagues. By providing

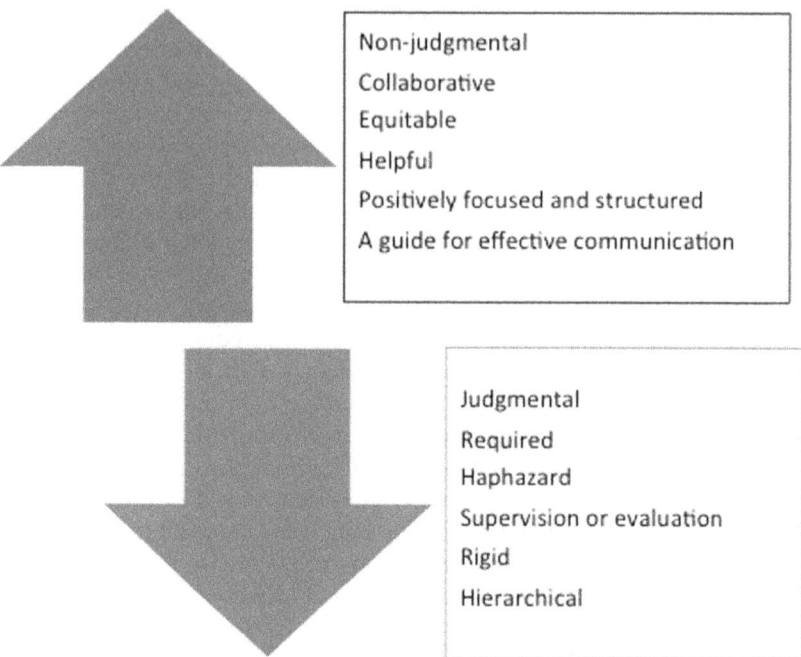

Figure 2.1 Supporting teachers of English Learners: Approaches to the classroom observation process

a framework for looking at instructional practices and classroom interactions within a set timeframe of 20 to 30 minutes, OPAL users can learn to 'see' broadly where, when, how and with whom instruction occurs and to couple observations with support for teachers of English Learners. With the foundation and purposes outlined for the OPAL, we next turn to learning to actually 'see what is there' without judgment.

What does it mean to observe in classrooms?

The field of education draws from several disciplines and classroom observation research that is still evolving (Douglas, 2009). As one of the central data collection methods of qualitative research, the gathering of observational data offers a firsthand account of the phenomenon being investigated (Merriam, 1998). Ethnographic field notes are designed to avoid bias, and they are used to represent reality versus what the researcher imagines is occurring. As Emerson *et al.* (1995: 167) asserted:

> Writing ethnographic field notes that are sensitive to members' meanings is primarily a matter not of asking but of inferring what people are concerned with from the specific ways in which they talk and act in a variety of natural settings.

Using ethnographic note taking in teacher observation has become more widely studied in the last 15 years, and the practice has been applied across a variety of contexts and student populations, including English Learners (Waxman *et al.*, 2009). The most common tools for data-gathering in classrooms are observations that document teacher behaviors – that is, note-taking that documents what teachers and students are actually *doing*. The development and use of classroom observation instruments or protocols typically allow for more reliable data compared to teacher self-reports, interviews, questionnaires and surveys (Hoge, 1985; Matsumura *et al.*, 2002; Pianta & Hamre, 2009). The results from brief notes can subsequently be rated according to levels of pre-identified practices observed to develop numeric scores of the activities occurring in the classroom. Written observation notes serve as *selective coding* into each of the OPAL domains (Strauss & Corbin, 1990) during a single observation (or teaching session), or across several observations that are pre-determined by the observers, teachers and school or district.

Before any actual OPAL observation takes place, the observer and teacher must agree on the observation protocols as illustrated in Figure 2.2. See also Appendix B for a complete set of observation guidelines.

The OPAL's research-based constructs provide a comprehensive approach to measuring teaching and learning in all content areas in diverse pre-K–12th grade classrooms. The next sections introduce the OPAL form, the research-based key terminology used in the development of the 18 OPAL indicators, and how those indicators are aligned to the four domains.

Planning the Observation: Observer and Teacher Agreements

	Content of Instruction (Learning Focus)
	• Both teacher and observer should be aware of learning focus; • Identify content area (i.e. math, English Language Development, language arts, science, social studies, art, music and movement); and • Identify topic of the lesson (i.e. fractions, idiomatic expressions, inferencing skills).
	Scoring or Not Scoring with the OPAL Form
	• An OPAL form is used to record each observation; • Anecdotal notes are recorded during observations; and • If both teacher and observer agree, anecdotal notes can serve as sources of evidence for scoring on the 6-point Likert-scale.
	Time and Date
	• Each observation is scheduled in advance; • Observation details include stated beginning and ending times; and • A total observational timeframe is between 20-30 minutes.

Figure 2.2 Planning the observation: Observer and teacher agreements

The OPAL Form

The OPAL instrument is a two-sided form listing the 18 indicators that are part of the four OPAL domains described in Chapter 1. As illustrated in Figure 2.3, the OPAL form comprises three columns: the first column shows the six-point Likert scale with which to score the evidence; the second column is used to take anecdotal notes from the observation; and the third column is used to flag ideas for discussion in the debrief conversation with the teacher. The 18 indicators are clustered within 4 domains – *rigorous and relevant curriculum, connections,*

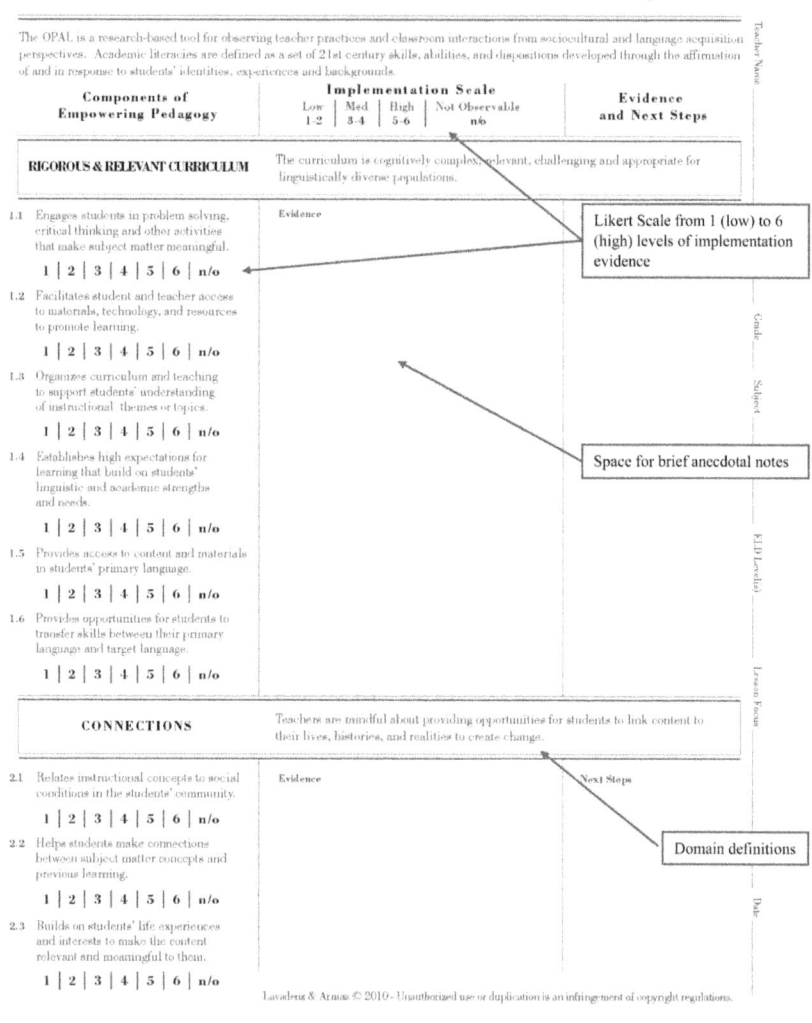

Figure 2.3 The OPAL form

comprehensibility and *interactions* – and the indicators were statistically determined through the multi-step validation process to measure practices that represent that domain. The full OPAL instrument form can be found in Appendix D.

The format of the OPAL form is designed to facilitate note-taking and the subsequent scoring of the levels of evidence that are represented in the six-point Likert scale. Each indicator may be scored low (one and two), middle (three and four) or high (five and six). We have found that these ranges have been useful for OPAL users as they gain familiarity with the form and with scoring and noting evidence. By using these low, middle and high ranges of implementation OPAL users can narrow down the range of evidence observed.

Gaining familiarity with the OPAL indicators

Table 2.1 contains the key terms for research-based practices that were used to develop the OPAL instrument. An OPAL user's first task is to gain familiarity with the OPAL indicators by looking for evidence of those practices in real time, whether it is a visit to a classroom of a welcoming teacher or in a virtual/video observation. The complete OPAL form appears in Appendix D. New users should carefully review the form, taking a moment to highlight the key terms that appear on Table 2.1. This table extracts the key terms from the 18 indicators to develop OPAL users' familiarity with the tool. More detailed practice with all four OPAL domains and their respective indicators is provided through the vignettes in Chapters 3–6.

Over the years, our OPAL Institute participants have gained familiarity with the OPAL instrument by engaging in a variety of activities in which they can practice taking anecdotal notes. They also practice scoring the OPAL using the six-point Likert scale accompanied by the OPAL descriptor rubric (Table 2.2).

The OPAL descriptor rubric provides an overview of each of the levels described in the OPAL's six-point Likert scale; Appendix C includes

Table 2.1 Key terms used in the OPAL indicators

Rigorous and relevant curriculum	Connections	Comprehensibility	Interactions
1.1 Problem solving/ critical thinking	2.1 Relates to students' social realities	3.1 Scaffolds instruction	4.1 Facilitates student autonomy
1.2 Access to materials, technology, resources	2.2 Helps students make connections	3.2 Amplifies student input	4.2 Modifies procedures to support learning
1.3 Organized curriculum and teaching	2.3 Makes learning relevant and meaningful	3.3 Explains key terms	4.3 Communicates subject matter knowledge
1.4 High expectations		3.4 Feedback/ checks for comprehension	
1.5 Access to content in L1		3.5 Informal assessment to adjust instruction	4.4 Uses flexible groupings
1.6 Transfer of skills			

Table 2.2 Overview of the OPAL descriptor rubric: Levels of practice as they correspond to the six-point Likert scale

Rating	Label	Description
6	Expert	The observed teacher behaviors, classroom context and interactions reflect an exceptional level of understanding of students' academic, developmental and linguistic needs. An extensive knowledge of the content area(s) is evidenced by thoughtful, integrated instructional planning, resulting in the consistent use of highly effective instructional practices that allow all students to access rigorous and relevant curriculum, culturally responsive methods and materials and equitable classroom interactions.
5	Accomplished	The observed teacher behaviors, classroom context and interactions reflect a consistent level of understanding of students' academic, developmental and linguistic needs. An in-depth knowledge of the content area(s) is evidenced by thoughtful, integrated instructional planning, resulting in the consistent use of effective instructional practices that allow all students to access rigorous and relevant curriculum, culturally responsive methods and materials and equitable classroom interactions.
4	Capable	The observed teacher behaviors, classroom context and interactions often reflect a sufficient level of understanding of students' academic, developmental and linguistic needs. A good working knowledge of the content area(s) is evidenced by thoughtful, integrated instructional planning, often resulting in the use of effective instructional practices that allow all students to access rigorous and relevant curriculum, culturally responsive methods and materials and equitable classroom interactions.
3	Developing	The observed teacher behaviors, classroom context and interactions sometimes reflect a sufficient level of understanding of students' academic, developmental and linguistic needs. A developing working knowledge of the content area(s) is evidenced by thoughtful, integrated instructional planning, sometimes resulting in the use of effective instructional practices that allow all students to access rigorous and relevant curriculum, culturally responsive methods and materials and equitable classroom interactions.
2	Apprentice	The observed teacher behaviors, classroom context and interactions reflect basic attempts towards understanding students' academic, developmental and linguistic needs. A basic working knowledge of the content area(s) is evidenced by disjointed instructional planning, often resulting in the limited use of effective instructional practices that allow all students to access rigorous and relevant curriculum, culturally responsive methods and materials and equitable classroom interactions.
1	Novice	The observed teacher behaviors, classroom context and interactions rarely or never reflect sufficient understanding of students' academic, developmental and linguistic needs. A minimal level of knowledge of the content area(s) is evidenced by disjointed instructional planning, consistently resulting in the limited use of effective instructional practices that allow all students to access rigorous and relevant curriculum, culturally responsive methods and materials and equitable classroom interactions.
N/O	Not observable	The skill or concept is not applicable in the context of this lesson/activity. It may be evident during another observation, but it was not observable or not applicable during this classroom visit.

the entire descriptor rubric, including specific levels of evidence for each of the indicators within the four OPAL domains. Chapters 3–6 will include activities for learning how to note and score evidence for the indicators in each specific domain. Table 2.2 introduces and defines the six levels of teacher expertise in the OPAL descriptor rubric.

Noting evidence on the OPAL form

Taking notes in the OPAL form's evidence column during observations *is not* like conducting ethnographic research. Nonetheless, there are several principles of ethnographic research that we adapt here so that observers can gather evidence from their 20–30 minute observations that they can use subsequently to score the numeric portion of the OPAL, should they and the observed teachers agree. These principles are:

- **Brevity:** In contrast with traditional forms of evidence-gathering, we recommend brief, even bulleted, examples of evidence gathered in the room, not scripted/verbatim notes of what teachers and/or students said, or exact moment-by-moment descriptions of classroom actions.
- **Accuracy:** If an OPAL user has not taken notes for a while, he or she might want to practice (either using a video or taking notes briefly in another setting) before conducting an actual observation. Once the observer and teacher have agreed on an observation time there will usually not be an opportunity to repeat that exact observation. Therefore, getting into the practice of note taking quickly is key. If the technology is available, observers may also type notes into an OPAL writeable form, such as online word, PDF or Excel formats.
- **Preparation:** Users should plan ahead to bring what is needed for their preferred manner of taking notes (e.g., pencils [with erasers], pens, laptop), as well as sufficient copies of the OPAL form and the observation schedule, if there will be more than one OPAL observation that day. They should also decide on a plan of action. Will they shift between the two pages of the OPAL? Will they start taking notes right away or practice 'reading the room' first? Users should also be sure to fill out the classroom information section prior to entering the room.
- **Precision:** OPAL users should use precise and descriptive words to document what they observe. For example, instead of writing 'classroom library', they might note the type and quantity of books in the library (e.g., 'large classroom library [200 + books] in several languages'); similarly, instead of 'computers', they might note 'computer section with 6 laptops'. Observers should be both brief and precise so that they will not need to rely on memory.
- **Focus:** The purpose of the OPAL observation is to observe instruction for English Learners in the context of a previously agreed-upon portion of a lesson in a specific content area. It might be easy to get

distracted by a fascinating conversation taking place between two students near the observation location, or to get caught up reading student essays on bulletin boards (as part of reading the room). Observers should maintain awareness of the short duration of the observation to make sure that they have enough time to observe instruction.

It is important to keep these key evidence-gathering 'techniques' in mind while gathering evidence with the OPAL tool. Our approach for gathering evidence of practices for English Learners is based on ensuring that observers enter the classroom with a *neutral stance*; that is to say, the observer has made no predetermined opinion about the nature of the classroom, the teacher or the students. The next section provides additional guiding strategies for OPAL observers.

Seeing what's there – The observation

Table 2.3 (The observation guide for OPAL domains) provides an overview of the central questions that observers need to keep in mind before, during and after the observation process.

Table 2.3 Observation guide for OPAL domains

OPAL domain	Description	Sources of evidence and guiding questions while observing
Rigorous and relevant curriculum	The curriculum is cognitively complex, relevant, challenging and appropriate for linguistically diverse populations.	The observer captures evidence of teaching and learning and scores implementation on the rating scale, ranging from one (low) to six (high). (See OPAL indicator descriptors.) Observer writes anecdotal notes stating what was seen, heard and said by either the teacher or the students. *Questions to guide the observation*: • What evidence indicates that the instructional practice is appropriate for students' grade level and/or language development level? • How are goals and objectives communicated to students? • How does the teacher communicate expectations to students? • What is the teacher's demeanor when approaching the class? Does he or she communicate respect and value for diversity? • What instructional program is offered in this classroom (Structured English Immersion? Mainstream English? Transitional Bilingual Program? Dual Language?) • What materials and sources are evident in the classroom? Are they in use? How is this determined? • How is language allocated in this classroom? Are there opportunities for students to use their primary language? If this is a BCLAD teacher, how does he or she use knowledge of the students' primary language to enhance and support delivery of the lesson?

Table 2.3 (Continued)

OPAL domain	Description	Sources of evidence and guiding questions while observing
Connections	Teachers are mindful about providing opportunities for students to link content to their lives, histories and realities.	The observer captures evidence of teaching and learning practices and scores implementation on the rating scale, ranging from low to high. (See OPAL indicator descriptors.) *Questions to guide the observation*: • What evidence exists in the classroom that students have had the opportunity to relate concepts to their social conditions and the realities of their community (evidence might include bulletin boards, posters, journals, teacher/student comments, etc.)? • What techniques elicit students' prior knowledge and/or learning and invite this to be part of the current lesson and/or activity? • How is students' previous learning acknowledged and utilized as a resource for the lesson? • What connections are made to capitalize on students' interests and experiences? • How are lessons/activities structured to increase student motivation?
Comprehensibility	Instruction allows for maximum student understanding and teachers utilize effective strategies to help students access content.	The observer captures evidence of teaching and learning practices and scores implementation on the rating scale, ranging from low to high. (See OPAL indicator descriptors.) *Questions to guide the observation*: • How does the teacher scaffold instruction so that all students can access the material? • How does the teacher 'recast' student language to validate response and extend student language ('i + 1' concept)? • How are graphic organizers or other visuals used so that students are part of the process and use these devices to practice language and skills in oral and written contexts? • What evidence exists in the classroom that shows how key terms and concepts are illustrated for students? • What type of questions and comments are provided to students as ongoing feedback during the lesson/activity? How do these questions help elicit student thinking and give the classroom teacher an understanding of whether students have grasped concepts? • What assessments are used during the lesson/activity? • What evidence exists that shows the teacher has made adjustments to the lesson/activity to accommodate for students' linguistic, cognitive and developmental needs?
Interactions	Varied participation structures allow for interactions that maximize engagement, leadership opportunities and access to the curriculum.	The observer captures evidence of teaching and learning practices and scores implementation on rating scale, ranging from low to high. (See OPAL indicator descriptors.) • The observer makes note of table and chair configuration, including independent and small group centers available in the classroom. • The observer looks for evidence of cooperative grouping (charts with roles and tasks for group work, group projects, group folders, baskets or bins to store ongoing group projects, etc.). • The observer looks for evidence of differentiated, small group instruction (list of small groups, list of group tasks, list of students working on planned, targeted mini-lessons, etc.). *Questions to guide the observation*: • What evidence exists that students are engaged in varied groupings? • How is lesson delivery sequenced to allow for student participation and interaction? • How are students given an opportunity to take leadership roles in the classroom?

Observing students during the OPAL observation

It is important to note that while the OPAL is focused primarily on teacher practices, the observer also watches for student engagement in the lesson, activity or tasks. All 18 indicators reflect that teachers are closely monitoring, interacting with and responding to the English Learners in their classrooms. As such, the observation guide in Table 2.3 identifies the ways in which the observer is also actively looking for evidence of students' engagement in and across the evidence of teachers' practices. Key questions to guide the observation of student engagement include:

- What evidence is there about students' comprehension of teacher talk/instructions/activities?
- How are students encouraged to be active listeners?
- How do students practice and interact with content in all four language domains: listening, speaking, reading and writing?
- How is the teacher monitoring student engagement?

Observer dispositions

The previous sections identify processes that develop the observational abilities and evidence-gathering abilities of OPAL observers. This section augments the 'nuts and bolts' adapted from the science of observing with consideration of the 'human' elements that make up the psychological stance of observers. These human elements are equally if not more important to gathering evidence, as a neutral dispositional stance builds a relationship of trust with the observed teachers – and this trust will be central to the conversations that happen *after* the observations. The planning meetings in which the observations are scheduled lay the foundation for subsequent professional development opportunities, including coaching, content-specific training and other forms of dialogue that contribute to expanding teacher professional learning about practices for English Learners.

OPAL observation etiquette

Ideally, the observation is scheduled by mutual agreement far in advance. This entails that the observer and the observed teacher have had prior conversations to determine the focus, intent and purpose of the observation. Based on conversations between the observer and the teacher, the teacher reflects upon and identifies the key practice area(s) that would be the focus and purpose of the observation, the potential OPAL domain(s) that they would like to prioritize and their intended outcome of the observation. The OPAL is intended to capture elements of instruction, classroom environment and student-to-teacher, teacher-to-student and student-to-student interactions regardless of where the teacher is in the lesson delivery. The OPAL does not require the observer to remain in the classroom for the entire duration of the lesson; rather it allows an observer to glean a quick impression of a particular lesson sequence as mutually agreed upon beforehand. Planning for the time/schedule and purpose of the observation eliminates conflicts in scheduling with the teacher and will allow teachers to tell students about the purpose of the visitation.

Prior to visiting the classroom, the observer should have information about the grade level(s), English Language Development (ELD) level(s) and the type of program (structured English immersion, transitional bilingual program, Dual Language program, mainstream English program). This information should be noted on the appropriate section of the OPAL form. Because the duration of the actual observation is very short (20–30 minutes), completing this section of the form in advance will save valuable observation time.

We use a 'detached' observer technique, whereby the observer enters the room and finds an unobtrusive place to sit and take notes; the observer should remain silent during the teacher's lesson so as not to interrupt instruction. Depending on where the teacher is in the lesson, we recommend limited interaction between the observer and the students or the teacher during the observation period, although a brief informal acknowledgement or greeting may take place at the beginning or end of the visit. *However, this introduction must be initiated by the teacher; even then it should not interrupt the lesson/activity.* The most important consideration is to dedicate the observation time to rating items on the OPAL and taking anecdotal notes as evidence of implementation.

Reading the room

An important part of the evidence in the observation period exists not only in what the teacher says and does, but also in the classroom environment itself. This means that the observer 'reads the room' as soon as he or she enters. Specific classroom evidence should be written in the anecdotal note section of the OPAL under the appropriate domain.

Questions to guide gathering evidence by 'reading the room':

- How are tables and chairs arranged (sign of group interactions)?
- What materials are available – books (core and supplemental), classroom library, technology (computers, teaching aids)? Are materials available in students' primary language(s)?
- What student work is visible – on bulletin boards/walls, in cubbies, on desk, in student notebooks?
- What teacher-generated text is displayed on bulletin boards or walls?
- What evidence is there of standards, goals and objectives communicated to students?
- What evidence is visible denoting long-term planning? What evidence is visible to inform the observer of the teaching and learning that have taken place in the classroom?

In the preceding pages, we have reviewed the key elements for beginning to observe teachers of English Learners. Next, we can begin to implement these key observation skills by applying them to a vignette.

Putting OPAL into Practice: Noting Evidence with a Vignette

Before we begin to identify the evidence from our first vignette, it is important to clarify the California context from which these classroom examples are drawn and to outline the structure of the vignettes. Because these classroom observations occurred in California, content standards are specific to those adopted by the California State Board of Education: (1) Common Core State Standards (CCSS) for English Language Arts and Literacy in History/Social Studies, Science and Technical Subjects and Mathematics (CDE, 2010/2013); (2) Next Generation Science Standards (CDE, 2013); (3) History Social Science Content Standards (CDE, 1998/2000); and (4) English Language Development (ELD) Standards (CDE, 2012). As identified in Chapter 1, each state determines the standards that are taught in schools, and most have adopted the same or similar Common Core standards for English language arts and math. As such, we expect that readers will (1) recognize similarities in the content *and* language standards connections presented for each vignette and (2) engage in the proposed 'reading and scoring' steps to examine practices for English Learners using the OPAL indicators.

Ms Mack's[1] vignette identifies the grade level, the specific California Common Core State Standard (2010), and the specific California English Language Development Standard (CDE, 2012) that correspond to the lesson observed for the vignette. It is important to note that all the vignettes and/or snapshots are taken from actual classrooms.

Process for noting evidence with Ms Mack

Now we will use the OPAL resources to note evidence with Ms Mack, our first vignette. As you 'enter' into Ms Mack's classroom by reading the vignette, you (the 'observer/reader') can note evidence by *underlining* practices that are aligned to key words in the OPAL indicator. Using the OPAL form while noting evidence will help you gain familiarity with the OPAL instrument.

To begin, return to the OPAL form that you used to underline the key terms (use it either electronically or print it out), and review the underlined key terms for each of the indicators. For Ms Mack's vignette, in addition to underlining some of the practices, we have also numbered the practices and coded them in the 'anecdotal notes' margin. Thus, the number that immediately follows an underlined practice can be tracked with a key word that is associated with an OPAL indicator or indicators. This activity is intended to provide practice in noting evidence and 'seeing' the evidence in the vignette. Chapters 3–6 will provide more in-depth practice with each of the four domains and the indicators associated with them.

Context for the vignette

Content Area: English Language Development (ELD), Vocabulary Development/Idiomatic Expressions
Grade: 2

State Standards

California Common Core State Standards – Grade 2

Reading Standards for Literature: **RL2.7**
Speaking and Listening: **SL2.1.a**
Language Standards: **Anchor Standard 5**

California English Language Development Standards – Grade 2

Part I: Interacting in Meaningful Ways: **2.I.A.1, 2.I.A.4, 2.I.B.5, 2.I.B.6 2.I.C.9, 2.I.C.11, 2.I.C.12**
Part II: Learning About How English Works: **2.II.B.3**

The Common Core State Standards and the English Language Development Standards listed above were considered in the design of this lesson. Please see *Notes* after the lesson for the complete text of all these components.

School context

This is an urban fringe school with a total of 730 students enrolled in grades K–eight. The student population is 99.7% Hispanic. Of the students enrolled, 49% are English Learners (ELs), 29.9% are Fluent-English Proficient (FEP) and 20.7% are ELs Redesignated Fluent-English Proficient (RFEP); 99% of the students receive free/reduced-price meals. This is a school-wide Title I program.

Lesson context

Students are part of the Spanish Transitional Bilingual Program. Students are in Early Intermediate and Intermediate English proficiency levels. ELD instruction is provided through team teaching with a focus on social studies/science content vocabulary followed by a daily ELD focus. The focus of the lesson is on vocabulary development and idiomatic expressions. Note: idiomatic expressions appear in the ELD standards at the third grade level, however, Ms Mack decided to modify her designated ELD lesson for her second grade students when she noticed that there was confusion regarding specific English idioms that appeared in the core English Language Arts text.

Classroom vignette: Ms Mack

<u>Students have access to a Spanish and English classroom library, leveled readers, bilingual place value charts,</u>[1] and science sets. Math and science centers are available to students. There is a read-along rug in one corner of the room where students sit during whole group instruction. <u>Bilingual word walls, bilingual place value charts,</u>[2] idiomatic expression charts, word analysis charts, student work and interactive charts are displayed throughout the classroom. <u>The seating arrangement is organized to allow students to have access to multiple groupings.</u>[3] There is a <u>projector/document reader</u>[1] in the front of the classroom.

As students sit on the read-along rug, *Ms Mack* <u>begins her lesson by reviewing</u>[4] what they have been learning on idiomatic expressions and shares with the students that they will read a book with examples of idiomatic expressions. The teacher asks the students, 'What do we know about idiomatic expressions?' One student shares, 'When I was watching T.V., I saw a show and it had the idiomatic expression, 'Cut to the chase'. Ms Mack extends on the student's response by asking the rest of the students to explain what 'Cut to the chase' means. Several of the students respond orally in unison to her prompt using Choral Response, <u>'To get to the point'. Ms Mack reminds the students that every time they find, share, remember, and use idiomatic expressions in their writings, they will receive credit in the Academic Language Proficiency Chart: L1 and L2.</u>[5] She writes down the names of the students who shared examples of idiomatic expressions during whole group instruction. She remembers that in yesterday's lesson one student shared an idiomatic expression in Spanish. Ms Mack asks the student to share the idiomatic expression in Spanish. The student shares, '<u>Deja el gato ir de la bolsa. (Let the cat out of the bag.)</u>'[2] Ms Mack expands on this example and asks the students, 'What does this mean? Does it mean you are really getting a cat and pulling it out of the bag?' The students share out loud, 'No, let a secret out'. Ms Mack responds, 'To let out a secret. Very good! <u>So he was able to use his Spanish to help him.</u>[2] That's excellent. So it means, to let out a secret'. After the students share examples of idiomatic expressions, Ms Mack begins reading the book, *More Parts* by Tedd Arnold. She asks the students, 'Can we use our knowledge of idiomatic expressions to make predictions?' <u>She engages the students in making predictions about the book based on the illustrations.</u>[6] They focus on an illustration of a boy with an image of an X-ray machine showing a broken heart. Ms Mack asks with questions to *encourage students justify their predictions*[5] about what is happening in the illustration. Students chorally respond that there is a broken heart in the X-ray machine. Ms Mack asks follow-up questions to elicit student input on, 'Why would the heart be broken?' She poses a question to the students:

Student: Because he fell.

Teacher: Okay. When he fell he broke his heart? What do you think? Could that really happen?

Students: No!

Teacher: So, what is he doing now? Very quickly, you will turn to your partner to make a prediction about what you think this book is going to be about. It is called, *More Parts*. How do we start a prediction?

Student: I predict ...

Teacher: Good! I predict ...

Ms Mack kneels down on the read along rug to work individually with a pair to elicit their predictions about the book. <u>She engages in a one-on-one teacher-student discussion</u>[3, 5] with one of the students:

Student: All of his parts will fall down and, and the doctor's going to fix him.

Anecdotal notes:

Coding for key practices aligned with OPAL indicators

[1] access to materials/technology
[2] access to primary language
[3] partner/multiple grouping
[4] assessing for prior knowledge
[3, 5] partner work with critical thinking
[6] scaffolding
[7] Adjusts instruction

Teacher: Oh! What gave you the idea that it was going to be about broken parts?

Student: Because at first hmmm, it was his heart and then it was his hand.

Teacher: Very good! <u>Is there anything else in the text that helped you infer that this is going to be about parts?</u>[6]

Student: Yeah, the title of the book.

Teacher: [*addressing all students*] Remember, does the title help us make predictions? <u>What else helps us make predictions? The title, the illustrations, pictures, and anything else you have with you that you carry with you every day ... your what?</u>[6]

Students: [*choral response*] Prior knowledge.

Teacher: Yes, your prior knowledge. Very good!

After the prediction activity, Ms Mack begins reading the book. She <u>pauses after reading a page to ask questions for student input to check on students' understanding of the story and clarify vocabulary used in the book.</u>[5] After reading a couple of pages of the book, she transitions into another activity related to idiomatic expressions. The teacher reviews the idiomatic expression of the week. Using <u>a projector to display the idiomatic expression on the white board,</u>[1] she shares, 'Draw the line'. Ms Mack elicits students' input by asking questions to explain the image related to the idiomatic expression. She instructs the students that they will '<u>read and look at context clues to come up with what we infer this idiomatic expression</u>[5] means'. One student shares, 'I think that the idiomatic expression "draw the line" means that you're hmm, get your own personal space. Because they are drawing a line between each other to stay back'. Ms Mack involves the students in <u>a choral reading of the idiomatic expression of the week and asks the students to 'read with fluency'.</u>[3,5] After reading the prompt, she instructs the students to turn to their partners to make inferences of what the expression means. She reminds the students to use *sentence frames* to discuss the idiomatic expression with their partners. <u>Ms Mack makes adjustments to support the learning of a new student who recently joined the class by providing him with a list of sentence frames to guide his discussion of the idiomatic expression with his partner</u>.[3,4,7] After the pair debrief, the students return to their small group tables to develop a quick write on an occasion when they used idiomatic expressions. The teacher reiterates the use of sentence frames to begin their quick write, 'An example of a time when ... One occasion when ... ' Ms Mack <u>walks around the classroom to provide one-on-one support to students writing their quick write.</u>[3,5,7]

Anecdotal notes:

Coding for key practices aligned with OPAL indicators

[1] access to materials/technology
[2] access to primary language
[3] partner/multiple grouping
[4] assessing for prior knowledge
[3,5] partner work with critical thinking
[6] scaffolding
[7] Adjusts instruction

Note: Below is the complete text of the Common Core State Standards English Language Arts (2010) and English Language Development Standards (2012) that are relevant to the lesson designed by Ms Mack.

California Common Core State Standards

- **Reading Standards for Literature – Grade 2 (RL)**
  RL2.7: Use information gained from the illustrations and words in a print or digital text to demonstrate understanding of its characters, setting or plot.

- Speaking and Listening Standards – Grade 2 (SL)

  SL2.1.a: Participate in collaborative conversations with diverse partners about grade 2 topics and texts with peers and adults in small and larger groups.

  a. Follow agreed-upon rules for discussions (e.g., gaining the floor in respectful ways, listening to others with care, speaking one at a time about the topics and texts under discussion).

- Language Standards – Grade 2 (L)

  Anchor Standard 5: Demonstrate understanding of word relationships and nuances in word meanings.

California English Language Development Standards – Grade 2

Part I: Interacting in Meaningful Ways

- A. Collaborative
  - 2.I.A.1: Exchanging information and ideas
    Contribute to class, group and partner discussions, including sustained dialogue by listening attentively, following turn-taking rules, asking relevant questions, affirming others and adding relevant information.
  - 2.I.A.4: Adapting language choices
    Adjust language choices (e.g., vocabulary, use of dialogue and so on) according to purpose (e.g., persuading, entertaining), task and audience (e.g., peers versus adults), with moderate support from peers or adults.
- B. Interpretive
  - 2.I.B.5: Listening actively
    Demonstrate active listening to read-alouds and oral presentations by asking and answering detailed questions, with oral sentence frames and occasional prompting and support.
  - 2.I.B.6: Reading/viewing closely
    Describe ideas, phenomena (e.g., how earthworms eat) and text elements (e.g., setting, events) in greater detail based on understanding of a variety of grade-level texts and viewing of multimedia, with moderate support.

- C. Productive
  - **2.I.C.9: Presenting**
    Plan and deliver brief oral presentations on a variety of topics (e.g., retelling a story, describing an animal).
  - **2.I.C.11: Supporting opinions**
    Support opinions by providing good reasons and increasingly detailed textual evidence (e.g., providing examples from the text) or relevant background knowledge about the content.
  - **2.I.C.12: Selecting language resources**
    a. Retell texts and recount experiences using complete sentences and key words.

Part II: Learning About How English Works

- A. Expanding and Enriching Ideas
  - **2.II.B.3.a: Using verbs and verb phrases**
    a. Use a growing number of verb types (e.g., doing, saying, being/having, thinking/feeling) with increasing independence.

Reviewing and revising anecdotal notes

Now that you have reviewed the evidence noted in Ms Mack's vignette, you can return to the notes and check for accuracy as well as for any missed evidence. This is a good practice to keep in mind in the later chapters and particularly in 'real time' observations, as the 20–30 minutes go by very quickly. Then, return to the OPAL form to do another quick scan of the key terms associated with the OPAL indicators. You will continue and expand on this process in Chapter 3, which focuses on the domain of *comprehensibility*.

Note

(1) All teachers' names are pseudonyms, as are the schools. Teachers have granted formal permission to be video recorded. Vignettes and snapshots in this book are based on the transcriptions of the video-recorded lessons.

3 OPAL Domain 3: Comprehensibility

> *It was very powerful to be able to examine and discuss how teachers provide opportunities for students to understand and access content. [The OPAL] allowed us to look for specific evidence and identify what's happening in classrooms to help refine instruction for English Learners.*
> *– OPAL Institute participant (English Learner Specialist: Teacher on Special Assignment)*

Educators work diligently to plan for and prepare curricular units, lessons and activities. When meeting the needs of a culturally and linguistically diverse group of learners, it is imperative to ensure that what is being taught is accessible to all students so that it results in maximum processing, comprehension and application of conceptual knowledge. Two focus questions will prepare us for the content of this chapter:

> **FOCUS QUESTIONS:**
>
> 1. What does *comprehensibility* mean in the context of teaching English Learners?
> 2. How is maximum *comprehensibility* for English Learners evidenced in the classroom? What information can be recorded and analyzed using the OPAL *comprehensibility* domain indicators?

Introduction

In this chapter we provide the reader with background information and examples of research-based practices that exemplify elements and indicators for the OPAL comprehensibility domain. Although this is the third of the four OPAL domains (see Figure 3.1), we introduce *comprehensibility* first because it has been emphasized the most in teacher preparation programs, site- and district-level training sessions and resource materials for teachers of English Learners.

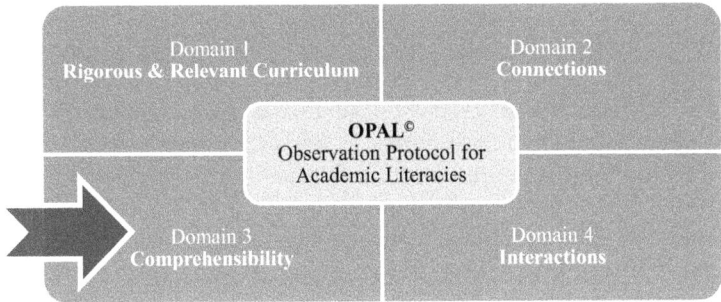

Figure 3.1 The Observation Protocol for Academic Literacies (OPAL) domains

First, we provide background information for each indicator, including brief classroom snapshots highlighting how key characteristics for each indicator might be evidenced in a classroom context. Next, we present teacher reflection questions and an OPAL descriptor rubric to assist educators in exploring how different levels of implementation of each of the OPAL indicators for Domain 3 (Comprehensibility) might appear from lower to higher levels of classroom practice. Finally, the reader will practice using the OPAL instrument using written vignettes, descriptions of lessons from our actual classroom observations. These vignettes will give the reader the opportunity to identify objective sources of evidence (anecdotal notes), to determine level(s) of implementation of the various indicators and to mark these on the OPAL Descriptor Rubric. The OPAL can be used by a teacher to reflect on their practice during the lesson planning stage or after delivering a lesson. Teachers can cite sources of evidence and provide a self-rating or seek opportunities to refine lesson planning by reflecting on each of the indicators identified for this domain. Additionally, an external observer or coach may document sources of evidence while observing classroom practice to rate levels of implementation based on each indicator. The vignettes, coupled with the foundational content presented in this chapter, will allow the user to begin to build proficiency toward ascertaining inter-rater reliability and confidently describing classroom practices and student–teacher actions and interactions related to this domain.

What Does *Comprehensibility* Mean in the Context of Teaching English Learners?

As defined in the OPAL tool, *comprehensibility* for English learners is attained when *instruction allows for maximum student understanding and teachers utilize effective strategies to help students access content*. To ensure English Learners *comprehend and apply* instructional concepts and skills, educators design instructional cycles that include ample opportunities for developing and explaining concepts. These cycles include engaging students in productive questioning and ample opportunities to practice academic language to describe and interpret concepts orally and in writing. Additive approaches to learning content and language are essential characteristics of equitable and differentiated instruction for English Learners. They include building on students' academic and linguistic strengths based on their English learner profiles and language proficiency levels to amplify their contributions to academic discussions and tasks. Five key indicators of comprehensibility for English Learners are outlined in Table 3.1. As you review Table 3.1, we invite the reader to engage in the 'Eliciting Prior Knowledge Activity' (Box 3.1) to conduct a quick preview of the domain and its corresponding indicators.

Table 3.1 Key Indicators for OPAL Domain 3: Comprehensibility

Opal domain	Indicators
Domain 3: Comprehensibility	3.1 Uses scaffolding strategies and devices (e.g., outlines, webs, semantic maps, compare/contrast charts, 'Know/Want to Know/Learned' chart) to make subject matter understandable.
	3.2 Amplifies student input by: questioning/ restating/ rephrasing/expanding/contextualizing.
	3.3 Explains key terms, clarifies idiomatic expressions, uses gestures and/or visuals to illustrate concepts.
	3.4 Provides frequent feedback and checks for comprehension.
	3.5 Uses informal assessments of student learning to adjust instruction while teaching.

BOX 3.1. ELICITING PRIOR KNOWLEDGE ACTIVITY

✓ Individually, *list* of as many strategies or approaches you can think of for making content comprehensible for English Learners.
✓ *Compare* your list with a colleague *and record* ideas that extend your thinking, or questions that arise as you review your lists.
✓ Next, *read* each OPAL indicator for Domain 3: Comprehensibility (Indicators 3.1–3.5).
✓ *Highlight* or underline key words/phrases for each of the indicators.
✓ Make a *list of any questions* you have about the indicators or key terms.

Getting to Know Each Indicator for the Comprehensibility Domain

In the sections that follow we explore each indicator in detail and introduce illustrative classroom snapshots. Expand and deepen your knowledge about each OPAL Domain 3 (Comprehensibility) indicator as you read each description below.

Indicator 3.1: Uses scaffolding strategies and devices

Teaching builds on learners' existing strengths and targets new learning goals based on an identification of a student's zone of proximal development (ZPD), or the learning space that exposes students to skills and knowledge that have not yet been learned, yet are within reach (Van Lier, 1996; Vygotsky, 1978). A scaffold for learning can be defined as a temporary device or strategy that supports learners in developing new knowledge and skills to transfer them to other contexts with increased levels of independence as evidenced by examples underlined in Figure 3.2. Additional examples include the use of outlines, webs, semantic maps, compare/contrast charts or know/want to know/learned chart to make subject matter understandable. Supports can be provided by adults or more capable peers and include verbal, procedural or instructional scaffolding (Bruner, 1983; Echevarria & Short, 2004; Gibbons, 2015, 2018; Walqui & Van Lier, 2010; Zwiers *et al.*, 2014).

Effective strategies for providing strategic support for English Learners include the use of appropriately scaffolded instruction according to

---

Classroom Snapshot
Grade Level: 2
Content Area: Mathematics (Structured English Immersion Program)
English Language Proficiency Level(s): Expanding (Intermediate)

Ms. Gomez is completing a unit on fractions with her students. She has <u>used many graphic organizers throughout the unit</u> to scaffold and capture students' conceptual understanding prior to beginning the unit and through its progression. Additionally, she has consistently <u>used interactive writing strategies to record and model the structure of informative/explanatory texts</u> in order to explain learned concepts. Together, the class recorded transition words for this type of text. As she presents a closing lesson, <u>students refer to the multiple organizers to verbalize how their understanding of fractions has changed over time and how they recorded their learning using organizers</u>. During this closing lesson, <u>students work with partners to create a four-quadrant idea map to synthesize their learning</u> by explaining and comparing fractions, orally and in writing.

Figure 3.2 Classroom snapshot/OPAL Indicator 3.1

students' developmental, linguistic and academic levels (Bruner, 1983; Cazden, 1986, 2001; Gibbons, 2009, 2015, 2018; Walqui & Van Lier, 2010). The end goal is to move learners toward independence so that they no longer need scaffolds to access and comprehend content. As such, educators intentionally plan for and maximize the use of scaffolding strategies and devices to allow for maximum comprehension of subject matter, and carefully consider what students already know, including their cultural knowledge and primary language. Conceptual organizers such as diagrams, compare/contrast charts, cognitive dictionaries and other graphic organizers provide opportunities for students to preview or review content. Additionally, they promote ways to synthesize information and represent concepts or new learning in multiple forms, including oral rehearsal of information as a bridge to writing.

Indicator 3.2: Amplifies student input by questioning/restating/rephrasing/expanding/ contextualizing

An interactive and responsive learning environment not only provides students with extensive language input, but also allows for maximum student output, allowing a teacher to analyze oral and written language production and gauge students' understanding of content (Gibbons, 2006, 2015; Zwiers *et al.*, 2014). As a result, a teacher can mediate instruction and elaborate on student input *and* output through questioning, rephrasing, expanding and/or contextualizing for students (see Figure 3.3).

Classroom Snapshot
Grade Level: 8
Content Area: Mathematics (Structured English Immersion Program)
English Language Proficiency Level: Expanding (Intermediate)

Mr. Cobbs has just asked his students to complete a written metacognitive reflection to record their understanding in response to the question: 'How is solving for a system of inequalities different from solving a system of equation?' He provides independent writing time while <u>he walks around to hear students' oral responses to the question in order to mediate what they will write.</u> As he listens to individual responses, <u>he asks follow-up questions that develop students' conceptual understanding but also challenge them to use the precise academic vocabulary</u> to describe their learning, both orally and in writing. He <u>rephrases responses he hears and asks students to repeat the precise or expanded version orally prior to incorporating it in their written response</u>.

Figure 3.3 Classroom snapshot/OPAL Indicator 3.2

This 'just-in-time scaffolding' is responsive to English Learners' needs as they are engaged in learning and making sense of content. Because this real-time micro-level scaffolding is dependent on how a specific learning episode unfolds, a teacher cannot plan explicitly for how to respond. We provide several important guidelines for best practice focused on uplifting student's academic and linguistic strengths while maximizing their opportunities to process, deepen and extend content learning. These include:

- Analyze students' oral or written input and output to listen for intended meanings in order to extend their understanding of a concept.
- Reword (or recast) students' responses using an appropriate academic or technical term to provide a more precise explanation of the concept to be learned. Expect that students repeat or recast the information with a partner or a small group using the precise academic language so that they rehearse it orally and continue to appropriate the language or clarify the concept.
- Provide wait time for students to think and respond to questions. Monitor and vary who responds to questions.
- Ask questions that allow students to extend their oral or written responses in order to make meaning of what they are learning.
- Keep questions that monitor level of comprehension, or understanding of content, at an appropriate level of difficulty so that most students can experience a high degree of success.
- Ask students to comment or elaborate on one another's answers.

All of the above occurs within a learning environment that engages students in interpretive, productive and collaborative opportunities to develop expertise in all domains of language: listening, speaking, reading and writing, with an explicit emphasis on metacognitive and metalinguistic processes. Metacognition and metalinguistic processes are two distinct yet interrelated constructs that facilitate opportunities for students to engage with oral, written and multimodal texts to maximize comprehensibility. Metacognition refers to one's ability to recognize, monitor and act on information by thinking about learning processes, planning, monitoring and evaluating (Chamot & O'Malley, 1994; Cohen, 1998). Strategies to develop metacognition include predicting/inferring, self-questioning, monitoring/clarifying, evaluating, summarizing and visualizing. Metalinguistic awareness includes an understanding of and ability to analyze and compare language use and features, including grammatical, syntactic, phonological or morphological rules and vocabulary (Achugar et al., 2007; National Academies of Sciences, Engineering and Medicine, 2017).

Indicator 3.3: Explains key terms, clarifies idiomatic expressions, uses gestures and/or visuals to illustrate concepts

In addition to using visuals, graphic organizers and manipulatives, other practices also increase comprehensibility and access to content for English Learners across differing language proficiency levels. Teachers should identify key vocabulary for content and language development to ensure understanding of these concepts or terms (see Figure 3.4). It is critical to provide multiple opportunities for students to use and internalize academic vocabulary as well as language structures. These must be taught in meaningful contexts and with purposeful opportunities to examine language use in oral and written text. In addition, it is important to emphasize metalinguistic processes related to vocabulary development, such as analysis of semantic features, word associations, figurative language or multiple-meaning words (Enright, 2013; Fang & Schleppegrell, 2010; Zipke *et al.*, 2009). Explicit teaching of key terms should be balanced with ample opportunity to study words in context in order to make meaning of text. This maximizes comprehensibility during directed instruction and scaffolds comprehension during independent reading (Brinton *et al.*, 1989; Carlo *et al.*, 2004; Krashen, 1982).

Classroom Snapshot
Grade: K
Content Area: History/Social Studies (Structured English Immersion Program)
English Language Proficiency Level: Emerging (Beginning)

Students in Mrs. Garcia's classroom are seated on the rug. They've just returned from taking a walk around their school to identify roles of different school personnel. Mrs. Garcia tells the class that they will be exploring how a school community works together to help each other. <u>She adds the word 'community' to the class word chart and proceeds to follow her routine for introducing key vocabulary</u> *where she pronounces the word. She asks the students to repeat the word to identify sounds they hear and know how to write. Then, she draws lines on the chart that represent each letter of the word. She pronounces the word again and writes it on the chart. She* <u>asks the Spanish-speaking English Learners in her class if any of them have heard of the word in Spanish</u> *'comunidad.' She praises students for making the connection to the English word 'community' and tells them they are brilliant for noticing the similarities of the words. Next, she proceeds to complete* <u>her routine for introducing vocabulary – (1) identify the word; (2) recall where the word may have been heard before and predict what it may mean; (3) write a brief definition using language elicited from the students; and (4) generate a sample sentence, together with students.</u> *Mrs. Garcia transitions to the next part of the lesson where she asks students to work in small groups to draw pictures of the different school personnel and brainstorm ideas of how each person helps support the school community.*

Figure 3.4 Classroom snapshot/OPAL Indicator 3.3

When a teacher establishes consistent language learning routines that embed intentional reflection of language use, it heightens English Learners' awareness of their application of language skills in context. Furthermore, it allows students to analyze and talk about language and helps draw their attention to differences and similarities between written and spoken discourse. Oral discourse includes specific dimensions such as nonverbal communication, tone, intonation, audience and purpose; whereas written discourse requires additional skills to develop and interpret written communication such as the ability to recognize, anticipate and/or use text structure (e.g. sequencing, cause/effect, compare/contract), cohesive devices (e.g. transitional words) and discipline-specific language. Teachers benefit from being aware of their discourse behaviors and how they may support or impede comprehensibility for English learners.

Indicator 3.4: Provides feedback and checks for comprehension

When explicit learning goals are shared with students, both teacher and learner can engage in a cycle of feedback and checks for comprehension that help determine and advance progress toward achieving learning goals (see Figure 3.5). A context conducive to feedback and checks for comprehension includes the following:

- Makes clear the purpose of comprehension checks so that students understand the benefits of monitoring their ongoing learning.
- Offers all students, especially culturally and linguistically diverse learners, a safe space for receiving and responding to feedback, both from the teacher and other students.
- Chunks information or input to incorporate consistent checks for comprehension by stopping at regular intervals for students to process content.
- Establishes routines to equalize how comprehension checks are conducted and who receives feedback.
- Distinguishes between comprehension checks and procedural tasks. The main focus is on the clarification of content processing and language use. When needed, the teacher provides corrective feedback to eliminate misconceptions about content or language learning.
- Includes teacher-guided as well as student self-checks (metacognitive checks) for comprehension.

A critical consideration for teachers of English Learners is how to differentiate expected student output during checks for comprehension based on students' language proficiency while simultaneously maintaining expectations for conceptual understanding. One research-based approach is referred to as the 'preview-review' method (Ovando *et al.*,

> *Classroom Snapshot*
> *Grade: 7*
> *Content Area: English Language Arts (Structured English Immersion Program)*
> *English Language Proficiency Level(s): Expanding (Intermediate)*
>
> *Over the course of the first semester Mr. Hidalgo has introduced and developed Reciprocal Teaching to help students interpret and discuss text. He has explicitly modeled, and developed students' skills in each of the four steps of this process: (1) Predict; (2) question; (3) clarify; and (4) summarize. In planning for instruction <u>Mr. Hidalgo determines how to chunk text passages to maximize opportunities for feedback on comprehension of the text by BOTH himself and peers.</u> During each learning episode <u>Mr. Hidalgo listens to the type of questions students are generating about the text and mediates accuracy of responses and depth of questioning.</u> When misconceptions occur, <u>he prompts students to re-read a section of the text</u>. Additionally, Mr. Hidalgo <u>records words or phrases from the text that are unclear</u> to many students in the class. He <u>keeps a word wall that includes Spanish cognates</u> that is responsive to students' needs. He expects students to utilize these key words/phrases when summarizing the text, orally and in writing.*

Figure 3.5 Classroom snapshot/OPAL Indicator 3.4

2003). In this method, new concepts are previewed, or introduced, at the beginning of a unit or lesson, using the English Learner's primary language. This increases the English Learner's comprehension of content presented in English during the lesson. At the completion of a lesson or unit, a review of what was learned is conducted using the student's primary language; this review may be either teacher-directed or student-led. The preview-review method provides an excellent method of checking for comprehension and is more effective than translating concepts or content during lesson delivery because it helps students become familiar with the content prior to the presentation of the lesson. Consequently, it allows students to concentrate on understanding the lesson which leads to increased comprehensibility and language learning.

Indicator 3.5: Uses informal assessments of student learning to adjust instruction while teaching

Another key element in monitoring and supporting maximum student comprehensibility is the use of informal assessments to adjust instruction while teaching (see Figure 3.6). We define informal assessment as teacher-mediated, ongoing opportunities during a learning episode to determine the extent of students' learning. Teachers can develop informal assessments and create opportunities to assess English Learners based on their level(s) of English proficiency with an emphasis on the ability to communicate content knowledge both orally and in writing.

> *Classroom Snapshot*
> *Grade Level: 10*
> *Content Area: Science (Structured English Immersion Program)*
> *English Language Proficiency Level(s): Emerging (Beginning) thru Expanding (Intermediate)*
>
> *For the duration of the unit on DNA and Protein Synthesis, Mr. Pierce implements the <u>use of Interactive Notebooks</u> wherein students record information in two ways: (1) Input (left side of notebook): notes, pictures, highlights from the text; and (2) personal connections (right side of notebook): Predictions, reactions, and synthesis of information.*
>
> *<u>As part of his daily routine, Mr. Pierce interacts with small groups of students, reviews notebook entries, and identifies students' conceptual understandings/misunderstandings.</u> Based on this information <u>he conducts mini-lessons or review sessions to ensure that students comprehend key concepts</u> and are able to synthesize information orally and in writing.*

Figure 3.6 Classroom snapshot/OPAL Indicator 3.5

Examples of informal assessments include:

- Teacher observations.
- Anecdotal notes of student progress.
- Visual, oral or written prompts that ask students to provide a synthesis of information.
- Cloze sentence completion to synthesize a key idea.
- Informal check-ins with individual students or small groups.
- Quick writes.
- Oral or written summaries.
- Whiteboard or technology-based 'in the moment' quiz responses.
- Metacognitive self-reflection journals or logs.

The California English Language Arts/English Language Development Framework (2014) details two purposes for assessment: (1) Formative (assessment *for* learning) defined as the provision of 'information about student learning minute-by-minute, day-to-day and week-to-week so that teachers continuously adapt instruction to meet students' specific needs and secure progress'; and (2) summative (assessment *of* learning) intended to 'provide information on students' current levels of achievement after a period of learning has occurred' (CA ELA/ELD Framework, 2014: 822–823).

Teachers of English Learners utilize informal assessments as part of their formative assessment approach, to identify and act upon evidence about students' acquisition of knowledge and skills as well as their language use during the learning process (Heritage, 2010; Swaffield, 2011; Walqui & Heritage, 2012). Alvarez *et al.* (2014) examine how formative assessment can be used to bolster instructional experiences for English Learners in the era of Common Core and other 'next generation' standards. Additionally, they propose the following research-based guiding principles for effective formative assessment for English Learners:

- Promotes student learning.
- Elicits evidence of learning through a variety of tasks.
- Changes the roles of teachers and students.
- Uses learning progressions to anchor learning goals and monitor learning.
- Results in meaningful feedback and adjustments to improve instruction for students.
- Enables students to become self-regulated and autonomous learners.

These principles serve to anchor the importance of OPAL Indicator 3.5: *uses informal assessments of student learning to adjust instruction while teaching.* This is at the heart of planning for, delivering, monitoring and supporting English Learners to obtain maximum comprehensibility.

How Can We Determine What Evidence We See in Observing for the OPAL Comprehensibility Domain?

In this section we will explore two classrooms using written vignettes. The reader is asked to think about each of the OPAL Domain 3 (Comprehensibility) indicators while reading the vignette. Use the right-hand margin to note detailed anecdotal evidence observed in each classroom vignette. For a review of how to identify and record objective anecdotal evidence, see Chapter 2. The following steps are recommended when engaging in this learning experience:

Before reading the vignettes focused on the comprehensibility domain:

- Review the overall definition of this domain, along with the specific indicators (Table 3.1).
- Underline the key words/phrases for each indicator.

Reading and scoring:

- Step 1: Read each written vignette and record anecdotal evidence.
- Step 2: Review the criteria delineated in the OPAL scoring rubric for this domain and use your anecdotal evidence to assign a rating.

After scoring:

- Compare your scores to those provided in this text.
- Identify additional sources of evidence for each indicator.
- Discuss results and implications for classroom practice.

OPAL Domain 3: Comprehensibility – Reflection Questions

Several questions can guide the reader in examining how teaching and learning are occurring in these classroom contexts in order for students to obtain maximum comprehensibility. In particular, *how does the classroom context ...*

- Include frequent checks for understanding?
- Deliver instruction that scaffolds the task by using visuals, graphic organizers and demonstrations to clarify concepts?
- Clarify and expand students' oral and written output?
- Provide multiple opportunities for students to use and appropriate academic discourse?
- Provide linguistically appropriate instruction by questioning and identifying tasks appropriate to each student's level of language proficiency?
- Informally assess students' understanding during lesson delivery to adjust instruction based on this formative assessment?

Reading and Scoring STEP 1: Read Each Vignette and Note Anecdotal Evidence Focused on OPAL Domain 3: Comprehensibility

Context for vignettes

The vignettes presented here were developed based on actual classroom observations. Pseudonyms are used to respect each teacher's commitment to creating opportunities for transparent, objective and reflective examination of classroom practices for English Learner students. The context for each set of vignettes is provided to give the reader an overall picture of factors that may have influenced decision-making processes, delivery of instruction and classroom practices. These include content area, grade level, English Learner language proficiency level(s) and focus content standards.

Because these classroom observations occurred in California, content standards are specific to those adopted by the California State Board of Education: (1) Common Core State Standards (CCSS) for English Language Arts and Literacy in History/Social Studies, Science and Technical Subjects and Mathematics (CDE, 2010, 2013); (2) Next Generation Science Standards (CDE, 2013); (3) History Social Science Content Standards (CDE, 1998, 2000); and (4) English Language Development (ELD) Standards (CDE, 2012). Nationally, each state determines the standards that are taught in schools. A number of states across the nation have adopted the same or similar Common Core standards for English and math while others have revised, edited or created other versions to respond to their state context. As such, we expect that readers will (1) recognize similarities in the content *and* language standards connections presented for each vignette and (2) engage in the proposed 'reading and scoring' steps to examine practices for English Learners using the OPAL indicators.

Content focus and factors

> **Content area:** Science, Integrated ELD[1]
>
> **Grade:** 3
>
> **Language proficiency level:** Expanding (Intermediate)[2]

STANDARDS CONNECTION

Next Generation Science Standards for California Public Schools[3] – Grade 3

Disciplinary Core Idea: 3-PS2.B: Types of Interactions (Physical Science):

3-PS2.B: Types of interactions: Electric and magnetic forces between a pair of objects do not require that the objects be in contact. The sizes of the forces in each situation depend on the properties of the objects and their distances apart and, for forces between two magnets, on their orientation relative to each other (3-PS2-3), (3-PS2-4).

Standard: 3-PS2-3. Ask questions to determine cause and effect relationships of electric or magnetic interactions between two objects not in contact with each other.

Science and engineering practices:
Practice 1: Asking Questions and Defining Problems
Practice 3: Planning and Carrying Out Investigations
Practice 4: Analyzing and Interpreting Data
Practice 7: Engaging in Argument from Evidence

Crosscutting concept:
Cause and Effect, 3-PS2-3

Connections to nature of science:
Science Knowledge is Based on Empirical Evidence. Science findings are based on recognizing patterns (3-PS2-2).
Scientific Investigations Use a Variety of Methods
Science investigations use a variety of methods, tools and techniques (3-PS2-1).

California English Language Development Standards[4] – Grade 3

I.A.1 **Exchanging information and ideas.** Contribute to class, group and partner discussions, including sustained dialogue, by following turn-taking rules, asking relevant questions, affirming others and adding relevant information.

I.B.5 **Listening actively.** Demonstrate active listening to read-alouds and oral presentations by asking and answering detailed questions, with occasional prompting and moderate support.

I.C.12 **Selecting language resources.** Use a growing number of general academic and domain-specific words in order to add detail, create an effect (e.g., using the word *suddenly* to signal a change) or create shades of meaning (e.g., *scurry* versus *dash*) while speaking and writing.

School context

The vignettes in this chapter take place in an elementary school that is a Science, Technology, Engineering and Mathematics (STEM) magnet school in a large urban school district. The pre-K–five school is in a high poverty area and has a dual language program with an excellent, long-standing reputation. The principal has been at that school for 28 years and knows many of the students' parents because they were students at the same elementary school. The school is sponsored by several science and engineering-related businesses and prestigious universities and there is a waiting list of students from around the district whose parents want them to attend. The teaching force has been fairly stable for the last eight years. Teachers with bilingual skills or math and science background receive a stipend after their second year at the school. The student population of the classrooms in these vignettes is comprised primarily of third-grade English Learner students at the Expanding Level.

Lesson context

As part of a series of lessons focused on the NGSS Disciplinary Core Idea 3 (Physical Science), teachers designed lessons that would allow students to explore and make conclusions about electric and magnetic forces between a pair of objects (3-PS 2-3). Specifically, the third-grade teachers created lessons on magnetism and polarity to support students' engagement in inquiry, increase conceptual understanding and promote an applied use of the Scientific Practices. Each teacher determined how they would present the lesson and selected procedures and routines to be used during their lesson.

Classroom Vignette 1: Dr Makar – Room 4–2 (Grade 3)

Dr Makar begins class by reminding students that scientists inquire, observe, record and question and are precise in asking questions and defining problems using evidence from investigations. He extends his thought by stating, 'In this class we will strive to use precise language to describe our scientific work'. He discourages the use of unscientific jargon maintaining a word wall of imprecise unscientific words that are not allowed – like 'thing', 'stuff', 'you know' and 'lots'. To illustrate his point Dr Makar tells the class that when he worked in a science lab of a chemical company, he needed to be able to communicate clearly with the other scientists. 'In our class we will prize objectivity and questions are not only welcome, they will be rewarded with extra credit because scientists emphasize the work by removing doubts'. Dr Makar further reinforces his expectations in the classroom by addressing students formally by their last names. He asks students to think of the classroom as a type of laboratory by giving them name tags to wear while they are in class. Students demonstrate their knowledge of this daily classroom routine. When they enter the class, they put on their name tags, which each student designed at the beginning of the semester. Dr Makar gives students the opportunity to build their understanding about the nature of science by having them learn how to collect empirical data. To do so, he begins by distributing lab sheets for students to take notes. Although they consistently use the lab sheets, he reinforces his expectations by restating their purpose and points to each of the lab sheet components while asking students to follow along. He walks around to monitor that all students are doing so. He asks questions and redirects students who need additional support. The lab templates include a box for key vocabulary and a space for students to jot down the word meanings as the lesson progresses. He mentions that the lab sheet has a place to write the step-by-step directions for the activity of the day and it has a section for them to copy the objectives, to write in their observations and a space at the bottom of the sheet for them to summarize the lesson at the end of the period and evaluate their claims. He reminds students that the reason he consistently asks them to orally rehearse and write a summary is so that they can monitor their comprehension and how they synthesize scientific information. It also helps him monitor and gives him an opportunity to adjust his instruction as well as give students written feedback on their lab sheets.	Anecdotal notes:

Students can plan and investigate collaboratively as Dr Makar hands each table team a small bag of assorted objects. The bags contain common items like screws, aluminum cans, bottle caps, name tags, copper pennies, a metal spoon, aluminum foil, a dollar bill, paper clips, an old video or audio-tape cassette and a ballpoint pen which serve as variables for their experiment. Students appear to know what is expected of them and have a routine for how to use realia and science materials. The materials monitor immediately takes charge of the items. He tells the rest of the students to jot down their hypothesis about which items will be attracted to the magnet. He asks students to turn to a partner to explain what hypothesis is. Dr Makar walks around listening to the students' conversations. He asks questions and redirects students' conversations where needed. After a few minutes he calls on three students to share the results of their partner discussion on defining what a hypothesis is. He expands on what they say by reminding them that a hypothesis is a possible explanation created by investigating a topic, gathering information and hypothesizing – or predicting – what might occur in a given situation. On the white board he provides them with a sentence frame for writing like a scientist to explain the cause and effect relationship between the different materials.

'If _____ [I do this] _____, then _____ [this] _____ will happen'.

He then tells them to work as a group to sort the objects into two categories, those made of steel, those that contain iron and those that are neither. They are to write their rationale for placing each item in a particular category on a Post-It note by that item. They must also complete a three-column graphic organizer on their lab sheet by listing the objects they predict will be attracted to the magnet, those that will be not be attracted and any that will be repelled. Dr Makar points to other graphic organizers in the rooms and reminds students that this is a familiar structure they use to facilitate conversation, investigation and organization of thinking around a topic. He gives them five minutes to work. As students work in small groups, Dr Makar circulates through each group listening to the discussion, clarifying and asking redirecting questions to help build conceptual understanding. He explains the terms 'attract' and 'repel' in various ways and probes to see that all students are comprehending the concept. He then asks the groups to rotate to every table to observe their colleagues' predictions. When they finish, he asks them to report on similarities and differences they observed from group to group, pointing out how scientists learn a great deal from one another. He also returns to the use of the word 'hypothesis' and the process they used to predict and hypothesize.

Next, Dr Makar instructs the groups to formally share out their predictions by reading their hypothesis using the now completed sentence frame he provided. Then, he distributes a strong bar magnet to each student and asks them to test their hypothesis, record their observations and note if there are any surprises. If so, they are to write a quick prediction about why they think the unexpected object was attracted to the magnet. Dr Makar models the first one for them, so they know what to do. He thinks aloud as he jots his prediction about why he thinks the paper ten-dollar bill is attracted to the magnet.

He tells students to pair up at their tables and try to make their magnets attract to each other. What do they observe? He says, 'Show me the magnets repelling, show me the magnets attracting'. He explains that each end of the bar magnet is called a pole, just like the earth has a north pole and a south pole. The poles that repel are alike or the same so the North Pole on one magnet and the North Pole on the other magnet repel, or push away, because they have the same polarity. The poles that attract are unlike, they are the opposites so north and south attract.

He has students repeat the terms as they physically make magnets attract and repel. He insists that partners monitor each other and utilize the scientific vocabulary so that he can see who has understood the terms and is able to use them in context.

Anecdotal notes:

Classroom Vignette 2: Miss Gustafson – Room 4–3 (Grade 3)

The weekly schedule posted on the front bulletin board shows that there is a half hour per week scheduled for science in Miss Gustafson's classroom. There is a library corner in the room with fiction and non-fiction leveled books that are color coded with a sign that reminds students to only select books at their readability level. There is also a small half-shelf of books in Spanish. On her desk, Miss Gustafson has a stack of magnet worksheets for distribution that have a paragraph at the top of the page and multiple-choice questions with bubble-in answers at the bottom.

    She begins class by telling students that they will need to work quickly today to get through the science lesson. She warns them that if they are off task, they will need to skip the hands-on experiment part of the lesson to move on to textbook reading time. She reminds them that in school and beyond, 'If you can't read, you can't do anything'. Miss Gustafson tells them that since they are the class with the lowest reading scores on the state achievement test she has designed today's lesson so that they can kill two birds with one stone by reading about the science topics in the standards they are required to cover this year. She begins the lesson by saying, 'Today students we are going to read about magnets and how they attract and repel'. She holds up a mini-book so that all students can see the picture on the cover and she asks, 'What will we learn today?' Several students giggle and whisper that today the teacher is going to kill some birds with a stone. Miss Gustafson overhears them and tells the two students to put their heads down on their desks for being smarty pants.

    She points to a list of ten vocabulary words related to the lesson that are written on the board. She previews them with the group by reading each one and telling students to repeat. She tells them they will need to look up the definitions for homework. She projects a transparency with three sentences that each have grammatical mistakes or an error in conventions. She tells students to read each sentence silently and copy it correctly onto a piece of paper. The sentences say: 1. Today we study magnets. 2. Magnets attractive and repellent. 3. They got to poles, north and south. After students copy the sentences and make the corrections and edits, she randomly calls on one student to come up and correct the first sentence by writing it on the white board. Miss Gustafson then asks the class if everyone else got the same answer. Some students nod their heads in assent. Then she invites another student to write the corrected sentence number two. The student's correction was Magnets are attractive and repellent. Miss Gustafson said, 'No, that is not the correct answer. It is, magnets attract and repel'. Then a third student comes up to write the corrected third sentence. The class discussion becomes one or two students calling out changes. The rest of the class gets noisy but is no longer engaged in actively correcting the sentences. She asks students to settle down and get ready for the next part of the lesson.

    Miss Gustafson tells them to get out their leveled reading texts. The books are mostly pictures with very limited print. Each group reads the eight-page paperback picture book on magnets while Miss Gustafson corrects papers at her desk. Students read the book twice, then Miss Gustafson asks if they have any questions. Students shake their heads 'no'. They fidget and glance at the clock. Since it is only a few minutes until recess, Miss Gustafson distributes an exit slip to each student and tells them to write a sentence about magnets and hand it in before they go out the door when the bell rings.

Anecdotal notes:

Reading and Scoring STEP 2: Examine Evidence and Assign an OPAL Rating

Now that you have had an opportunity to read each of the classroom vignettes and note anecdotal evidence, review the sources of evidence and OPAL ratings. Review the overall definition of this domain to determine how the classroom context performs on each of the indicators related to promoting maximum comprehensibility for English Learners. Review each of the descriptors on the scoring rubric (Table 3.2). Use your anecdotal notes to determine a rating for each of the OPAL indicators included in OPAL Domain 3: Comprehensibility (Indicators 3.1–3.5).

After Scoring

Review your OPAL ratings for Domain 3: Comprehensibility. Reflect on what you recorded as you analyzed the written vignettes. Compare your scores to those proposed in Table 3.3. Note anecdotal evidence and rationale for each rating. Discuss observations about sources of evidence and ratings with a colleague.

Summary

Attaining maximum comprehensibility for English Learners requires a teacher to intentionally plan for the use of scaffolding strategies that are responsive to English Learners' developmental, academic and linguistic levels. A key aspect of this is the identification of concepts and academic discourse, including key vocabulary with ample opportunities for introduction, review and use of language in tandem with content learning. Iterative cycles of formative assessment and feedback promote responsive teaching and dynamic learning.

Reflection

Think about the content of this chapter and the focus questions for comprehensibility. Reflect on the following: How has my knowledge in identifying and supporting practices maximum comprehensibility for English Learners increased? What can I do to continue to explore ways of supporting comprehensibility for English Learners? Are there comprehensibility practices that are more realistic than others? What support do I need to work toward enhancing my repertoire of comprehensibility practices?

Table 3.2 Descriptor rubric for OPAL Domain 3: Comprehensibility

OPAL Domain: Comprehensibility

Instruction allows for maximum student understanding and teachers utilize effective strategies to help students access content.

Opal indicators	1 Novice [rarely or never]	2 Apprentice [basic attempts]	3 Developing [sometimes]	4 Capable [often]	5 Accomplished [consistent]	6 Expert [exceptional]	N/O Not Observable
3.1 Uses scaffolding strategies and devices (i.e. outlines, webs, semantic maps, compare/ contrast charts, KWL) to make subject matter understandable	Teacher *rarely or never* uses a variety of learning experiences and strategies that make complexity and depth of subject matter understandable	Teacher *makes basic attempts* to use a variety of learning experiences and strategies that make complexity and depth of subject matter understandable	Teacher *sometimes* uses a variety of learning experiences and strategies that make complexity and depth of subject matter understandable	Teacher *often* uses a variety of learning experiences and strategies that make complexity and depth of subject matter understandable	Teacher *consistently* uses a variety of learning experiences and strategies that make complexity and depth of subject matter understandable	Teacher shows *exceptional ability to consistently* use a variety of learning experiences and strategies that make complexity and depth of subject matter understandable	The skill or concept is not applicable in the context of this lesson/activity. It may be evident during another observation, but it was not observable during this classroom visit
3.2 Amplifies student input by: questioning/ restating/ rephrasing/ contextualizing	Teacher *rarely or never* asks questions and/ or facilitates discussions to clarify and extend student oral or written output	Teacher *makes basic attempts* to ask questions and/or facilitates discussions to clarify and extend student oral or written output	Teacher *sometimes* asks questions and/or facilitates discussions to clarify and extend student oral or written output	Teacher *often* asks questions and/or facilitates discussions to clarify and extend student oral or written output	Teacher *consistently* asks questions and/ or facilitates discussions to clarify and extend student oral or written output	Teacher shows *exceptional ability to consistently* ask questions and/or facilitate discussions to clarify and extend student oral or written output	The skill or concept is not applicable in the context of this lesson/activity. It may be evident during another observation, but it was not observable during this classroom visit

OPAL Domain 3 57

3.3 Explains key terms, clarifies idiomatic expressions, uses gestures and/or visuals to illustrate concepts	Teacher *rarely or never* makes concepts comprehensible and provides a context for students to understand key terms through the use of demonstrations, concrete objects or visuals	Teacher *makes basic attempts to* make concepts comprehensible and provides a context for students to understand key terms through the use of demonstrations, concrete objects or visuals	Teacher *sometimes* makes concepts comprehensible and provides a context for students to understand key terms through the use of demonstrations, concrete objects or visuals	Teacher *often* makes concepts comprehensible and provides a context for students to understand key terms through the use of demonstrations, concrete objects or visuals	Teacher *consistently* makes concepts comprehensible and provides a context for students to understand key terms through the use of demonstrations, concrete objects or visuals	Teacher shows *exceptional ability to consistently* make concepts comprehensible and provides a context for students to understand key terms through the use of demonstrations, concrete objects or visuals	The skill or concept is not applicable in the context of this lesson/activity. It may be evident during another observation, but it was *not* observable during this classroom visit
3.4 Provides frequent feedback and checks for comprehension	Teacher *rarely or never* asks incisive questions during instruction to determine how well every student understands central ideas and concepts. Teacher *rarely or never* provides positive, constructive feedback to students guide next steps	Teacher *makes basic attempts* to ask incisive questions during instruction to determine how well every student understands central ideas and concepts. Teacher *makes basic attempts to* provide positive, constructive feedback to students guide next steps	Teacher *sometimes* asks incisive questions during instruction to determine how well every student understands central ideas and concepts. Teacher *sometimes* provides positive, constructive feedback to students guide next steps	Teacher *often* asks incisive questions during instruction to determine how well every student understands central ideas and concepts. Teacher *often* provides positive, constructive feedback to students guide next steps	Teacher *consistently* asks incisive questions during instruction to determine how well every student understands central ideas and concepts. Teacher *consistently* provides positive, constructive feedback to students guide next steps	Teacher shows *exceptional ability to consistently* ask incisive questions during instruction to determine how well every student understands central ideas and concepts. Teacher shows *exceptional ability to consistently* provide positive, constructive feedback to students guide next steps	The skill or concept is not applicable in the context of this lesson/activity. It may be evident during another observation, but it was *not observable* during this classroom visit
3.5 Uses informal assessments of student learning to adjust instruction while teaching	Teacher *rarely or never* makes formative assessment an integral part of the learning process to provide all students information about their progress as they engage in activities	Teacher *makes basic attempts to* make formative assessment an integral part of the learning process to provide all students information about their progress as they engage in activities	Teacher *sometimes* makes formative assessment an integral part of the learning process to provide all students information about their progress as they engage in activities	Teacher *often* makes formative assessment an integral part of the learning process to provide all students information about their progress as they engage in activities	Teacher *consistently* makes formative assessment an integral part of the learning process to provide all students information about their progress as they engage in activities	Teacher shows *exceptional ability to consistently* make formative assessment an integral part of the learning process to provide all students information about their progress as they engage in activities	The skill or concept is not applicable in the context of this lesson/activity. It may be evident during another observation, but it was *not observable* during this classroom visit

Table 3.3 Anecdotal evidence and scores for written vignettes

OPAL Domain 3 Comprehensibility	Vignette 1 Dr Makar (Grade 3)	Vignette 2 Miss Gustafson (Grade 3)
Indicator 3.1	Anecdotal evidence: Lab sheet templates provide support for students to prioritize areas of focus. Dr Makar consistently uses a variety of strategies, including realia, to make the complex subject matter understandable. Students test their ideas and conceptual understanding in small and whole group. They sort the objects and use a 3-column chart graphic organizer to record the contents of each category. Other charts/graphic organizers are evident in the room and Dr Makar reminds students that these devices are familiar to them.	Anecdotal evidence: Although the brief leveled reading books have many pictures, there is minimal discussion of the books or content with students prior to the independent reading. No evidence of other scaffolding strategies or devices.
	OPAL Score: 5	OPAL Score: 1
Indicator 3.2	Anecdotal evidence: Dr Makar tells students to write their hypotheses but then expands his instructions with a brief reminder of what a hypothesis is. He asks students to do a partner share, invites three students to report and amplifies responses. When he tells students that the north poles on two magnets are alike he amplifies by saying they are similar, and when he says repel, he extends by saying push away. Dr Makar provides written feedback on their summaries.	Anecdotal evidence: Miss Gustafson asks students if they have any questions but rarely explores their understanding or helps them extend their responses. She simply moves on when they ask no questions. When students respond by giggling and telling her that she is going to kill two birds with a stone, she punishes them rather than using the opportunity to extend student understanding of the meaning of this idiomatic expression.
	OPAL Score: 5	OPAL Score: 1
Indicator 3.3	Anecdotal evidence: During the lesson Dr Makar provides a sentence frame to help students use the formal reporting language he requires. He rephrases and restates definitions and terms to target various language levels for one key term, prediction – hypothesis. He uses visuals and realia during the lesson to promote comprehensibility. He asks students to explain key terms to each other as well as to him. Students record key vocabulary on their lab sheets.	Anecdotal evidence: The vocabulary words are listed, but not explained. Students are expected to look up the definitions. Miss Gustafson uses the idiomatic phrase 'to kill two birds with one stone' without anticipating that students might misunderstand and without providing any kind of explanation or clarification. When it becomes clear that students don't understand, she makes them put their heads down.
	OPAL Score: 4	OPAL Score: 1

Table 3.3 (Continued)

OPAL Domain 3 Comprehensibility	Vignette 1 Dr Makar (Grade 3)	Vignette 2 Miss Gustafson (Grade 3)
Indicator 3.4	Anecdotal evidence: Dr Makar encourages students to ask questions in class by giving extra credit for questions. He monitors this for every student. He also structures his instruction for student self-discovery and designs his experiments to give students feedback on the science concepts and processes. Student feedback is provided orally and in writing by both the teacher and peers. Dr Makar also reinforces the scientific importance of asking questions and has routines that consistently allow for frequent feedback and checks for comprehension. OPAL Score: 4	Anecdotal evidence: The daily language exercise is corrected in class so she may get some idea of what students know about spelling and grammar but minimal information about their comprehension of science and magnets. Miss Gustafson rarely asks incisive questions during instruction to determine how well every student understands central ideas and concepts. OPAL Score: 1
Indicator 3.5	Anecdotal evidence: As students work in partners and small groups, Dr Makar circulates through each group listening to the discussion, clarifying and asking redirecting questions. He provides students information about their progress so they know if they are on track and clarifies if they have misunderstood. He records their use of scientific language to provide individual feedback. In addition, he routinely uses consistent structures, such as lab sheets, partner discussions, group discussion and oral and written summaries to assess student knowledge and understanding of the concepts. OPAL Score: 5	Anecdotal evidence: At the end of class, students are told to complete an exit ticket about magnets so Miss Gustafson may get some input about what students know and don't know. The topic is vague and it is unclear what the exit slip is assessing in relation to the objective set for the lesson. OPAL Score: 1

Notes

(1) The California English Language Arts/English Language Development Framework uses the term Integrated ELD to describe instruction for English Learners in content areas guided by the ELD and ELA standards. This new term encompasses previously used terms such as sheltered instruction or specially designed academic instruction in English (SDAIE).

(2) *Expanding Proficiency Level:* Students at this level are challenged to increase their English skills in more contexts and learn a greater variety of vocabulary and linguistic structures, applying their growing language skills in more sophisticated ways that are appropriate to their age and grade level. California Department of Education (CDE) English Language Proficiency Level Definition in English Language Development Standards Publication (2012). www.cde.ca.gov/sp/el/er/documents/eldstndspublication14.pdf.

(3) California Department of Education (2013). *Next Generation Science Standards for California Public Schools, Kindergarten through Grade Twelve (CA NGSS).* www.cde.ca.gov/pd/ca/sc/ngssstandards.asp.

(4) California Department of Education (2012). *English Language Development Standards Kindergarten through Grade 12.* www.cde.ca.gov/sp/el/er/documents/eldstndspublication14.pdf.

4 OPAL Domain 4: Interactions

> *Creating dynamic interactions for English Learners is more than just collaborative groups. By exploring this OPAL Domain, I learned so much about the role that classroom culture and decisions I make about interactions play in maximizing opportunities for students to engage, especially my English Learners.*
> *– OPAL Institute Participant (Classroom Teacher)*

English Learners benefit from maximum engagement, interactions and ownership of learning content and processes. This chapter examines how educators can foster active learning for English Learners by using knowledge of students' learning processes and employing varied interactive structures that guide and empower students to advocate for and be active participants in their learning journey. Two focus questions will prepare us for the content of this chapter.

> **FOCUS QUESTIONS:**
> 1. What are *interactions* in the context of teaching English Learners?
> 2. How are *interactions* for English Learners evidenced in the classroom? What information can be recorded and analyzed using the OPAL interactions domain indicators?

Introduction

In Chapter 3 we provided background information and examples of research-based practices that exemplify elements and indicators for the OPAL comprehensibility domain and what it looks like when *instruction allows for maximum student understanding and teachers utilize effective strategies to help students access content*. Although each of the OPAL domains is interrelated (see Figure 4.1), this chapter will build on the knowledge gained from examining each domain individually and will

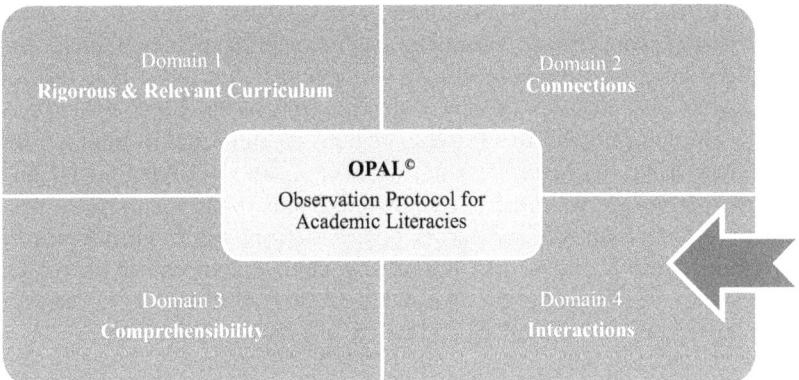

Figure 4.1 The Observation Protocol for Academic Literacies (OPAL) domains

couple this with opportunities to explore evidence of classroom practice focused on OPAL Domain 4: Interactions.

First, we provide background information for each indicator, including brief classroom snapshots highlighting how key characteristics for each indicator might be evidenced in a classroom context. Next, we present teacher reflection questions and an OPAL descriptor rubric to assist educators in exploring how different levels of implementation of each of the OPAL indicators for Domain 4 (Interactions) might appear from lower to higher levels of classroom practice. Finally, the reader will practice using the OPAL instrument using written vignettes, descriptions of lessons from our actual classroom observations. These vignettes will give the reader the opportunity to identify objective sources of evidence (anecdotal notes), to determine level(s) of implementation of the various indicators and to mark these on the OPAL Descriptor Rubric. The OPAL can be used by a teacher to reflect on their practice during the lesson planning stage or after delivering a lesson. Teachers can cite sources of evidence and provide a self-rating or seek opportunities to refine lesson planning by reflecting on each of the indicators identified for this domain. Additionally, an external observer or coach may document sources of evidence while observing classroom practice to rate levels of implementation based on each indicator. The vignettes, coupled with the foundational content presented in this chapter, will allow the user to begin to build proficiency toward ascertaining inter-rater reliability and confidently describing classroom practices and student–teacher actions and interactions related to this domain.

What Are *Interactions* in the Context of Teaching English Learners?

A teacher plans for and engages students in multiple opportunities for interactions in formal and informal learning spaces. The fourth domain of the OPAL instrument defines *interactions* as the use of *varied participation structures to maximize student engagement in content and language, increase opportunities to enact leadership roles that bolster interactions and to amplify access to the curriculum.* English Learners require ample opportunities for engagement in high-quality interactions that allow for rehearsing, sharing, expanding and applying social and academic language to construct knowledge and make meaning of academic content. Four key indicators of interactions for English Learners are delineated in Table 4.1. As you review Table 4.1, we invite the reader to engage in the 'Eliciting prior knowledge activity' (Box 4.1) to conduct a quick preview of the domain and its corresponding indicators.

Table 4.1 Key Indicators for OPAL Domain 4: Interactions

Opal Domain	Indicators
Domain 4: Interactions	4.1 Facilitates student autonomy and choice by promoting active listening, questioning and/or advocating. 4.2 Modifies procedures and rules to support student learning. 4.3 Effectively communicates subject matter knowledge in the target language. 4.4 Uses flexible groupings to promote positive interactions and accommodations for individual and group learning needs.

BOX. 4.1 ELICITING PRIOR KNOWLEDGE ACTIVITY

- ✓ *Read* each indicator above (Indicators 4.1–4.4).
- ✓ *Highlight* or underline key words/phrases for each of the indicators.
- ✓ *Draw* a visual representation of the interactions construct based on an initial review of the key terms included in each of the indicators.
- ✓ Next, *label* your visual representation with the key terms you have identified.
- ✓ Make a *list of any questions* you have about the indicators or key terms.

Getting to Know Each Indicator in the Interactions Domain

In the sections that follow we explore each indicator in detail and introduce illustrative classroom snapshots. Expand and deepen your knowledge about each OPAL Domain 4 (Interactions) indicator as you reach each description below.

Indicator 4.1: Facilitates student autonomy and choice by promoting active listening, questioning and/or advocating

Bruner (1978), like Vygotsky, focused on the social and cultural aspects of learning. He suggested that people understand better when the subject has personal significance for them, not just through attention to 'the facts' (Bruner, 1978). Knowledge, memory and language learning are constructed through meaningful interactions with peers and adults in their environments. Learning is intended to be a process of discovery in which learners build their own knowledge, through conversations, questioning and dialogue with teachers and peers (Kibler *et al.*, 2020; Swain & Watanabe, 2013; Van Lier, 2004; Van Lier & Walqui, 2012). Furthermore, learners are more likely to be active participants in their own learning when (1) actions are perceived to be initiated and monitored by the learner; and (2) learning tasks are connected to personal interest or importance (de Charms, 2013; Kibler *et al.*, 2020; Patall *et al.*, 2013). Student autonomy is a critical component of the language learning context that includes the learner exercising control over their own learning and focusing attention on interpersonal actions and development of self-monitoring skills (Benson, 2011) (see Figure 4.2).

In a culturally and linguistically diverse classroom, teachers can employ techniques to balance opportunities for teacher-to-student, student-to-teacher and student-to-student interactions. For each of these interaction structures, the teacher facilitates and models the affirmation of students' contributions to the learning context and employs procedures for students to take ownership of content learning and engage actively in instructional processes. For example, a teacher anticipates a theme or

---

Classroom Snapshot

Grade Level: 6

Content Area: Science – Urban Ecology (Structured English Immersion Program)

English Language Proficiency Level: Expanding (Intermediate)

Mrs. Kang's students have been working on a unit focused on Patterns of Urban Land Use. The class has learned about cities as ecosystems, microhabitats and community relationships, and <u>city and land use policies in their local context</u>. In groups of five, students <u>conduct several site-evaluation cycles for an identified section of their school yard</u>. They <u>collect data and ask critical questions about</u>: (1) land use; (2) surface temperature variation; (3) assessing tree health; and (4) evaluation of types of surfaces. Based on this investigation, <u>each group identifies an issue in their local school yard that they feel is urgent to address</u>. They work collaboratively to <u>create a Land Use Proposal and a Land Use Model to communicate their recommendations for improving land use in their setting</u>.

Figure 4.2 Classroom snapshot/OPAL Indicator 4.1

topic to be covered in an upcoming unit. The teacher has knowledge of their students' backgrounds and experiences and can connect with a student or groups of students to gain insight or gather questions about the content or related topics. This can be done prior to beginning a unit using an anticipatory set, small group discussion or class survey. Based on this information, a teacher can structure whole group, small group, partner and individual learning experiences that promote choice and ownership of content knowledge. Interactions and engagement can be maximized when the teacher couples the use of varied grouping with the identification of learning and language goals that are responsive to students' academic, linguistic and other experiences that shape their identities (Lopez & Musanti, 2019).

Indicator 4.2: Modifies procedures and rules to support student learning

Teachers can structure academic and community-building components of classroom environments in ways that allow for targeted and supported student learning. Procedures are established classroom routines that help a classroom space be responsive to the learners and maintain a familiar balance and harmony in a learning community (Figure 4.3).

In addition to procedures such as transitioning to independent activities, submitting assignments and monitoring group work, a language learning classroom includes routines such as how students organize their learning, maintaining a learning log, pacing of the lesson or engaging

---

Classroom Snapshot

Grade Level: 2

Content Area: English Language Development (Designated ELD)

English Language Proficiency Level(s): Expanding (Intermediate)

As part of a Designated English Language Development (ELD) Lesson, Mrs. Mack's students are making inferences about idiomatic expressions to practice using prior knowledge and textual information to comprehend text. This will support their learning during their English Language Arts class. Mrs. Mack moves from whole group instruction to partner and small-group work with the expectation that students remain engaged 90–100% of the time. As she monitors the transition from a whole group to partner group activity, she acknowledges that one of her students has recently joined the class and is not familiar with the established classroom routines for using academic discussion sentence frames to share predictions or inferences about text. She modifies procedures for this student by (1) sitting him next to a peer who can model the routine; and (2) giving him a handout with the list of sentence frames.

Figure 4.3 Classroom snapshot/OPAL Indicator 4.2

in questioning, group discussions or collaborative conversations. Rules support positive learning spaces and are intended to promote respect for everyone's right to learn and to protect student safety, including socio-emotional well-being.

Creating a classroom environment that includes procedures responsive to the needs of the learners necessitates a classroom teacher differentiating instructional processes. Tomlinson's (2001) seminal work on differentiated instruction stresses that individual students' learning needs are based on adaptations to what is taught (content), how it is taught (process) and evidence of student learning (products).

Our work addresses specific aspects of content area instruction with the types of interactions/tasks (processes) that can yield maximum results for English Learners across language proficiency levels (emerging to bridging/beginning to advanced) and across the four language domains of listening, speaking, reading and writing (Lee, 2019). One way to do this is to model the steps of a process students will follow. This should include expectations for engagement, language and content application or use in an academic or social context. Such modeling will elucidate for students the expectations for maximum participation and production. Another example of differentiating processes and/or procedures is to preview and review material for students. This can be done in an English Learner's primary language and will increase the opportunity for maximum interaction and engagement.

As a teacher delivers a lesson or facilitates classroom activities, formative assessment and observation opportunities can be employed to make 'in the moment' decisions about modifying procedures or rules to increase student interaction and engagement. For example, if a student who is at a beginning language level is paired up with a student or group of students who are having difficulty engaging this student in the conversation or task, the teacher can pair the student with other students who speak his primary language. This will allow the struggling student to explain things or ask questions in his first language, feel like a part of the class, thereby maximizing learning.

Indicator 4.3: Effectively communicates subject matter knowledge in the target language

A classroom teacher is responsible for overseeing, managing and contributing to the advancement of subject matter knowledge in an instructional setting as evidenced by the communication of subject matter knowledge in the target language. The expectation is that educators have a developed pedagogic skill set, as well as a sophisticated level of content knowledge *and* the ability to plan and facilitate effective classroom interactions that allow students to meet academic and linguistic targets in the language of instruction.

Shulman (1987) argued that, in addition to content knowledge in their subject matter, teachers also need to develop pedagogic content knowledge, defined as 'that special amalgam of content and pedagogy that is uniquely the province of teachers, their own special form of professional understanding' (1987: 8). Box 4.2 highlights key components of Shulman's description of pedagogic content knowledge.

BOX. 4.2 PEDAGOGIC CONTENT KNOWLEDGE

- General pedagogical knowledge, with special reference to those broad principles and strategies of classroom management and organization that appear to transcend subject matter.
- Knowledge of learners and their characteristics.
- Knowledge of educational contexts, ranging from workings of the group or classroom, the governance and financing of school districts, to the character of communities and cultures.
- Knowledge of educational ends, purposes and values and their philosophical and historical grounds.
- Content knowledge.
- Curriculum knowledge, with particular grasp of the materials and programs that serve as 'tools of the trade' for teachers.
- Pedagogical content knowledge, that special amalgam of content and pedagogy that is uniquely the province of teachers, their own special form of professional understanding.

(Shulman, 1987: 8)

Teachers guide effective communication of subject matter and interactions by explicitly modeling the type of language required for specific genres, as well as providing structures that allow students to practice these orally and in writing. Varied interactions are required for students to develop communicative competence – this means that students need to be able to talk, question and use the discourse of various genres if they are to gain competency in both English and the content area (Celce-Murcia et al., 1993; Swain & Watanabe, 2012). The classroom teacher is the primary model of communicative competence, as well as facilitator of its development. In this role, the teacher can convey effective communication of subject matter in the target language, while simultaneously attending to English Learners' academic and linguistic needs (see Figure 4.4).

Interactions that are supported, monitored and facilitated by teachers and peers in the classroom allow for the creation of formal and

> *Classroom Snapshot*
>
> Grade: 11
>
> Content Area: English Language Arts – English 11, American Literature (Structured English Immersion Program)
>
> English Language Proficiency Level(s): Expanding (Intermediate and Early Advanced)
>
> Mr. Triggs uses Writer's Workshop to teach writing in his English 11, American Literature class. At the beginning of this class period, he reminds students that they have been using the STAR (Substitute, Take things out, Add things, and Rearrange) Writing Strategy to conduct peer editing sessions. As per his daily routine, he begins this learning episode with a mini-lesson responsive to his students' writing needs. Today, he conducts a 'Think Aloud' to model how to organize an essay about prominent figures in U.S. History by chronological order. To lead this session <u>Mr. Triggs displays his knowledge of historical figures in the United States, past and present.</u> Additionally, he is <u>explicit about the writer's craft required to introduce a reader to the essay</u> and <u>provides multiple examples</u> of how he could rewrite his introduction to improve this section. Next, Mr. Triggs transitions to framing the peer editing sessions. He asks students to identify the type of writing they are working on in order to best assign peer editing groups: autobiographical, expository-persuasive, or literary analysis. He uses <u>grade-level, discipline-specific discourse</u> and <u>provides extended examples about why the individual students' writing choice belongs to one of the three genres.</u> At the end of the class period, Mr. Triggs provides closure by <u>comparing and contrasting the approach to writing an introduction for each of the three types of writing.</u> He asks students to <u>record characteristics ('universal aspects') of lead sentences for each of the three types of writing</u> to serve as a resource for future writing.

Figure 4.4 Classroom snapshot/OPAL Indicator 4.3

informal spaces that welcome and affirm the experiences, languages and culture of all students while encouraging mutual accountability for engaging in academic contexts (de Jong, 2022). Schleppegrell (2012) contends that teaching linguistically and culturally diverse students academic registers is an equity issue, given that access to these registers outside of school varies. Often classroom opportunities are a critical space for English Learners to engage in the use of academic discourse appropriate to different contexts.

Indicator 4.4: Uses flexible groupings to promote positive interactions and accommodations for individual and group learning needs

Higher levels of student engagement are attained when collaborative practice and teamwork are evident throughout an instructional day (see Figure 4.5). Typically, this means that there is a decrease in teacher-led,

> *Classroom Snapshot*
>
> *Grade: 5*
>
> *Content Area: English Language Arts (Structured English Immersion Program)*
>
> *English Language Proficiency Level(s): Expanding (Intermediate)*
>
> Mr. Rico's 5th grade classroom houses individual student desks that are <u>arranged in pods of four.</u> On the upper right-hand corner of each desk is a <u>color-coded label and number, representing each student's role in collaborative group work</u>. Mr. Rico uses two coding systems to <u>vary collaborative group work based on individual academic, developmental and linguistic levels.</u> Additionally, these systems are used to <u>establish routines and accountability for collaborative group work</u>. As he begins a lesson on persuasive writing, he asks students to regroup according to their color groups. He asks the January class president to review the <u>roles according to colors</u>: Green: Recorder; Blue: Reporter; Yellow: Task Master; Red: Organizer/Document Collection. He begins the lesson by presenting a whole group mini-lesson on the art of persuasion and creating strong pro and con arguments. He proceeds to assign <u>collaborative group work where each member contributes and justifies ideas for and against a topic</u>. Based on students' English proficiency levels and background knowledge, students are provided with <u>differentiated academic discussion sentence frames</u> to capture and justify ideas, both orally and in writing.

Figure 4.5 Classroom snapshot/OPAL Indicator 4.4

whole-class instruction and more small groups, where students can process content, while practicing language with their peers in a facilitated, lower-risk setting.

Cooperative learning is a key instructional strategy for English Learners because it enhances interactions among students, promotes the development of positive academic and social support systems for English Learners, prepares students for increasingly interactive environments and allows teachers to manage large classes of students with diverse needs (Holt, 1993; Ovando & Combs, 2018).

Flexible student grouping and collaborative routines engage students in talking about content in relevant, meaningful and structured ways. These routines are scaffolds that allow students to be accountable for their own learning by increasing autonomy to build self-direction and individual responsibility, thus contributing to positive interdependence in their interactions, collaboration and collective language and content learning with partners or groups (Saunders & Goldenberg, 2010; Swain & Watanabe, 2012). From simple processes such as structured turn-taking, to individual roles/jobs or responsibilities in small group work, to

Assessment of Cooperative Group Work

INTERPRETIVE	COLLABORATIVE
Assess:	Assess:
Subject matter academic skills	Social skills and group interactions
Critical thinking and comprehension	Student advocacy

PRODUCTIVE	METACOGINITIVE/ METALINGUISTIC
Assess:	Assess:
General academic and discipline specific language use	Reflection on language
Oral and written language	Self-reflection on content or language learning

Figure 4.6 Assessment of cooperative group work

varying partners with 'bilingual buddies', students who actively participate in classroom discussions with others are more engaged in learning the content. Students are explicitly taught (and helped to find) language to interact respectfully with their peers, and the language to talk about their feelings, needs and intentions.

When we assess varied interaction structures, it is important to consider various dimensions of interactions. These dimensions are reflective of the modes of communication as specified in the California English Language Development Standards (California Department of Education, 2012). Considerations for assessment for each of these dimensions are based on the work of Hurley and Tinajero (2001) (see Figure 4.6).

How Can We Determine What Evidence We See in Observing for the OPAL Interactions Domain?

In this section we will explore two classrooms using written vignettes. The reader is asked to think about each of the OPAL Domain 4 (Interactions) Indicators as they read the vignette. Use the right-hand margin to note detailed anecdotal evidence observed in each classroom vignette. For a review of how to identify and record objective anecdotal evidence see Chapter 2. The following steps are recommended when engaging in this learning experience:

Before reading the vignettes related to the interactions domain:

- Review the overall definition of this domain, along with the specific indicators (Table 4.1).
- Underline the key words/phrases for each indicator.

Reading and scoring:

- Step 1: Read each written vignette and record anecdotal evidence.
- Step 2: Review the criteria delineated in the OPAL scoring rubric for this domain and use your anecdotal evidence to assign a rating.

After scoring:

- Compare your scores to those provided in this text.
- Identify additional sources of evidence for each indicator.
- Discuss results and implications for classroom practice.

OPAL Domain 4: Interactions – Reflection Questions

Several questions can guide the reader in examining how teaching and learning are occurring in these classroom contexts to promote opportunities for interactions. In particular, *how does the classroom context ...*

- Create classroom routines that promote student autonomy to build self-direction and self-monitoring skills?
- Assess students' linguistic, academic and social abilities in order to create flexible groupings?
- Modify classroom structures and procedures to include accountability as part of collaborative work?
- Model and provide time for students to participate in academic discourse within a given content area so that they apply these skills across other content areas?

Reading and Scoring STEP 1: Read Each Vignette and Note Anecdotal Evidence Focused on OPAL Domain 4: Interactions

Context for vignettes

The vignettes presented here were developed based on actual classroom observations. Pseudonyms are used to respect each teacher's commitment to creating opportunities for transparent, objective and reflective examination of classroom practices for English Learner students. The context for each set of vignettes is provided to give the reader an overall picture of factors that may have influenced decision-making processes, delivery of instruction and classroom practices. These include content area, grade level, English Learner language proficiency level(s) and focus content standards.

Because these classroom observations occurred in California, content standards are specific to those adopted by the California State Board of Education (1) Common Core State Standards (CCSS) for English Language Arts and Literacy in History/Social Studies, Science and Technical Subjects and Mathematics (CDE, 2010, 2013); (2) Next Generation Science Standards (CDE, 2013); (3) History Social Science Content Standards (CDE, 1998, 2000); and (4) English Language Development (ELD) Standards (CDE, 2012). Nationally, each state determines the standards that are taught in schools. A number of states across the nation have adopted the same or similar Common Core standards for English and math while others have revised, edited or created other versions to respond to their state context. As such, we expect that readers will (1) recognize similarities in the content *and* language standards connections presented for each vignette and (2) engage in the proposed 'reading and scoring' steps to examine practices for English Learners using the OPAL indicators.

Content focus and factors

> Content Area: Mathematics, Integrated ELD[1]
> Grade: 2
> Language Proficiency Levels: Emerging[2] (Beginning) to Expanding[3] (Intermediate)

Standards Connection
California Common Core State Standards – Mathematics[4] – Grade 2

Domain:
Measurement and Data (2MD)

Mathematical Content Standards for Measurement and Data:

2MD: Work with Time and Money
8. Solve word problems involving dollar bills, quarters, dimes, nickels and pennies, using $ and ¢ symbols appropriately.

Mathematical Practices:

- o MP1: Make sense of problems and persevere in solving them;
- o MP4: Model with mathematics;
- o MP6: Attend to precision.

California English Language Development Standards[5] – Grade 2:

I.A1 **Exchanging information and ideas.** Contribute to class, group and partner discussions, including sustained dialogue, by listening attentively, following turn-taking rules, asking relevant questions, affirming others and adding relevant information.

I.B5 **Listening actively.** Demonstrate active listening to read-alouds and oral presentations by asking and answering detailed questions, with oral sentence frames and occasional prompting and support.

I.C9 **Presenting.** Plan and deliver brief oral presentations on a variety of topics (e.g., retelling a story, describing an animal).

School context

The classrooms in these vignettes are located in an elementary school in a quiet suburban community where the school district is known for its high-test scores. This school has a combination of students from some of the wealthiest families in the area. The school also enrolls students from three trailer parks and three motels on the other side of Foothill Boulevard. These students are all on free lunch and almost all live with single mothers or grandmothers. The elementary school teaching staff have been in place for years and the school population is very stable with little transience.

Lesson context

Two second grade teachers present their lessons on US currency using combinations of coins and bills. There are a few English Learners in each class and their English language proficiency level ranges from emerging to expanding. The English Learners speak mostly Spanish but a variety of other languages including Mandarin, Korean, Farsi, Tagalog and Greek are also represented. These students are the children of visiting faculty from a prestigious university nearby.

Classroom Vignette 1: Ms Warner – Room 22 (Grade 2)

	Anecdotal notes:
Room 22 has a reading bulletin board that says *Reading Takes You Anywhere*. It is covered with book reports, student-made posters and projects in English and Spanish. There is a pocket chart that indicates what reading groups children belong to. Names are written on sentence strips and a strip at the top of the board reads 'Groups for the Month'. Another bulletin board shows history/social studies projects which were completed in groups. There is a group rubric stapled to each project with group members' names on it and a score for each component of the assignment. There is a math bulletin board that says *The Smart Money is on Room 22*. It displays pictures of price tags, world coins and currency, the price list for the school cafeteria and advertisements for local grocery stores.	
Class begins with students sitting on the rug in front of the classroom and Ms Warner reading aloud to the students the humorous Shel Silverstein poem 'Smart'. The poem is about a boy who trades his dollar bill for two quarters, because everyone knows that two is more than one, then continues to trade for coins of lesser value because there are more of them (five pennies for one dime, etc.). Ms Warner consistently communicates clearly, reads with fluency and good pronunciation. Ms Warner asks the class if they thought it was funny and a chorus of voices answers, 'Yes!' She then instructs them to turn to the person sitting closest to their shoulder [their 'shoulder partner'] and share what they think made the poem funny.	
After listening to a few of the pairs discuss, Ms Warner interrupts and models for students the kind of answer she is looking for. 'I asked if you think the poem is funny and you said, yes. Then I asked you to talk about what you think made the poem funny. So if I were answering the question, I would say it this way: I think the poem was funny because the boy thinks his father will be proud of him for trading his money for more money but he doesn't realize that having more coins does not mean he has more money'.	
Ms Warner then proceeds to provide scaffolds to support students' oral language output, 'Now when you talk to your partner, use this frame to summarize your thinking: *I think Silverstein's poem 'Smart' is humorous because* _____. After you practice telling your partner, work together to write your answer using the sentence frame'.	
Three pairs of student volunteers are selected to share their written responses and then are invited them to tack them to the bulletin board with the slogan that says, 'The Smart Money's on Room 22'.	
Ms Warner continues the lesson, reinforcing the idea that the value of money is not the same as the quantity of coins and bills.	
She then poses a question for the groups to discuss at their tables:	
'If we were going to help the boy in the poem be really smart with his dollar, what would we have suggested or advised him to do?' She gives them two minutes to discuss, then she calls the groups back together and projects a frame on the board with some words taken out and tells them that together we are going to re-write the poem so that the boy ends up with an amount of money worth a lot more than the boy in the poem. She models how to rewrite the first stanza with the whole group.	

> My dad gave me a dollar
> Because I'm his favorite daughter.
> I traded it for _____ quarters,
> Which is _____ cents more than a dollar.

Next, Ms Warner calls up a small group of English Learner students to work with her. While she is working with them, the rest of the class works in pairs on the coin concentration game, where they turn over two cards and if the value on one card matches the coins pictured on the other, they get to keep those cards. Whoever has the most cards in their possession at the end of the time, wins. Working with the small group, Ms Warner acknowledges that two of the students are already experts with money values and making change because they work with their parents at the swap meet on the weekends. She explains that they need only some additional help with the English words for the coins, and with counting in English. Two other students are less familiar with American currency because they only recently arrived in the United States. (Their parents tried to place them in kindergarten because they do not know English, despite the fact that they have already had two years of school in their home country.) Ms Warner pairs the two student 'experts' with the newcomers and encourages them to play the coin concentration game in their primary language. She adjusts the game by telling this group that in addition to matching, they need to explain how they know the value of the coins on the picture card. Together they practice counting to one hundred and then she gives each student a pronunciation practice CD to take home and listen to and recite the numbers along with the CD.

Anecdotal notes:

Classroom Vignette 2: Ms Rios – Room 26 (Grade 2)

In this classroom the desks are in rows and the bulletin boards have a poster with the class rules and consequences, and a slogan that says, 'Please work quietly so your classmates can concentrate'. There is a large class chart with stars for nightly homework, and a bulletin board displaying students' best work for past spelling tests they completed. There are two mismatched sets of encyclopedias on a bookshelf in the back, some dictionaries, bilingual dictionaries and three computers along the back wall.

    Ms Rios switches on the projector, gets out some U.S. coins, places them on the projector and covers them with a sheet of paper. She instructs all students to get out a sheet of paper and not to share their answers with anyone. When she uncovers the coins, each student is asked to write down the amount of money the coins represent. She models an example by writing the amount. There is no mention of the names of the coins or other mathematical terminology. She proceeds to do seven more reveals. When she is done, she tells students to look at the model displayed on the projector, and to use the answer key to correct their own work.

    Next, Ms Rios displays some picture cards of fruits and vegetables on the board. One by one she places a price tag next to each picture and students are to work individually to figure out the coins that would be needed to make the amount displayed. Finally, they are to write out word problems as if they were shopping for fruits and vegetables and were calculating the amounts needed to purchase. She tells students they would be trading word problems with other students, so that they could solve each other's word problems. Several students were confused and frustrated, but she tells them, 'Just do how best you can'. She then assigns the class two pages in their math books to complete, while she calls up the four students who were struggling. She reminds everyone to be very quiet, and promises extra points to the students that work quietly to complete the assignment. One student points to a picture on the page and asks the name of the objects. Another student jumps in to give the answer and Ms Rios says, 'In here, we encourage everyone to think and figure things out for themselves. There are good dictionaries in the back of the room and don't forget there is a glossary in back of your math text'.

    While students work on the exercises in the textbook, Ms Rios works with the English Learners to practice counting in English and saying the names of the coins. Two students ask, 'Ms Rios, can we just stay at our desks to complete the assignment? We already know how to count in English, we learned that in kindergarten'. She replies, 'No, you need to stay with the English Learner group because you are English Learners'. The students slump in their chairs and roll their eyes. Ms Rios leads the group in counting from one to one hundred, then reviews the names of the U.S. coins, using picture cards from the ELD program.

Anecdotal notes:

Table 4.2 Descriptor rubric for OPAL Domain 4: Interactions

OPAL Domain: Interactions

Varied participation structures allow for interactions that maximize engagement, leadership opportunities and access to the curriculum.

Opal Indicators	1 Novice [rarely or never]	2 Apprentice [basic attempts]	3 Developing [sometimes]	4 Capable [often]	5 Accomplished [consistent]	6 Expert [exceptional]	n/o Not observable
4.1 Facilitates student autonomy and choice by promoting active listening, questioning and/or advocating	Teacher rarely or never employs classroom structures that involve student choice and opportunities for students to critically interact with and examine content through diverse perspectives	Teacher makes basic attempts to employ classroom structures that involve student choice and opportunities for students to critically interact with and examine content through diverse perspectives	Teacher sometimes employs classroom structures that involve student choice and opportunities for students to critically interact with and examine content through diverse perspectives	Teacher often employs classroom structures that involve student choice and opportunities for students to critically interact with and examine content through diverse perspectives	Teacher consistently employs classroom structures that involve student choice and opportunities for students to critically interact with and examine content through diverse perspectives	Teacher shows exceptional ability to consistently employ classroom structures that involve student choice and opportunities for students to critically interact with and examine content through diverse perspectives	The skill or concept is not applicable in the context of this lesson/activity. It may be evident during another observation, but it was not observable during this classroom visit
4.2 Modifies procedures and rules to support student learning	Teacher rarely or never redirects students in a positive manner, with a focus on learning and modifying lesson sequence to accommodate student needs	Teacher makes basic attempts to redirect students in a positive manner, with a focus on learning and modifying lesson sequence to accommodate student needs	Teacher sometimes redirects students in a positive manner, with a focus on learning and modifying lesson sequence to accommodate student needs	Teacher often redirects students in a positive manner, with a focus on learning and modifying lesson sequence to accommodate student needs	Teacher consistently redirects students in a positive manner, with a focus on learning and modifying lesson sequence to accommodate student needs	Teacher shows exceptional ability to consistently redirect students in a positive manner, with a focus on learning and modifying lesson sequence to accommodate student needs	The skill or concept is not applicable in the context of this lesson/activity. It may be evident during another observation, but it was not observable during this classroom visit

(Continued)

76 The Observation Protocol for Academic Literacies

Table 4.2 (Continued)

OPAL Domain: Interactions

Varied participation structures allow for interactions that maximize engagement, leadership opportunities and access to the curriculum.

Opal Indicators	1 Novice [rarely or never]	2 Apprentice [basic attempts]	3 Developing [sometimes]	4 Capable [often]	5 Accomplished [consistent]	6 Expert [exceptional]	n/o Not observable
4.3 Effectively communicates subject matter knowledge in the target language	Teacher shows little or no use of appropriate target language, including pronunciation, articulation, tone and age-appropriate / level-appropriate language	Teacher makes basic attempts to use appropriate target language, including pronunciation, articulation, tone and age-appropriate / level-appropriate language	Teacher sometimes uses appropriate target language, including pronunciation, articulation, tone and age-appropriate / level-appropriate language	Teacher often models appropriate use of the target language, including pronunciation, articulation, tone and age-appropriate / level-appropriate language	Teacher consistently models appropriate use of the target language, including pronunciation, articulation, tone and age-appropriate / level-appropriate language	Teacher shows exceptional ability to consistently model appropriate use of the target language, including pronunciation, articulation, tone and age-appropriate / level-appropriate language	The skill or concept is not applicable in the context of this lesson/activity. It may be evident during another observation, but it was not observable during this classroom visit
4.4 Uses flexible groupings to promote positive interactions and accommodations for individual and group learning needs	Teacher rarely or never establishes classroom routines and structures that provide opportunities for varied collaborative work Teacher rarely or never supports and monitors equity-based student collaboration	Teacher makes basic attempts to establish classroom routines and structures that provide opportunities for varied collaborative work Teacher makes basic attempts to support and monitor equity-based student collaboration	Teacher sometimes establishes classroom routines and structures that provide opportunities for varied collaborative work Teacher sometimes supports and monitors equity-based student collaboration	Teacher often establishes classroom routines and structures that provide opportunities for varied collaborative work Teacher often supports and monitors equity-based student collaboration	Teacher consistently establishes classroom routines and structures that provide opportunities for varied collaborative work Teacher consistently supports and monitors equity-based student collaboration	Teacher shows exceptional ability to consistently establish classroom routines and structures that provide opportunities for varied collaborative work Teacher shows exceptional ability to consistently support and monitor equity-based student collaboration	The skill or concept is not applicable in the context of this lesson/activity. It may be evident during another observation, but it was not observable during this classroom visit

Reading and Scoring STEP 2: Examine Evidence and Assign an OPAL Rating

Now that you have had an opportunity to read each of the classroom vignettes and note anecdotal evidence, review the sources of evidence and OPAL ratings. Review the overall definition of this domain to determine how the classroom context performs on each of the indicators related to promoting interactions for English Learners. Review each of the descriptors on the scoring rubric (Table 4.2). Use your anecdotal notes to determine a rating for each of the OPAL indicators included in OPAL Domain 4: Interactions, Indicators 4.1–4.4.

After Scoring

Review your OPAL ratings for Domain 4: Interactions. Reflect on what you recorded as you analyzed the written vignettes. Compare your scores to those proposed in Table 4.3 below. Note anecdotal evidence and rationale for each rating. Discuss observations about sources of evidence and ratings with a colleague.

Summary

Educators create, facilitate and monitor learning environments that allow English Learners to benefit from maximum engagement, interactions and ownership of learning content and processes. The use of varied interactive structures empowers students to manage and employ content and language learning as active participants in their learning journey.

Reflection

Think about the content of this chapter and the focus questions posed to frame the content of this chapter. Reflect on the following: How has my knowledge in identifying and supporting *interactions* for English Learners increased? What can I do to continue to explore the construct of interactions for English Learners? What strategies for interaction do I presently use? What strategies do I need to observe before implementing in my classroom? Do interaction strategies differ depending on the content or genre of focus (e.g. social studies versus math)?

Table 4.3 Anecdotal evidence and scores for written vignettes

OPAL Domain 4 Interactions	Vignette 1 Ms Warner (Grade 2)	Vignette 2 Ms Rios (Grade 2)
Indicator 4.1	Anecdotal evidence: Throughout the lesson students are given the opportunity to work in pairs and small groups on tasks that elicit their ideas and best thinking rather than on tasks that are rote and fill in the blank with only one right answer. When students express their enjoyment of the poem she read aloud, she directs students to share what they think made it funny so that they learn to listen to and learn from diverse perspectives. The questions she poses respond to the poem. There is some questioning that requires questioning of mathematical concepts. OPAL score: 4	Anecdotal evidence: When Ms Rios models her warm-up activity she reminds students not to share their answers with anyone. Several students are confused during the independent practice and when they ask for help, Ms Rios tells them to do the best they can. There is no evidence that the independent practice activities are designed to promote questioning. OPAL score: 1
Indicator 4.2	Anecdotal evidence: Ms Warner adjusts the work when she is circulating through the pairs and listens to their discussion of what made the poem funny. She realizes there is some misunderstanding of the task and intervenes by providing a model of how to answer the question. When the English Learner students work with Ms Warner she adjusts the matching game to include an explanation of how they know the value of the coins on the picture card. OPAL score: 4	Anecdotal evidence: When working with the English Learner group, two students ask if they can stay at their desks to complete the assignment because they already know how to count in English, but Ms Rios requires that they come to the group. She does not change her procedures to allow these students to work independently despite the fact that they already know how to count in English. OPAL score: 1
Indicator 4.3	Anecdotal evidence: Ms Warner reads the poem aloud and communicates effectively during the lesson. The language that is highlighted throughout the lesson is focused on the literary connection. There is some inconsistency in the use and reinforcement of vocabulary and subject matter terminology for students. OPAL score: 4	Anecdotal evidence: This lesson is taught in English. There are limited opportunities where Ms Rios explained and expands on subject matter knowledge for students. There are also several inconsistencies in language during the delivery of the lesson: e.g., 'Just do how best you can'. OPAL score: 3
Indicator 4.4	Anecdotal evidence: Throughout the lesson, students work in pairs and small groups. Problem solving is done actively and pair groupings are both random (the person sitting nearest your shoulder) and intentional (those in their fixed, regular work groups). During the independent work time, Ms Warner forms a small, flexible group of English Learner students to work with her to assure they understand both the concept and the vocabulary. She recognizes that two of the students are experts with money values and she reinforces the value of that knowledge by encouraging them to mentor their peers in the home language. Evidence around the room shows charts and rubrics indicative of small group work outside of the math time. OPAL score: 5	Anecdotal evidence: The bulletin board slogan 'Please work quietly so your classmates can concentrate' emphasizes the priority of silence and independent work in the classroom. The homework charts highlight individual efforts. When one student answers the question raised by another student and gives the name of a picture on the page, Ms Rios discourages students from helping one another and reminds students 'In this classroom, we encourage everyone to think and figure things out for themselves.' There are plenty of dictionaries in the back of the room and don't forget there is a glossary in the back of your math text'. Ms Rios reinforces students' individual efforts by promising extra points for working quietly on the assignment. She does not permit students to take the initiative to collaborate with other students. OPAL score: 1

Notes

(1) The California English Language Arts/English Language Development Framework uses the term Integrated ELD to describe instruction for English Learners in content areas guided by the ELD and ELA standards. This new term encompasses previously used terms such as sheltered instruction or specially designed academic instruction in English (SDAIE).
(2) **Emerging Proficiency Level:** Students at this level typically progress very quickly, learning to use English for immediate needs as well as beginning to understand and use academic vocabulary and other features of academic language. California Department of Education (CDE) English Language Proficiency Level Definition in English Language Development Standards Publication (2012) www.cde.ca.gov/sp/el/er/documents/eldstndspublication14.pdf.
(3) **Expanding Proficiency Level:** Students at this level are challenged to increase their English skills in more contexts and learn a greater variety of vocabulary and linguistic structures, applying their growing language skills in more sophisticated ways that are appropriate to their age and grade level. California Department of Education (CDE) English Language Proficiency Level Definition in English Language Development Standards Publication (2012) www.cde.ca.gov/sp/el/er/documents/eldstndspublication14.pdf.
(4) California Department of Education (2013, 2014) *California Common Core State Standards: Mathematics*. www.cde.ca.gov/be/st/ss/documents/ccssmathstandardaug2013.pdf.
(5) California Department of Education (2012) *English Language Development Standards Kindergarten through Grade 12*. www.cde.ca.gov/sp/el/er/documents/eldstndspublication14.pdf.

5 OPAL Domain 1: Rigorous and Relevant Curriculum

> *We loved the exercise where we were asked to (re)define what a rigorous learning environment looks like in our district, especially for English Learners. If it means different things to different people we can't support and guide our teachers to refine instruction for our students.*
> – OPAL Institute Participant (District-Level Administrator)

Educators have a moral and legal obligation to provide educational access and opportunity for English Learners based on the same rigorous content standards expected of all students. The implementation of the Common Core State Standards (CCSS) across the United States has required a significant shift in the way programs, curriculum and instruction are provided to this diverse group of language learners. Walqui and Heritage (2012) contended that 'Every teacher will now need to be a teacher of the language and literacies that all their students, including English Learners, must possess to act in disciplinary valued ways in their classes'. This chapter examines how educators can provide a learning context that promotes high expectations for English Learners by planning, organizing and implementing an aligned curriculum that challenges students to think critically, problem solve, innovate and adapt ideas as they engage in relevant and interdisciplinary content learning. Two focus questions will prepare us for the content of this chapter.

FOCUS QUESTIONS:

1. What is *rigorous and relevant curriculum* in the context of teaching English Learners?
2. How is a *rigorous and relevant curriculum* for English Learners evidenced in the classroom? What information can be recorded and analyzed using the OPAL rigorous and relevant curriculum domain indicators?

Introduction

Chapters 3 and 4 provided the reader with an opportunity to examine two research-based constructs essential to effective instruction for English Learners. Chapter 3 focused on the OPAL Comprehensibility Domain, in which *instruction allows for maximum student understanding and teachers utilize effective strategies to help students access content*. In Chapter 4 we explored the OPAL interactions domain and discussed opportunities for *varied participation structures to allow for interactions that maximize engagement, leadership opportunities and access to the curriculum* in content and language learning. In this chapter we present the elements necessary for all students to experience a *rigorous and relevant curriculum* (see Figure 5.1).

First, we provide background information for clusters of indicators in this domain, including brief classroom snapshots highlighting how key characteristics for each indicator might be evidenced in a classroom context. Next, we present teacher reflection questions and an OPAL Descriptor Rubric to assist educators in exploring how different levels of implementation of each of the OPAL indicators for Domain 1 might appear from lower to higher levels of classroom practice. Finally, the reader will practice using the OPAL instrument using written vignettes, descriptions of lessons from our actual classroom observations. These vignettes will give the reader the opportunity to identify objective sources of evidence (anecdotal notes), to determine level(s) of implementation of the various indicators and to mark these on the OPAL Descriptor Rubric. The OPAL can be used by a teacher to reflect on their practice during the lesson planning stage or after delivering a lesson. They can cite sources of evidence and provide a self-rating or seek opportunities to

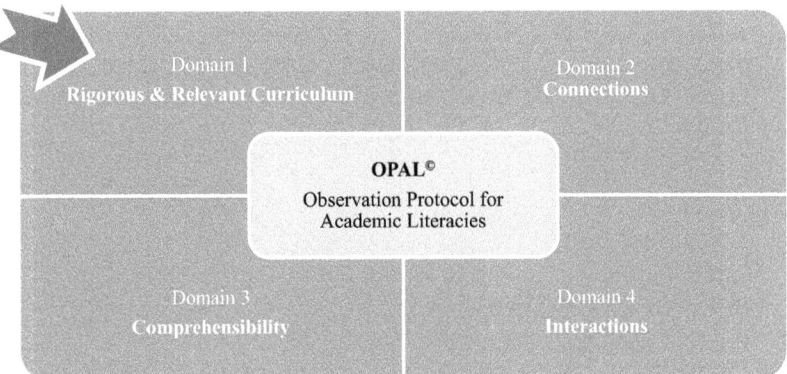

Figure 5.1 The Observation Protocol for Academic Literacies (OPAL) domains

refine lesson planning by reflecting on each of the indicators identified for this domain. Additionally, an external observer or coach may document sources of evidence while observing classroom practice to rate levels of implementation based on each indicator. The vignettes, coupled with the foundational content presented in this chapter, will allow the user to begin to build proficiency toward ascertaining inter-rater reliability and confidently describing classroom practices and student–teacher actions and interactions related to this domain.

What Is the *Rigorous and Relevant Curriculum* in the Context of Teaching English Learners?

A teacher designs instruction based on grade-level academic and language standards, alignment of core content and knowledge of who the students are in their classroom. The first OPAL domain of rigorous and relevant curriculum purports that, for English Learners to attain maximum educational outcomes, *the curriculum [must be] cognitively complex, relevant, challenging and appropriate for linguistically diverse populations.* How can we develop a common definition of rigor? How is relevance achieved? To explore these questions, we ask the reader to engage in the activity described in Figure 5.2.

Activity: Defining rigor

1. **Record personal definition of rigor.** Think of as many words or phrases that describe critical elements of rigorous instruction for English Learners. Record this information.
2. **Read video transcript: Rigor, expectations and interactions (Walqui, 2010).** The transcript below features an excerpt from Dr Aida Walqui's address focused on describing critical elements of the Quality Teaching for English Learners (QTEL) project.[1] The excerpt presents a discussion of rigor in the classroom. As you read the transcript, write down key words and ideas that help define rigor and characteristics of rigorous instruction for English Learners.

Defining Rigor

Figure 5.2 Defining rigor *acrostic poem: A type of poem where the first, last or other letter in each line together spell a word or phrase. Most acrostic poems use the first letter of each line to spell out the word or phrase

... academic rigor can manifest itself in multiple different instantiations but if you walk into a class and you see rigor it doesn't need to look in exactly the same way as if you walk into a different class. But key elements in rigor are that the ideas that are being discussed are central in the discipline so they are kernel ideas and that these ideas are woven, connected to others in clusters of meaning. This is the essence of rigor. Many times in education people think, if it's rigorous then it must be very difficult, or if it's rigorous then it must be almost impossible to understand. That is not the case. Rigorous is: we go for central ideas and we interconnect them in the kinds of relationships in which, in the discipline, we typically find them. Rigorous is also using higher-order thinking skills ... And high expectations in teaching – in teaching English Learners or in teaching any students – is always manifested by engaging students in activities that provide them with high levels of support. So in education high expectations and high levels of support are two sides of the same coin and they are inseparable. Don't ever allow anybody to say 'I have high expectations and my students are not doing well', because the high expectations will only be proven by the kinds of the supports that the teacher brings to the students so that they can truly engage in those interactions. Furthermore, the secret of those interactions are privy to the students. They are aware of what they are doing. They can name it, and they know what it's useful for because unless they do all of that, they cannot own these tools to use them in the future. There has to be a lot of explicit teaching of why we do this, what's the purpose and we have to have clear criteria.

(Walqui, 2010: 0:05–3:25)

3. **Synthesize information using an acrostic poem format.** Next, use your list of ideas to synthesize your knowledge by creating an acrostic poem to convey the idea of rigor for English Learner students. Below are a few examples written by OPAL Institute participants that serve English Learners in different program types such as: (a) Structured English Immersion (SEI) that includes instruction primary in English with sheltered English approaches and primary language support; (b) bilingual programs that use primary language instruction as a vehicle to obtaining English proficiency; and (c) dual language programs where English Learner and English-only students learn content and literacy in two languages to attain sociocultural, bilingual/biliteracy and academic competencies.

When experiencing rigorous and relevant curricula, all students receive the opportunity to engage in and develop 21st-century skills: (1) critical thinking and problem solving; (2) collaboration and leadership; (3) agility and adaptability; (4) initiative and entrepreneurialism; (5)

OPAL Institute Participant Acrostic Poems

Resources of high quality	**R**elevant &	**R**elevant resources build knowledge in two or more languages
Investment in the classroom as a community of learners	**i**nquiry-based	
Grouping conceptual learning	**g**reatness occurs through	**I**nteractions are purposeful and occur in multiple languages
Open-ended questions & thinking skills	**O**rganized, yet spontaneous dialogue about complex	**G**row confidence in language(s) and literacies to support high-level challenges
Reconstructing knowledge for application and expansion	**r**elationships and quality interactions.	**O**ral rehearsal for meaningful dialogue
-Frances Kidwell	-Pablo Cornejo	**R**elationships foster cross-cultural understanding
		-Camila Acosta

Figure 5.3 OPAL institute participant acrostic poems

Table 5.1 Key indicators for OPAL Domain 1: Rigorous and Relevant Curriculum

Opal domain	Indicators
Domain 1: Rigorous and Relevant Curriculum	1.1 Engages students in problem solving, critical thinking and other activities that make subject matter meaningful. 1.2 Facilitates student and teacher access to materials, technology and resources to promote learning. 1.3 Organizes curriculum and teaching to support students' understanding of instructional themes or topics. 1.4 Establishes high expectations for learning that build on students' linguistic and academic strengths and needs. 1.5 Provides access to content and materials in students' primary language. 1.6 Provides opportunities for students to transfer skills between their primary language and target language.

effective oral and written communication; (6) accessing and analyzing information; and (7) curiosity and imagination (Wagner, 2008). Table 5.1 details six key indicators for a rigorous and relevant curriculum that make 21st-century teaching and learning robust for English Learners. As you review Table 5.1, we invite the reader to engage in the 'making connections activity' (Box 5.1) to conduct a quick preview of the domain and its corresponding indicators.

BOX. 5.1 MAKING CONNECTIONS ACTIVITY

- ✓ *Read* each indicator above (Indicators 1.1–1.6);
- ✓ *Highlight* or underline key words/phrases for each of the indicators;
- ✓ *Draw arrows* between the indicators that you believe most connect to one another;
- ✓ *Reflect* on why you believe these relationships exist;
- ✓ Make a *list of any questions* you have about the indicators or key terms.

Once you've completed the 'making connections activity' (Box 5.1), think further about how you can identify connections to *other* indicators in OPAL Domain 3: Comprehensibility or Domain 4: Interactions? Why do you believe connections to the other OPAL Domains exist? See Appendix A (OPAL Technical Report) to explore the statistical analyses on inter-relatedness across domains.

Getting to Know Each Indicator in the OPAL Domain 1: Rigorous and Relevant Curriculum

In the sections that follow we explore each indicator in detail and introduce illustrative classroom snapshots. Expand and deepen your knowledge about the indicators as you read the descriptions for each cluster of indicators presented below.

Indicators 1.1 and 1.3

The first cluster of indicators focuses our attention on what teachers do to promote and provide high quality, intellectual instruction that uplifts the potential of interdisciplinary teaching approaches to deepen and expand students' content knowledge through meaningful learning. Read and consider these two indicators:

1.1 Engages students in problem solving, critical thinking and other activities that make subject matter meaningful
1.3 Organizes curriculum and teaching to support students' understanding of instructional themes or topics

Critical thinking and problem-solving skills require students to use knowledge, facts and data to solve problems by making judgments and decisions about what they have learned (National Research Council, 2012). Teachers facilitate, develop and guide students' ability to synthesize, analyze and apply what they have learned or read across integrated learning contexts. Critical thinking and problem solving (Indicator 1.1) represent one of the learning and innovation skills delineated in the Framework for 21st-Century Learning (Partnership for 21st-Century Learning, A Network of Battelle for Kids, 2019). These skills are also known as the 'Four Cs': (1) Creativity and innovation; (2) Critical thinking and problem solving; (3) Communication; and (4) Collaboration. For teachers of English Learners, providing equitable access to environments that foster these skills requires maintaining high expectations, differentiating instruction and supporting student learning while organizing curriculum and instruction that builds students' understanding of universal themes (Indicator 1.3). See Figure 5.4 for a classroom snapshot that illustrates this. Universal themes are central ideas that transcend cultures, disciplines and geographic locations. Themes can be used to create cross-disciplinary connections and provide an excellent way of organizing a unit of study. Examples of universal themes include:

- Courage.
- Effects of the past.
- Perseverance.
- Change.
- Friendship conflict.
- Loyalty.
- Exploration.
- Relationships.
- Community.
- Survival.
- Force.
- Patterns.
- Interdependence.
- Justice.

Expanding on the idea of universal themes, the Partnership for 21st-Century Learning (2019) argues that 21st-century initiatives should focus on core academic subject mastery *and* 21st-century skills outcomes. The following interdisciplinary themes can be addressed through key subject areas (e.g. reading or language arts, world languages, arts, mathematics, economics, science, geography, history, government and civics):

- Global awareness.
- Financial, economic, business and entrepreneurial literacy.
- Civic literacy.

- Health literacy.
- Environmental literacy.

Furthermore, when developing units of study for English Learners, careful consideration should be given to essential questions, learning goals, assessment and differentiated learning activities, including the pacing and organization of short-term and long-term learning goals in curricular and instructional planning (Gibbons, 2015, 2018; Tomlinson & McTighe, 2006).

Indicator 1.2: Facilitates student and teacher access to materials, technology and resources to promote learning

To create supportive, rigorous and relevant classroom contexts, teachers ensure that English Learners have equitable access to appropriate materials and resources, beyond core texts (Indicator 1.2). These resources are selected for the academic and affective value they bring to students' learning environment. Additionally, they are meant to create a language-rich environment so that English Learners can benefit from exposure to print and language throughout the instructional day. Examples may include:

- List of essential questions and learning goals
- Charts related to development of content, or conversational and academic language structures to support students' oral and written output
- Student-centered work products
- Home–school connection procedures
- Learning logs
- Word work charts or booklets
- Bilingual dictionaries or apps on technology devices
- Multi-genre resources in multiple languages (representative of student demographic): primary source documents, online resources, visual text media, culturally relevant text
- Community-based resources
- Authentic realia

A critical examination of text can be conducted as an additional consideration for text selection. Freeman and Freeman (2007) created a 'cultural relevance' rubric for teachers and/or students to pose questions around cultural relevancy of texts. Box 5.2 offers an adapted version of these questions.

BOX 5.2 CULTURAL RELEVANCE RUBRIC

1. Are the characters in the story like you and your family?
2. Have you ever had an experience like one described in this story?
3. Have you lived in or visited places like those in the story?
4. Could this story take place this year?
5. How close do you think the main characters are to you in age?
6. Do the main characters in the story represent gender variety?
7. Do the characters talk like you and your family do?
8. How often do you read stories like these?

In addition to creating robust learning environments reflective of the diversity in the classroom, teachers can advocate for adapted texts for Emerging Level (beginning) English Learners, including versions in students' primary languages, as well as access to bilingual dictionaries and technology/multi-media to enhance/augment learning. For other language proficiency levels, teachers can explore having excerpts of texts, leveled texts and differentiated texts that allow students to access the same content through different forms and perspectives.

Technology is an integral component of 21st-century learning classrooms. For English Learners, access to technology affords opportunities to develop technology skills through the engagement of digital and multimedia texts. Technology resources can provide forums for additional investigation of topics or authors, sharing/synthesizing information about a topic or text, or locating and using information to justify, persuade, inform or extend knowledge on a given focus area (California Department of Education, 2014; Hopkins, 2017). These meaningful experiences with technology, texts, materials and other resources help engage English Learners in rigorous and relevant learning. See Figure 5.4 for this indicator in action.

Indicator 1.4: Establishes high expectations for learning that build on students' linguistic and academic strengths and needs

Expectations are established based on content and performance standards as well as knowledge of students' academic, developmental and linguistic needs (Indicator 1.4). Teacher expectations of students may be held either consciously or subconsciously but are overtly demonstrated through classroom/school learning experiences and teacher-student interactions, including questioning, assigned tasks, expected output and dialogue and classroom structures. Student academic performance is influenced by a teacher's expectations and goals for student achievement and there are differences in expectations for ethnic, linguistic and socio-economically diverse students (Hopkins, 2017; Rosenthal & Jacobson, 2000; Rubie-Davies *et al.*, 2006; Tenenbaum & Ruck, 2007; Van den Bergh *et al.*, 2010). Awareness of these patterns of behavior becomes an important component of professional development and action in diverse communities.

Classroom Snapshot: Indicators 1.1–1.4
Grade Level: 5
Content Area: Science/Urban Ecology (Structured English Immersion)
English Language Proficiency Level: Expanding (Intermediate)

A scan of Mr. Michael's classroom reveals that students have access to an <u>extensive classroom library. Texts,</u> including magazines and newspapers, are <u>categorized by topic and language</u> (English, Spanish). Also evident throughout the classroom are <u>story maps, graphic organizers, dictionaries, student portfolios, Google Chromebooks</u> at students' desks, and <u>bilingual word walls.</u>

Currently, students are working in groups of four to complete their script for the filming of a Public Service Announcement (PSA). They are writing collaboratively using the Google Docs online platform. The unit's <u>guiding question</u> is posted on the bulletin board: <u>What can we do to create healthy and sustainable ecosystems where we live?</u> A classroom concept chart includes <u>student-written entries that summarize key understandings</u> from lessons in this unit: (a) a city is an urban ecosystem; (b) ecosystems contain biotic, abiotic and human-made elements; (c) humans impact the urban ecosystem; (d) the study of urban ecology is intended to inform environmental action to maintain healthy and sustainable neighborhoods. Each student has an Interactive Science Notebook where they have <u>recorded predictions, synthesized information from oral and written texts, recorded data from field site evaluations, drawn plans for their proposed community solution, and recorded discipline-specific and general academic vocabulary and language structures.</u>

Mr. Michael sits with a group of students to conduct a mini-lesson in support of their development of a script for their PSA. He explains that his goal is to assist them in <u>strengthening their explanation</u> of the problem they identified in order to include sufficient data to <u>justify their proposed solution</u>. He reminds them that the purpose of the PSA is to (1) inform their community about an ecological problem in their city; and (2) explain the importance of their proposed solution. To begin, he asks students to review two sections in their Interactive Science Notebooks and, <u>with a partner, synthesize the information</u> collected during their field site evaluations. Partners report on what they discussed and Mr. Michael asks the group to <u>compare what they hear with what they've already included in their PSA script</u>. Together, Mr. Michael and the group members <u>generate a list of additional, relevant information that can be included in the PSA.</u> They <u>prioritize what should be included</u> and Mr. Michael <u>models different language structures and text connectors for conveying facts in a PSA.</u> He specifically <u>points out the difference in how to structure the PSA script to then be translated into a media text.</u> Students apply what they've learned during their independent group work.

Figure 5.4 Classroom snapshot/OPAL Indicators 1.1–1.4

One approach to establishing high expectations is to couple standards-based efforts with an emphasis on academic language development based on knowledge of students' English proficiency levels. This allows for the differentiation of instruction, while maintaining the delivery of grade-level content as the primary focus (Bunch & Martin, 2021; Chamot & O'Malley, 1994; Heritage *et al.*, 2015; Lee, 2019; Saunders & Goldenberg, 2010). Lessons should be differentiated to incorporate language and content-based learning activities (see Figure 5.4). Heightening awareness of classroom interactions and expectations is critical. It is also essential to develop and use assessment results to inform teaching practices that lead to English Learners' success.

Indicators 1.5 and 1.6

The next cluster of indicators allows us to consider how we leverage students' primary language. In this section we provide background information and research evidence intended to build and extend the understanding of how the use of primary language as well as attention to cross-linguistic transfer can support English Learners. Read and underline key terms in the following indicators:

1.5 Provides access to content and materials in students' primary language
1.6 Provides opportunities for students to transfer skills between their primary language and target language

To meet federal and civil rights requirements, pre-K–12 English Learner students are enrolled in services and programs that enable them 'to attain both English proficiency and parity of participation in the standard instructional program within a reasonable amount of time' (U.S. Department of Education, Office of English Language Acquisition, 2017: 1). For our purposes we focus on three main types of language programming for ELs which include: (1) bilingual; (2) dual language; or (3) Structured English Immersion (SEI). The first two programs use primary language instruction to develop literacy skills and content knowledge in the student's primary language, while simultaneously leveraging English Learners' primary language skills and knowledge to accelerate English language development and academic achievement, the difference being that transitional bilingual programs focus on transitioning students to an all English setting whereas dual language programs focus on primary language (L1) maintenance and bilingual/biliteracy development. In contrast, SEI programs provide instruction overwhelmingly in English and do not develop or maintain English Learners' primary language. Nonetheless, SEI programs can use primary language support as an essential tool for developing English proficiency and academic learning.

Regardless of program type, research affirms that the use of primary language instruction or support for English Learners has a positive impact on learning (Dolson & Burnham-Massey, 2011; Francis *et al.*, 2006; Genesee *et al.*, 2006; National Academies of Sciences, Engineering and Medicine, 2017; Thomas & Collier, 2003). Therefore, it is essential to ensure that *both access to content and materials in students' primary language* (Indicator 1.5) *and* opportunities for students to *transfer skills between their primary language and target language* (Indicator 1.6) are present in the classroom (see Figure 5.5).

Classroom Snapshot: Indicators 1.5 – 1.6
Grade Level: 10
Content Area: Biology (Structured English Instruction)
English Language Proficiency Level: Expanding (Early Intermediate, Intermediate and Early Advanced)

Mr. Pierce begins an end-of-unit lesson where <u>students are asked to write an explanatory/informational text synthesizing the key elements/processes of protein synthesis.</u> Protein synthesis is the process by which a cell combines amino acids to create a polypeptide, or protein. The process is divided into two main stages: transcription, in which the information on a strand of DNA is used to create mRNA; and translation, in which amino acids join to the mRNA to produce a polypeptide. Throughout the unit students have worked in whole group, small groups, and partner groups to create models that detail the process. Posters and drawings of the models they created are found around the room and in their Science Notebooks. Students labeled the stages of the process in English. Students also benefitted from <u>labeling in their primary language (L1),</u> after they had a <u>preview and review of the content in their primary language by either the paraprofessional (</u>for Spanish-speaking English Learners) or a <u>peer</u> (for the Vietnamese-speaking English Learners). Mr. Pierce uses differentiated close reading techniques to help English Learners read, comprehend, and summarize information on protein synthesis from the Biology text as well as other supplemental resources. Although Mr. Pierce does not speak either Spanish or Vietnamese, <u>he has worked with his colleagues to locate material in students' primary language as well as to have in-classroom resources</u> in L1 to help support students' conceptual understanding. To <u>support the transfer of skills</u> between L1 (student's first language)and L2 (target language – English), Mr. Pierce identified <u>characteristics of the text type (explanatory/informational)</u> and worked with the World Language teachers to develop a <u>writing outline that students could use in both classes.</u> In this way, students could <u>transfer their learning from their L1 World Language class to writing in English in their science class.</u> Furthermore, Mr. Pierce expanded the <u>word work section of their Science Notebook to include the recording of cognates for Spanish speaking English Learners.</u> During class, he encourages both Spanish and Vietnamese-speaking English Learners to <u>explain the concept of protein synthesis to their family in L1.</u> After they did this, he asks them to <u>record HOW they were able to use two language systems to communicate content knowledge.</u>

Figure 5.5 Classroom snapshot/OPAL Indicators 1.5–1.6

As noted above, research supports the use of primary language for English Learners in all program types. Within SEI program models, a key strategy is to provide primary language support by using the student's home language to facilitate understanding of core content that is taught in English. Bilingual teachers are uniquely qualified to provide access to the core curriculum through primary language support. However, as described in Figure 5.5, this support can also be provided by paraprofessionals, community members or cross-age/peer tutors. There are numerous primary language strategies that provide access to the core curriculum in English-language classrooms, including, but not limited to:

- Bilingual dictionaries for vocabulary development.
- Bilingual or primary language trade and content area books/texts across a variety of genres (e.g. expository, fiction).
- Cognate charts*.
- Cross-age tutoring.
- Encouraging thinking (cognition) and responses in students' primary language.

*Most relevant for languages that share a common linguistic ancestor.

Furthermore, students' primary languages can be used to preview, or introduce, new concepts at the beginning of a unit or lesson. This increases English Learners' comprehension of content presented during the lesson delivered in English. At the completion of a lesson or unit, a review of what was learned (either teacher-directed or student-led) is conducted using the student's primary language. This is a method of checking for comprehension and is referred to as the 'preview-review' method (Mercuri, 2015; National Academies of Sciences, Engineering and Medicine, 2017; Ovando *et al.*, 2003). This preview-review method is more effective than translating concepts or content during lesson delivery because it helps students become familiar with the content prior to the presentation of the lesson.

Primary language instruction differs from primary language support and is a key element in bilingual and dual language programs. It provides access to the core curriculum by using the student's primary language (e.g. Spanish, Mandarin, Vietnamese) as the medium of instruction. Primary language instruction helps students master grade-level standards in the content areas while simultaneously attending to the acquisition of English proficiency. An additional goal

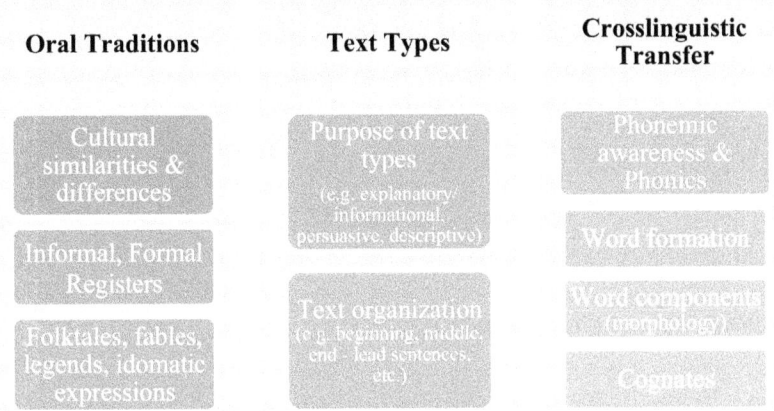

Figure 5.6 Forms of cross-linguistic transfer for English Learners

of target language instruction is for students to develop bilingualism and biliteracy.

To differentiate instruction for English Learners, teachers should encourage students to actively transfer skills between their first language and English (Lucas & Beresford, 2010). This can range from simply pointing out cognates in both languages to explicitly teaching differences in the phonologies (sound systems) and/or grammars between the first and second language. To do this, teachers need to have some basic understanding of the features of the languages spoken by their students. For example, knowing that there are no consonant blends in Vietnamese can help teachers address this feature in oral language or writing instruction. In addition, teachers need to create opportunities for metalinguistic awareness, defined as the ability to monitor and reflect on the use of language with attention to word choice, discourse, grammatical structures, sentence construction, text cohesion and text type and purpose. There are documented benefits of increased levels of metalinguistic awareness for English Learners (Carlo *et al.*, 2004; Ginsberg *et al.*, 2011; Zipke, 2007; Zipke *et al.*, 2009). Teachers can explicitly support the transference of concepts and skills, and identification of English-specific elements, in each of the following areas:

OPAL Domain Indicators 1.5 and 1.6 challenge educators to reflect on and maximize opportunities to strategically capitalize on students' primary language assets as part of the overall delivery and orchestration of a rigorous and relevant curriculum for English Learners.

How Can We Determine What Evidence We See in Observing for the OPAL Domain 1: Rigorous and Relevant Curriculum?

In this section we will explore two classrooms using written vignettes. The reader is asked to think about each of the OPAL Domain 1 (Rigorous and Relevant Curriculum) Indicators as they read the vignettes. Use the right-hand margin to note detailed anecdotal evidence observed in the vignettes. For a review of how to identify and record objective anecdotal evidence see Chapter 2. The following steps are recommended when engaging in this learning experience:

Before reading the vignettes:

- Review the overall definition of this domain, along with the specific indicators (Table 5.1).
- Underline the key words/phrases for each indicator.

Reading and scoring:

- Step 1: Read each written vignette and record anecdotal evidence.
- Step 2: Review the criteria delineated in the OPAL scoring rubric for this domain and use your anecdotal evidence to assign a rating.

After scoring:

- Compare your scores to those provided in this text.
- Identify additional sources of evidence for each indicator.
- Discuss results and implications for classroom practice.

OPAL Domain 1: Rigorous and Relevant Curriculum – Reflection Questions

Several questions can guide the reader in examining how teaching and learning are occurring in these classroom contexts to promote implementation of rigorous and relevant curriculum. In particular, *how does the classroom context ...*

- Engage students in problem solving and critical thinking?
- Use curricular materials that represent cultural perspectives?

- Present lessons and units of study to promote cross-curricular understanding based on cognitive *and* language proficiency levels?
- Identify learning objectives that address language and content standards?
- Establish high expectations based on content and English Learner standards to address students' linguistic and academic needs?
- Provide access to materials and content in students' primary language?
- Provide opportunities for students to transfer what they know from their first language to English?

Reading and Scoring STEP 1: Read Each Vignette and Note Anecdotal Evidence Focused on OPAL Domain 1: Rigorous and Relevant Curriculum

Context for vignettes

The vignettes presented here were developed based on actual classroom observations. Pseudonyms are used to respect each teacher's commitment to creating opportunities for transparent, objective and reflective examination of classroom practices for English Learner students. The context for each set of vignettes is provided to give the reader an overall picture of factors that may have influenced decision-making processes, delivery of instruction and classroom practices. These include content area, grade level, English Learner language proficiency level(s) and focus content standards.

Because these classroom observations occurred in California, content standards are specific to those adopted by the California State Board of Education: (1) Common Core State Standards (CCSS) for English Language Arts and Literacy in History/Social Studies, Science and Technical Subjects and Mathematics (CDE, 2010, 2013); (2) Next Generation Science Standards (CDE, 2013); (3) History Social Science Content Standards (CDE, 1998/2000); and (4) English Language Development (ELD) Standards (CDE, 2012). Nationally, each state determines the standards that are taught in schools. A number of states across the nation have adopted the same or similar Common Core Standards for English and math while others have revised, edited or created other versions to respond to their state context. As such, we expect that readers will (1) recognize similarities in the content *and* language standards connections presented for each vignette and (2) engage in the proposed 'reading and scoring' steps to examine practices for English Learners using the OPAL indicators.

Content focus and factors – Vignette 1

> **Content Area:** Mathematics
> **Grade:** 6
> **Language Proficiency Level:** Expanding[2] (Intermediate)

STANDARDS CONNECTION

California Common Core State Standards – Mathematics[3] – Grade 6

Domain:

Expressions and Equations (6EE)

Mathematical Content Standards for Expressions and Equations:

6EE: Apply and extend previous understandings of arithmetic to algebraic expressions

2c. Evaluate expressions at specific values of their variables. Include expressions that arise from formulas used in real-world problems. Perform arithmetic operations, including those involving whole-number exponents, in the conventional order when there are no parentheses to specify a particular order (**Order of Operations**).

3. Apply the **properties of operations** to generate equivalent expressions.

Mathematical Practices:

- MP1: Make sense of problems and persevere in solving them;
- MP2: Reason abstractly and quantitatively;
- MP3: Construct viable arguments and critique the reasoning of others;
- MP6: Attend to precision.

California English Language Development Standards[4] – Grade 6

I.A1 Exchanging information and ideas. Contribute to class, group and partner discussions by following turn-taking rules, asking relevant questions, affirming others, adding relevant information and paraphrasing key ideas.

I.B5 Listening actively. Demonstrate active listening in oral presentation activities by asking and answering detailed questions, with occasional prompting and moderate support.

I.C9 Presenting. Plan and deliver longer oral presentations on a variety of topics and content areas, using details and evidence to support ideas.

School context

This vignette is from a sixth–eighth grade-span school in a small pre-K–eight school district located in a highly impacted community with many families with parents who are first-generation immigrants to the United States and children who were born in the United States. For most US-born students, their first language at home was Spanish; many have become conversant in English but are still classified as English Learners because they have not scored proficient on the required English proficiency test and have been stagnant at the *expanding* level for several years.

Lesson context

Grade six teachers plan and present lessons on the order of operations to provide opportunities for students to apply and extend previous understandings of arithmetic to algebraic expressions (see standards identified above). Sixth-grade students are expected to 'apply algebraic order of operations and the commutative, associative and distributive properties to evaluate expressions; and justify each step in the process'. Each teacher has prepared her own lesson for the introduction of this concept. About half of the students in these two classes are classified as English Learners with Expanding English proficiency. They all have varying levels of Spanish language proficiency. Most do not read or write Spanish.

Classroom Vignette 1: Mrs Nguyen – Room 101 (grade 6)

	Anecdotal notes:
The seating arrangement in Room 101 is organized in double rows of desks so that students are paired at all times. There is a whiteboard in the front of the class and bulletin boards on one side and in the back of the room. The side bulletin board reflects the current topic of study, including completed student tests and a slogan that reads **Room 101 is > Ever.** The back bulletin board displays a number of large charts with lists of Spanish and English cognate patterns related to mathematics. On the bookshelf along the back wall is a class set of dictionaries, including math glossaries and Spanish/English bilingual dictionaries.	

-ive	-ivo, -iva
additive	aditivo
distributive	distributivo
associative	asociativo
multiplicative	multiplicativo
negative	negativo
positive	positivo

Mrs Nguyen warms up the class for the lesson by quickly walking them outside to the front of the school where the busses and cars drop off and pick up students each day. She asks students to sketch the entrance and exit and to indicate some kind of sign or symbol to let the vehicles know which way they must proceed. Mrs Nguyen asks students to talk with their partners and predict what might happen if there were no clear routine about which driveway is the entrance and which the exit is. She asks them to use the sentence frame:

> If there were no clear directions about which driveway to enter, then_____.

She then directs the pairs to come up with as many different scenarios as they can think of to analyze what might happen if the vehicles do not have a clear direction that shows how to enter. She then points to the four-way stop at the corner in front of the school and asks, 'What happens when four cars stop at the same time, which car goes first? How do people know that? What happens if a car goes out of order?'

Mrs Nguyen asks students to sit down on the grass and pull out their notebook and pencil. She holds up her individual whiteboard for the class to see. It has the following written on it:

$$2 + 9 \div 3 - 5 + 6 \times 5 \div 2 = ?$$

Mrs Nguyen reads this aloud and asks students to copy it down and work with their partner to figure out the answer. She circulates through the group to listen to their problem-solving conversations. Next, she tells each pair to partner with another pair and share their answer and justify how they got the answer. She tells them to be prepared to explain to the whole group what their partner pair did to get their answer. She gives them a sentence frame to use to report their answer <u>and</u> how they arrived at their answer:

> Our partners' answer is _____. They found the answer by_____.

She has each group display the problem with the answer written in the blank space. Students are challenged to huddle with their partners and discuss why some groups came up with different answers. Mrs Nguyen asks them to come back into the classroom to share their ideas. After each group reports out, Mrs Nguyen summarizes by indicating that without applying rules to tell us which operation to complete first, we ended up with different possible ways to solve the equation and several different answers. She then points out to students how she gave her summary, the language she used and how important it is for them to have the flexibility to speak in academic language as well informal conversational language.

Mrs Nguyen asks students questions to help them discover the connection between the math problem and the chaos that would develop in the parking lot if there were no rules or order for drivers to follow. In the same way, the students determine, a number sentence needs a set of rules for the order of operations to get consistent answers. Mrs Nguyen writes a new equation on the board and reviews the order of operations by writing the mnemonic device PEMDAS vertically on the board. Next to each letter she writes the step in the order of operations and draws the related symbol such as the parenthesis or plus or minus sign. As she demonstrates each step, she encourages teams to look again at their problem and determine how to solve it by using the order of operations. She challenges students to think about the implications for addition and subtraction versus multiplication and division.

On the exit slip at the end of the period, Mrs Nguyen asks students to explain the order of operations and to tell why mathematicians use it.

Complete Step 1 – 'Read and record anecdotal evidence' for Vignette 1 and turn your attention to Vignette 2 which offers a second opportunity to look for evidence related to the OPAL Domain 1: Rigorous and Relevant Curriculum. Begin by previewing the content focus and factors for this vignette. Be sure to note anecdotal evidence for this vignette as well. Once you complete Step 1 for both Vignettes you'll examine your evidence and score both vignettes using the descriptor rubric (Table 5.2).

Content focus and factors – Vignette 2

> **Content Area:** American Literature – Writer's Workshop
> **Grade Level:** 11
> **Language Proficiency Level(s):** Expanding/Bridging (Intermediate and Early Advanced)[5]

STANDARDS CONNECTION

English Language Arts Common Core State Standards[6] – Grades 11–12

Speaking and Listening: Comprehension and Collaboration: SL1a-d

1. Initiate and participate effectively in a range of collaborative discussions (one-on-one, groups and teacher-led) with diverse partners on grade 11–12 topics, texts and issues, building on others' ideas and expressing their own clearly and persuasively.
   a. Come to discussions prepared, having read and researched material under study; explicitly draw on that preparation by referring to evidence from texts and other research on the topic or issue to stimulate a thoughtful, well-reasoned exchange of ideas.
   b. Work with peers to promote civil, democratic discussions and decision-making, set clear goals and deadlines and establish individual roles as needed.
   c. Propel conversations by posing and responding to questions that probe reasoning and evidence; ensure a hearing for a full range of positions on a topic or issue; clarify, verify or challenge ideas and conclusions; and promote divergent and creative perspectives.
   d. Respond thoughtfully to diverse perspectives; synthesize comments, claims and evidence made on all sides of an issue; resolve contradictions when possible; and determine what additional information or research is required to deepen the investigation or complete the task.

Writing: Text Types and Purposes: W1d, 2a; Production and Distribution of Writing: W4, W5

W1d: Establish and maintain a formal style and objective tone while attending to the norms and conventions of the discipline in which they are writing.

W2a: Write informative/explanatory texts to examine and convey complex ideas, concepts and information clearly and accurately through the effective selection, organization and analysis of content.
  a. Introduce a topic **or thesis statement**; organize complex ideas, concepts and information so that each new element builds on that which precedes it to create a unified whole; include formatting (e.g., headings), graphics (e.g., figures, tables) and multimedia when useful to aiding comprehension.

W4: Produce clear and coherent writing in which the development, organization and style are appropriate to task, purpose and audience.

W5: Develop and strengthen writing as needed by planning, revising, editing, rewriting or trying a new approach, focusing on addressing what is most significant for a specific purpose and audience. (Editing for conventions should demonstrate command of Language standards 1-3 up to and including grades 11-12.)

California English Language Development Standards[7] – Grades 11–12

I.A.1: Exchanging information and ideas. Contribute to class, group and partner discussions, sustaining conversations on a variety of age and grade-appropriate academic topics by following turn-taking rules, asking and answering relevant, on-topic questions, affirming others and providing coherent and well-articulated comments and additional information.

I.A.4: Adapting language choices. Adjust language choices according to the task (e.g., group presentation of research project), context (e.g., classroom, community), purpose (e.g., to persuade, to provide arguments or counterarguments) and audience (e.g., peers, teachers, college recruiter).

I.B.5: Listening actively. Demonstrate comprehension of oral presentations and discussions on a variety of social and academic topics by asking and answering detailed and complex questions that show thoughtful consideration of the ideas or arguments with light support

I.C.10a: Writing. a. Write longer and more detailed literary and informational texts (e.g., an argument about free speech) collaboratively (e.g., with peers) and independently by using appropriate text organization and register.

II.A.1: Understanding text structure. Apply analysis of the organizational structure of different text types (e.g., how arguments are organized by establish clear relationships among claims, counterclaims, reasons and evidence) to comprehending texts and to writing clear and cohesive arguments, informative/explanatory texts and narratives.

School context

This vignette is from a mid-size urban high school district. The student population is multilingual and multiethnic. The classroom is part of the PUENTE Project.[8] PUENTE is a national award-winning program that for more than 30 years has improved the college-going rate of tens of thousands of California's educationally underrepresented students. Its mission is to increase the number of educationally disadvantaged students who enroll in four-year colleges and universities, earn college degrees and return to the community as mentors and leaders to future generations. The program is interdisciplinary in approach, with writing, counseling and mentoring components.

Lesson context

Students receive instruction as part of the Structured English Immersion program. Students are at the Expanding/Bridging (Intermediate and Early Advanced) Proficiency levels. Students engage in revision and peer editing of the second drafts of their expository/persuasive, literary analysis and autobiographic writing.

Classroom Vignette 2: Mr Triggs – Room 203 (Grade 11)

Students have access to an authentic literature library that has grade-span texts, including a representation of culturally relevant books. Students use semantic mapping and writer's reference notebooks. Mr Triggs utilizes the STAR (**S**ubstitute, **T**ake out, **A**dd, **R**earrange) writing strategy and the PUENTE writing competencies as part of the writer's workshop. Mr Triggs uses a projector to display information on the whiteboard for students to follow along. Students have technology devices available to them and can access apps, dictionaries and search engines to research needed items to revise or expand written content. Mr Triggs begins his lesson by reviewing the STAR writing strategy for students to use as they revise the second draft of their papers and participate in peer editing with fellow students. Mr Triggs reviews an earlier lesson: 'We talked yesterday about "starring" your paper with revise. We substitute, we take things out, we add things and we rearrange them if we need to'. Mr Triggs provides an example of how he rearranged an introduction about prominent figures in U.S. history to organize his writing in chronological order. Mr Triggs provides English Learner support by modeling how to think aloud as he incorporates the STAR writing strategy into his writing. He elicits student input by asking if any other figures can be added in his writing and insists that students justify their responses. Mr Triggs makes connections to previous learning by reviewing the three types of writing genres they have done in class before: the autobiographical, the expository-persuasive and literary analysis. To support student learning, he asks the students, 'So, you are going to tell me what your topic is and which of those three you are writing and that will tell me how to group you guys'. The students share their topic and type of writing genre they selected. Mr Triggs expands on students' thinking by asking students to elaborate on the topic and writing genres they selected. **Student (Steven):** My essay is about how the author argues that with power comes greed, and also how – like the hierarchy of how the leader and then the people who work for him.	Anecdotal notes:

	Anecdotal notes:
Teacher (Mr Triggs): Okay. And that's going to be like a power hierarchy, I assume. Why did you make that decision?	
Student (Steven): Yes. This was one of the themes we discussed in our history class.	
Teacher (Mr Triggs): Okay. So you're doing literary analysis.	
Student (Steven): Yes.	
Teacher (Mr Triggs): Okay. Beautiful. Viviana.	
Student (Viviana): I'm doing an expository-persuasive on children stories.	
Teacher (Mr Triggs): Okay. So talk to me about that how – what is it that you are arguing that makes it persuasive or what is it that you are explaining that makes it expository?	
Student (Viviana): Like the pigs are trying to convince all the other animals that humans are bad and then, in the story, the teacher is trying to convince students that they shouldn't be doing things to other people.	
Teacher (Mr Triggs): So you are comparing how the two pieces of literature are similar?	
Student (Viviana): Yeah.	

To transition to the next phase of revision and peer editing, Mr Triggs reiterates that part of the process of getting drafts better is 'sharing your work with other people and getting their input, so that's what we are going to do right now'. He instructs the students to get into groups of three and turn their desks so that they all face each other. Once the students are grouped into pairs of three, Mr Triggs reviews the different roles students will engage in while peer reviewing the essays of other students in their groups. As he reviews the roles of the reader and responder listed on the whiteboard, he verbally provides the instructions: 'You are going to take turns – whoever is sitting closest to me is going to be the first reader, okay? The reader reads the essay slowly and clearly – you want to be able to go slowly enough so that your readers can understand you and think about what you are saying. If you are a responder, you are listening for strong lines. For me, when I do this, I've got to write down a couple of words, otherwise I'm going to forget it by the time I get to the end of the – listening to the essay. So listen for some strong lines and then think of one question. What's the question you can ask that might help the writer add more information or be more specific about the information. Okay? The reader underlines the strong lines on their own paper and then writes down the questions'. At the end of the instructions, Mr Triggs emphasizes, 'After you write down the questions that your reader asks, you say thank you, don't forget this – you say thank you and then somebody else becomes the reader and you do it again'. As the students read and share their feedback to improve the essays, Mr Triggs walks around the classroom to monitor students interacting during group time. He provides individual support to groups requesting additional classification on specific writing genres.

After the peer review, Mr Triggs reviews the different components of the PUENTE writing competencies strategy to transition into an activity in which students brainstorm the areas they need to improve on their essays, regardless of which type of the three writing types they selected. Mr Triggs explains, 'In other words, one of the things that no matter what you are writing you need to do well – you need to have a thesis and you need to stick to that thesis. So that's one thing that I would do. I gave you a thesis, what else do we need to have? No matter what kind of paper you are writing, what else do you need to have?' Mr Triggs applies the 'sequence' component of the PUENTE writing competencies strategy to review the degree of structure and coherence in a composition. The students work together to brainstorm areas to improve their essays. For the brainstorming activity, Mr Triggs writes down the three writing genres

	Anecdotal notes:
on the white board, along with an additional category, 'Universals', to visually display the similarities and differences in each writing genre. The students raise their hands to provide their input as Mr Triggs writes the areas on the white board for each of the three writing genres. One student shared starting an essay with a good lead. Mr Triggs expands on the idea of writing a good lead by comparing and contrasting how a lead will be written differently based on the specific writing genre. He explains, 'And that lead would be a little bit differently written – those of you that are doing the autobiographical, they would be a little differently written, but you guys will have the same'. Mr Triggs points to 'universals' and 'literacy analysis' on the whiteboard to emphasize the genres where the lead is written differently. After the brainstorming activity, Mr Triggs redirects the students to look at the lists and identify one or two areas they are struggling with, and to focus on those areas as they share with new partners outside of their groups. He also instructs students to develop open-ended questions on the two areas for their new peer partner to focus on as they read their drafts. Students work with other students to share their questions and provide their input on ways to improve their drafts. Students quietly read the essays and answer the open-ended questions. As the students finish sharing and getting ready to end the class, Mr Triggs asks the students to continue working on improving their drafts and bring in their revisions the next day to conference with him one-on-one about strengthening the content of their essays.	

Reading and Scoring STEP 2: Examine Evidence and Assign an OPAL Rating

Now that you've had an opportunity to read the classroom vignettes and note anecdotal evidence, review the sources of evidence and OPAL ratings. Review the overall definition of this domain to determine how the classroom context performs on each of the indicators related to providing a rigorous and relevant curriculum for English Learners. Review each of the descriptors on the scoring rubric (Table 5.2). Use your anecdotal notes to determine a rating for each of the OPAL indicators included in OPAL Domain 1: Rigorous and Relevant Curriculum (Indicators 1.1–1.6).

After Scoring

Review your OPAL ratings for Domain 1: Rigorous and Relevant Curriculum. Reflect on what you recorded as you analyzed the written vignettes. Compare your scores to those proposed in Table 5.3. Note anecdotal evidence and rationale for each rating. Discuss observations about sources of evidence and ratings with a colleague.

Summary

To provide access and equity for English Learners in 21st-century classrooms, educators create contexts and learning opportunities that promote high expectations by planning, organizing and implementing an aligned curriculum that challenges students to think critically, problem solve, innovate and adapt ideas as they engage in relevant and

104 The Observation Protocol for Academic Literacies

Table 5.2 Descriptor rubric for OPAL Domain 1: Rigorous and Relevant Curriculum

OPAL Domain 1: Rigorous and Relevant Curriculum
The curriculum is cognitively complex, relevant, challenging and appropriate for linguistically diverse populations.

Opal indicators	1 Novice [rarely or never]	2 Apprentice [basic attempts]	3 Developing [sometimes]	4 Capable [often]	5 Accomplished [consistent]	6 Expert [exceptional]	n/o Not observable
1.1. Engages students in problem solving, critical thinking and other activities that make subject matter meaningful	Teacher *rarely or never* engages students in problem solving activities and supports students in critically investigating subject matter through multiple approaches that make subject matter meaningful	Teacher makes *basic attempts to* engage students in problem solving activities and supports students in critically investigating subject matter through multiple approaches that make subject matter meaningful	Teacher *sometimes* engages students in problem solving activities and supports students in critically investigating subject matter through multiple approaches that make subject matter meaningful	Teacher *often* engages students in problem solving activities and supports students in critically investigating subject matter through multiple approaches that make subject matter meaningful	Teacher *consistently* engages students in problem solving activities and supports students in critically investigating subject matter through multiple approaches that make subject matter meaningful	Teacher shows *exceptional ability* to consistently engage students in problem solving activities and support students in critically investigating subject matter through multiple approaches that make subject matter meaningful	The skill or concept is not applicable in the context of this lesson/activity. It may be evident during another observation, but it was *not observable* during this classroom visit
1.2 Facilitates student and teacher access to materials, technology and resources to promote learning	Teacher *rarely or never* allows access to and incorporates the use of a variety of instructional materials, technology and supplemental resources that reflect diversity and support and enhance student learning	Teacher makes *basic attempts to* allow access to and appropriate the use of a variety of instructional materials, technology and supplemental resources that reflect diversity and support and enhance student learning	Teacher *sometimes* allows access to and incorporates the use of a variety of instructional materials, technology and supplemental resources that reflect diversity and support and enhance student learning	Teacher *often* allows access to and incorporates the use of a variety of instructional materials, technology and supplemental resources that reflect diversity and support and enhance student learning	Teacher *consistently* allows access to and incorporates the use of a variety of instructional materials, technology and supplemental ppropri that reflect diversity and support and enhance student learning	Teacher shows *exceptional ability* to consistently allow access to and incorporate the use of a variety of instructional materials, technology and supplemental resources that reflect diversity and support and enhance student learning	The skill or concept is not applicable in the context of this lesson/activity. It may be evident during another observation, but it was *not observable* during this classroom visit

1.3 Organizes curriculum and teaching to support students' understanding of instructional themes or topics	Teacher *rarely or never* selects and sequences units of study and lessons that promote student understanding of themes and topics and show relationships to other subject areas	Teacher *makes basic attempts to* select and sequence units of study and lessons that promote student understanding of themes and topics and show relationships to other subject areas	Teacher *sometimes* selects and sequences units of study and lessons that promote student understanding of themes and topics and show relationships to other subject areas	Teacher *often* selects and sequences units of study and lessons that promote student understanding of themes and topics and show relationships to other subject areas	Teacher *consistently* selects and sequences units of study and lessons that promote student understanding of themes and topics and show relationships to other subject areas	Teacher shows *exceptional ability to consistently* select and sequence units of study and lessons that promote student understanding of themes and topics and show relationships to other subject areas	The skill or concept is not applicable in the context of this lesson/ activity. It may be evident during another observation, but it was *not observable* during this classroom visit
1.4 Establishes high expectations for learning that build on students' linguistic and academic strengths and needs	Teacher *rarely or never* establishes high expectations and clearly explains learning goals that are academically, linguistically and developmentally appropriate	Teacher *makes basic attempts* to establish high expectations and clearly explain learning goals that are academically, linguistically and developmentally appropriate	Teacher *sometimes* establishes high expectations and clearly explains learning goals that are academically, linguistically and developmentally appropriate	Teacher *often* establishes high expectations and clearly explains learning goals that are academically, linguistically and developmentally appropriate	Teacher *consistently* establishes high expectations and clearly explains learning goals that are academically, linguistically and developmentally appropriate	Teacher shows *exceptional ability to consistently* establish high expectations and clearly explain learning goals that are academically, linguistically and developmentally appropriate	The skill or concept is not applicable in the context of this lesson/ activity. It may be evident during another observation, but it was *not observable* during this classroom visit
1.5 Provides access to content and materials in students' primary language	Teacher *rarely or never* uses the students' primary language (L1) as a teaching and learning tool to support all students in achieving learning goals	Teacher *makes basic attempts* to use the students' primary language (L1) as a teaching and learning tool to support all students in achieving learning goals	Teacher *sometimes* uses the students' primary language (L1) as a teaching and learning tool to support all students in achieving learning goals	Teacher *often* uses the students' primary language (L1) as a teaching and learning tool to support all students in achieving learning goals	Teacher *consistently* uses the students' primary language (L1) as a teaching and learning tool to support all students in achieving learning goals	Teacher shows *exceptional ability to consistently* use the students' primary language (L1) as a teaching and learning tool to support all students in achieving learning goals	The skill or concept is not applicable in the context of this lesson/ activity. It may be evident during another observation, but it was *not observable* during this classroom visit

(Continued)

Table 5.2 (Continued)

OPAL Domain 1: Rigorous and Relevant Curriculum
The curriculum is cognitively complex, relevant, challenging and appropriate for linguistically diverse populations.

Opal indicators	1 Novice [rarely or never]	2 Apprentice [basic attempts]	3 Developing [sometimes]	4 Capable [often]	5 Accomplished [consistent]	6 Expert [exceptional]	n/o Not observable
1.6 Provides opportunities for students to transfer skills between primary language and target language	Teacher rarely or never capitalizes on primary language (L1) skills that transfer to second language (L2) and uses student knowledge of L1 and L2 as learning tools, appropriate to instructional goals	Teacher makes basic attempts to capitalize on primary language (L1) skills that transfer to second language (L2) and uses student knowledge of L1 and L2 as learning tools, appropriate to instructional goals	Teacher sometimes capitalizes on primary language (L1) skills that transfer to second language (L2) and uses student knowledge of L1 and L2 as learning tools, appropriate to instructional goals	Teacher often capitalizes on primary language (L1) skills that transfer to second language (L2) and uses student knowledge of L1 and L2 as learning tools, appropriate to instructional goals	Teacher consistently capitalizes on primary language (L1) skills that transfer to second language (L2) and uses student knowledge of L1 and L2 as learning tools, appropriate to instructional goals	Teacher shows *exceptional ability* to consistently capitalize on primary language (L1) skills that transfer to second language (L2) and use student knowledge of L1 and L2 as learning tools, appropriate to instructional goals	The skill or concept is not applicable in the context of this lesson/ activity. It may be evident during another observation, but it was not *observable* during this classroom visit

Table 5.3 Anecdotal evidence and scores for written vignettes

OPAL Domain 1: Rigorous and Relevant Curriculum	Vignette 1 Mrs Nguyen (grade 6)	Vignette 2 Mr Triggs (grade 11)
Indicator 1.1	Anecdotal evidence: Throughout the lesson, Mrs Nguyen often engages students in problem solving activities and supports students in critically investigating subject matter through multiple approaches that make subject matter meaningful. Rather than begin the lesson with a rote introduction of the order of operations, Mrs Nguyen challenges students to explain how a real-life example is related to the need for a consistent approach for systems to follow. She then has students apply this to their thinking about math equations. She builds in opportunities for students to discover the importance of the order of operations and how it works by giving students an opportunity to examine and analyze how others in the class solved the equation. Score: 4	Anecdotal evidence: During the delivery of the lesson plan, Mr Triggs prompts students to ask questions and actively listen to strategies to use while sharing their first drafts with each other. Students are asked to reflect on and engage in discussion on the similarities and differences between the three different writing genres. Mr Triggs engages the students in an activity to identify universal themes and specific approaches related to expository/persuasive, literary analysis and autobiographic writing. Score: 3
Indicator 1.2	Anecdotal evidence: Even though this is a math class, Mrs Nguyen allows access to and incorporates the use of a variety of instructional materials that reflect diversity and support and enhance student learning. There are a number of reference materials available to students such as dictionaries, glossaries and bilingual dictionaries. Score: 5	Anecdotal evidence: Students have access to an authentic literature library. Students use semantic mapping and writer's reference notebooks. Mr Triggs utilizes the STAR writing strategy and the PUENTE writing competencies as part of the writer's workshop. Mr Triggs uses a projector to display information on the whiteboard for students to follow along. Students use technology devices to access apps, dictionaries/thesaurus. Additionally, students can research historical figures or other information needed to write their texts. Score: 4
Indicator 1.3	Anecdotal evidence: Mrs Nguyen is aware of the standards from previous grade levels and plans instruction to consistently provide a review of foundational knowledge to students to access grade-level content. She selects and sequences the lesson to promote student understanding of themes and topics and show relationships to other subject areas. She incorporates all language domains (listening, speaking, reading, writing). Score: 4	Anecdotal evidence: Mr Triggs provides students with opportunities to reflect on elements of revising and organizing essays by modeling and incorporating the STAR writing strategies and the PUENTE writing competencies as part of the writer's workshop. The universal themes are posted in the classroom and students keep a writer's notebook to monitor learning and progress over the semester. Students are also asked to reflect on elements for good writers. He provides step-by-step instructions for the editing process to support their role as peer responders and editors. Score: 4

(Continued)

Table 5.3 (Continued)

OPAL Domain 1: Rigorous and Relevant Curriculum	Vignette 1 Mrs Nguyen (grade 6)	Vignette 2 Mr Triggs (grade 11)
Indicator 1.4	Anecdotal evidence: Mrs Nguyen explains learning goals and the instructional steps throughout the lesson. The language and content goals for the lesson are listed on the whiteboard; some students have noted them in their notebooks. When providing problems for students during the lesson, there was not evidence of differentiation of problems, nor higher level mathematical academic language usage. She provides only one type of sentence frame, although she has various ELD levels represented in her classroom. Score: 3	Anecdotal evidence: Mr Triggs establishes the expectations of the writer's workshop to empower students to take ownership of the process. He provides instructions and defines the roles of readers and responders. As he reviews the roles listed on the whiteboard, he verbally provides the instructions: 'You are going to take turns – whoever is sitting closest to me is going to be the first reader, okay? The reader reads the essay slowly and clearly – you want to be able to go slowly enough so that your readers can understand you and think about what you are saying. If you are a responder, you are listening for strong lines. For me, when I do this, I've got to write down a couple of words, otherwise I'm going to forget it by the time I get to the end of the – listening to the essay. So listen for some strong lines and then think of one question. What's the question you can ask that might help the writer add more information or be more specific about the information. Okay? The reader underlines the strong lines on their own paper and then writes down the questions'. Score: 4
Indicator 1.5	Anecdotal evidence: Mrs Nguyen does not speak Spanish but includes resources in the room such as her chart of Spanish-language cognates to accompany the English terminology. Students keep a record of these in their math journals and student work shows this serves as a teaching and learning tool. She has resources available in Spanish. Score: 4	Anecdotal evidence: There are no opportunities for students to access content and materials in their primary language (L1). Score: 1
Indicator 1.6	Anecdotal evidence: Mrs Nguyen capitalizes on primary language skills that transfer from Spanish to English by encouraging students to think about the comparison and contrast between the terminology in English and in Spanish. She has a cognate word wall posted in the classroom to reinforce the connections between the two languages. Score: 3	Anecdotal evidence: There are no opportunities for students to transfer skills between their primary language (L1) and target language (L2). Score: 1

interdisciplinary content learning. Culturally relevant materials and resources responsive to students' academic, developmental and linguistic levels are used to leverage students' assets, including knowledge and transfer of primary language skills and resources. Carefully designed and orchestrated, the inclusion of all of these elements results in the provision of a rigorous and relevant curriculum for English Learners.

Reflection

Think about the content of this chapter and the focus questions that began it. Reflect on the following: how has my knowledge in identifying and supporting *rigorous and relevant curriculum* for English Learners increased? What can I do to continue to explore this construct to refine my work with English Learners?

Notes

(1) WestEd's Quality Teaching for English Learners (QTEL) works to provide both elementary and secondary educators with the tools they need to accelerate language development, academic literacy and disciplinary knowledge of all students, particularly English learners. For more information about QTEL visit www.qtel.wested.org/.
(2) *Expanding Proficiency Level:* Students at this level are challenged to increase their English skills in more contexts and learn a greater variety of vocabulary and linguistic structures, applying their growing language skills in more sophisticated ways that are appropriate to their age and grade level. California Department of Education (CDE) English Language Proficiency Level Definition in English Language Development Standards Publication (2012) www.cde.ca.gov/sp/el/er/documents/eldstndspublication14.pdf.
(3) California Department of Education (2013, 2014) *California Common Core State Standards: Mathematics.* www.cde.ca.gov/be/st/ss/documents/ccssmathstandaraug2013.pdf.
(4) California Department of Education (2012) *English Language Development Standards Kindergarten through Grade 12.* www.cde.ca.gov/sp/el/er/documents/eldstndspublication14.pdf.
(5) *Expanding Proficiency Level:* Students at this level are challenged to increase their English skills in more contexts and learn a greater variety of vocabulary and linguistic structures, applying their growing language skills in more sophisticated ways that are appropriate to their age and grade level. California Department of Education (CDE) English Language Proficiency Level Definition in English Language Development Standards Publication (2012) www.cde.ca.gov/sp/el/er/documents/eldstndspublication14.pdf.
(6) California Department of Education (2010) *California Common Core State Standards: English Language Arts & Literacy in History/Social Studies, Science, and Technical Subjects.* www.cde.ca.gov/be/st/ss/documents/finalelaccssstandards.pdf.
(7) California Department of Education (2012) *English Language Development Standards Kindergarten through Grade 12.* www.cde.ca.gov/sp/el/er/documents/eldstndspublication14.pdf.
(8) Visit the PUENTE program website for more information. http://puente.berkeley.edu/about.

6 OPAL Domain 2: Connections

> *Without connections, we don't engage our students, especially our English Learners. After observing each other on the connections portion of the OPAL, we know that we've focused on relating objectives to students' likes/dislikes and interests. The next step for our grade-level team is to link learning more to school wide community connections as well as environmental conditions outside the school.*
> *– OPAL Institute Participant (Lead Teacher)*

Fostering positive classroom relationships and promoting community building to engage and honor linguistically and culturally diverse students in our schools begins with recognizing, respecting and valuing the strengths of every student. This includes cultivating awareness of students' backgrounds, academic experiences, linguistic journeys, cultural knowledge and norms and political and social dimensions of their context. In this chapter we ask the reader to reflect on how to create and maximize opportunities to bridge connections for English Learners that are responsive to and reflective of who they are. Two focus questions will prepare us for the content of this chapter:

FOCUS QUESTIONS:
1. What are *connections* in the context of teaching English Learners?
2. How are *connections* for English Learners evidenced in a classroom? What information can be recorded and analyzed using the OPAL connections domain indicators?

Introduction

In Chapters 3–5 the reader was introduced to three of the four research-based constructs represented as domains in the OPAL Tool. Chapter 3 focused on the OPAL Comprehensibility Domain, in which *instruction allows for maximum student understanding and teachers utilize effective strategies to help students access content.* In Chapter

4 we explored the OPAL interactions domain and discussed opportunities for *varied participation structures to allow for interactions that maximize engagement, leadership opportunities and access to the curriculum* in content and language learning. Chapter 5 presented the OPAL rigorous and relevant curriculum domain and explored how English Learners can attain maximum educational outcomes through *a curriculum that is cognitively complex, relevant, challenging and appropriate for linguistically diverse populations*. In this chapter we present the concepts associated with creating *connections* for English Learners (see Figure 6.1).

First, we provide background information for each indicator, including brief classroom snapshots highlighting examples from the field in which each indicator can be observed. Next, we present teacher reflection questions and an OPAL descriptor rubric to assist educators in exploring how different levels of implementation of each of the OPAL indicators for Domain 2 (Connections) might appear from lower to higher levels of classroom practice. Finally, the reader will practice using the OPAL instrument through the use of written vignettes, descriptions of lessons from our actual classroom observations. These vignettes will give the reader the opportunity to identify objective sources of evidence (anecdotal notes), to determine level(s) of implementation of the various indicators and to mark these on the OPAL descriptor rubric. The OPAL can be used by a teacher to reflect on their practice during the lesson planning stage or after delivering a lesson. They can cite sources of evidence and provide a self-rating, or seek opportunities to refine lesson planning by reflecting on each of the indicators identified for this domain. Additionally, an external observer or coach may document sources of evidence while observing classroom practice to rate levels of implementation based on each indicator. The vignettes, coupled with the foundational

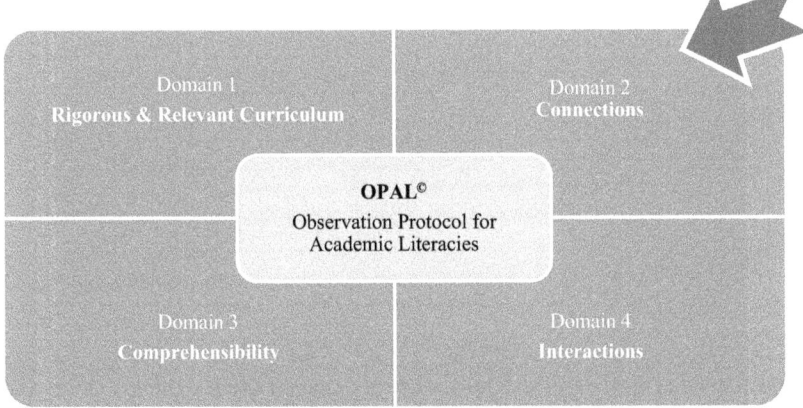

Figure 6.1 The Observation Protocol for Academic Literacies (OPAL) domains

content presented in this chapter, will allow the user to begin to build proficiency toward ascertaining inter-rater reliability and confidently describing classroom practices and student–teacher actions and interactions related to this domain.

What are *Connections* in the Context of Teaching English Learners?

We have defined the construct of connections in the OPAL tool as the explicit and intentional opportunities teachers build into instructional contexts that *provide opportunities for students to link content to their lives, histories and realities.*

These include more than just creating connections from one lesson to another or building on students' prior knowledge of a given subject. It requires teachers of English Learners to enact the integrated roles/functions focused on language teaching, as delineated by Fillmore and Snow (2018). See Figure 6.2 below and consider how these roles are evidenced in your context.

All teachers of English Learners are teachers of language. As such, the connections domain involves more than just content knowledge and connections across content areas. Educators must also be aware of the collective community knowledge and socio-political realities represented in students' daily lives. Three key indicators of connections for English Learners are delineated in Table 6.1. As you review Table 6.1, we invite the reader to engage in the 'Eliciting Prior Knowledge Activity' (Box 6.1) to conduct a quick preview of the domain and its corresponding indicators.

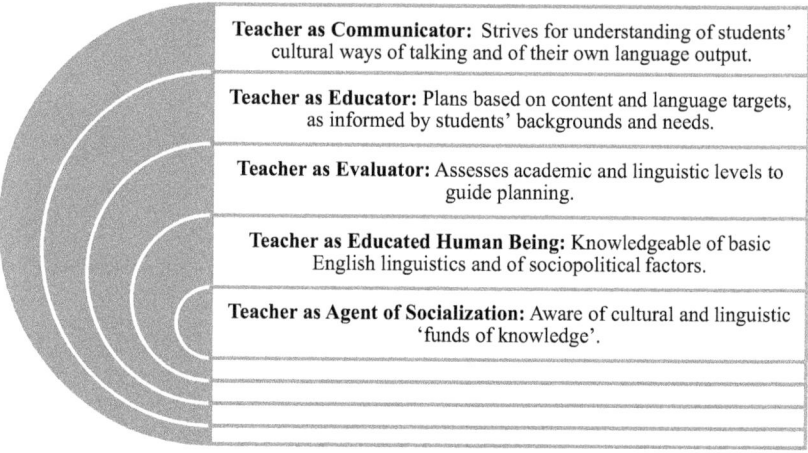

Figure 6.2 What teachers need to know about language (Adapted from Fillmore & Snow, 2018)

Table 6.1 Key indicators for OPAL Domain 2: Connections

Opal domain	Indicators
Domain 2: Connections	2.1 Relates instructional concepts to social conditions in the students' community. 2.2 Helps students make connections between subject matter concepts and previous learning. 2.3 Builds on students' life experiences and interests to make the content relevant and meaningful to them.

BOX. 6.1 ELICITING PRIOR KNOWLEDGE ACTIVITY

- ✓ *Read* each indicator above (Indicators 2.1–2.3).
- ✓ *Highlight* or underline key words/phrases for each of the indicators.
- ✓ *Think* about ways you make connections for English Learner students in your context based on an initial review of the key terms included in each of the indicators.
- ✓ Next, *categorize* your examples in a three-column chart that corresponds to each type of connection (see below).
- ✓ Make a *list of any questions* you have about the indicators or key terms.

To document your thinking, divide a piece of paper into three columns, label each column and categorize your examples as follows:

2.1 Connections to community, world	2.2 Interdisciplinary connections	2.3 Connections to self

Getting to Know Each Indicator in the Connections Domain

In the sections that follow we explore each indicator in detail and introduce illustrative classroom snapshots. Expand and deepen your knowledge about each of the indicators as you reach each description below.

Indicator 2.1: Relates instructional concepts to social conditions in the students' community

Instruction that values and cultivates the educational and personal experiences English Learners bring to the classroom, rather than ignoring or trying to replace these experiences, enables students to make meaningful connections with what is being taught and to apply or extend new learning to their community, history or social reality (Cummins, 2001; Llopart & Esteban-Guitart, 2018). As we explore Indicator 2.1, we consider how a unit or topic affects students in their community relative to what they have experienced as part of their social realities (e.g. daily routines, interactions, relationships, attitudes, cultural identities, religion, language status). Some examples of relevant classroom practice appear in Figure 6.3.

Depending on students' age and developmental levels, their social reality can be considered through one or multiple perspectives: classroom, school, local communities/neighborhoods, groups, national or global (Partnerships for 21st-Century Learning, a Network of Battelle for Kids, 2019). The goal of exploring content through multiple perspectives is to promote change at the individual level while simultaneously seeking to effect change in society.

Examples of Classroom Practice:

Conducting research/inquiry in one's community with a focus on action

Example #1: Students are engaged in a unit of study focused on the theme of survival. They <u>identify an issue in the community</u> related to the theme (e.g. homelessness) and <u>conduct research</u> on lessons learned about survival and the homeless population. Students <u>detail how they might empathize</u> with the homeless and also how they can <u>communicate their story</u> of survival and resiliency in order to <u>influence local policies in response</u> to this group of citizens.

Example #2: While engaging in a unit on economics, <u>students research trends for local economic indicators</u> such as earnings, unemployment rate, poverty rate, population. They <u>identify</u> potential <u>responses to how individuals and societies can make decisions to allow individuals in the community to (re)allocate resources.</u>

For younger learners, an <u>analysis of the prices of a select number of items in a large supermarket versus a community store</u> allows for an <u>analysis of cost factors and creation of a spending plan.</u>

Figure 6.3 Examples of classroom practice supporting Indicator 2.1

From a social justice perspective, educators focus attention on students' community, history and social realities to support English Learners and their families and help them to feel empowered with increased knowledge to advocate for themselves in school and community contexts (Mansilla & Jackson, 2011; Sleeter & Grant, 2009). A diverse classroom allows teachers to value and capitalize on multiple perspectives (Paris & Alim, 2014). Conversely, English Learners see their home cultures, languages and communities represented and being studied in their classroom. This validates their identity while fortifying the purpose for learning as an individual and collective change force.

Indicator 2.2: Helps students make connections between subject matter concepts and previous learning

Deep understanding of subject matter is predicated on the ability to transfer information in isolated areas into deeper level understandings that transcend contexts (Bransford *et al.*, 2000; Leseaux & Harris, 2015). When developing units of study for English Learners, teachers should give careful consideration to essential questions, learning goals, assessment and differentiated learning activities, including the pacing and organization of short-term and long-term learning goals in curricular and instructional planning (Gibbons, 2016, 2018; Tomlinson & McTighe, 2006). Central to this is the integration of skills across content areas to help students make connections between subject matter concepts and previous learning (Indicator 2.2); examples appear in Figure 6.4.

English Learners benefit from teachers' explanations and modeling of cognitive and metacognitive strategies and processes for tackling complex instructional learning (Chamot & O'Malley, 1994; Gersten & Baker, 2000; Hammond & Gibbons, 2005; Zwiers & Crawford, 2011).

Examples of Classroom Practice

- *Articulation of goals and objectives for students across disciplines*
- *Thematic instruction*
- *Know/Want to know/How will I learn it/Learned (KWHL) charts*
- *Integration of writing across the curriculum*
- *Charts or organizers that convey text type and purpose and how a text is organized, regardless of content area focus (e.g. informational/explanatory text)*
- *Metacognitive strategies instruction (e.g. planning, problem solving, monitoring, evaluation)*
- *Learning logs/journals*

Figure 6.4 Examples of classroom practice supporting Indicator 2.2

Indicator 2.3: Builds on students' life experiences and interests to make the content relevant and meaningful to them

Another important component of making connections for English Learners involves a raised consciousness on the part of educators to recognize and affirm that students and their families possess 'funds of knowledge' that can be incorporated into classroom instruction to build strengths, knowledge and diversity (Gonzalez et al., 2005). Making meaningful connections to students' cultures and life experiences by moving beyond core curricular materials (which often do not reflect students' lives) helps bridge school and household learning and allows students to make sense of abstract or complex concepts taught in schools (Dong, 2017; Dwordin, 2006; Hensley, 2005; Moje et al., 2004). Some examples of relevant classroom practice appear in Figure 6.5.

Prior knowledge, skills, interests and beliefs influence what English Learners attend to in the learning environment and how they organize and interpret their learning. Prior knowledge refers not just to information or skills previously acquired through school experiences, but also to the experiences that have shaped an English Learner's identity as a person and a learner. Attention to this indicator allows an educator to shift from a deficit perspective to one that celebrates and promotes awareness of students' backgrounds and prior experiences, including the challenges and opportunities English Learners experience when learning a second language. At the same time, attention to prior knowledge establishes transcultural norms and communication patterns and responds to political and social forces affecting students' daily lives.

Examples of Classroom Practice:

- *'I am' poems/Identity texts*
- *Family quilts featuring key family members, near or far*
- *Weekly reflections: Students share one positive event and one event that allowed them to learn from a mistake (not so positive)*
- *Creation of 'Me Bags' with objects that represent themselves*
- *'Find Someone Who': scavenger hunt to find someone who has experienced specific events in their live (e.g. birth of a sibling, loss of a family member, moved from one neighborhood-city-country to another, participated in a march for a cause, etc.)*
- *Student surveys: topics of interest, most helpful ways of learning content, perceptions on language learning*
- *Family home visits to uncover community skills and resources that can be brought to the classroom/school context*
- *Family interviews: students interview a member of their family to learn about their experience or opinion regarding a concept*

Figure 6.5 Examples of classroom practice supporting Indicator 2.3

How Can We Determine What Evidence We See in Observing for the OPAL Connections Domain?

In this section we will explore two classrooms using written vignettes. The reader is asked to think about each of the OPAL Domain 2 (Connections) indicators as they read the vignette. Use the right-hand margin to note detailed anecdotal evidence for each classroom vignette. For a review of how to identify and record objective anecdotal evidence see Chapter 2. The following steps are recommended when engaging in this learning experience:

Before reading the vignettes focused on the connections domain:

- Review the overall definition of this domain, along with the specific indicators (Table 6.1).
- Underline the key words/phrases for each indicator.

Reading and scoring:

- Step 1: Read the written vignettes and record anecdotal evidence.
- Step 2: Review the criteria delineated in the OPAL scoring rubric for this domain and use your anecdotal evidence to assign a rating.

After scoring:

- Compare your scores to those provided in this text.
- Identify additional sources of evidence for each indicator.
- Discuss results and implications for classroom practice.

OPAL Domain 2: Connections – Reflection Questions

Several questions can guide the reader in examining how teaching and learning are occurring in these classroom contexts to promote opportunities for *connections*. In particular, *how does the classroom context ...*

- Value and link students' personal experiences and previous learning to classroom instruction?
- Provide resources and activities that reflect students' cultural backgrounds and interests?
- Pose questions and elicit student thinking about their histories, communities, cultures and languages?

Reading and Scoring STEP 1: Read Each Vignette and Note Anecdotal Evidence Focused on OPAL Domain 2: Connections

Context for vignettes

The vignettes presented here were developed based on actual classroom observations. Pseudonyms are used to respect each teacher's commitment to creating opportunities for transparent, objective and reflective examination of classroom practices for English Learner students. The context for each set of vignettes is provided to give the reader an overall picture of factors that may have influenced decision-making processes, delivery of instruction and classroom practices. These include content area, grade level, English Learner language proficiency level(s) and focus content standards.

Because these classroom observations occurred in California, content standards are specific to those adopted by the California State Board of Education (1) Common Core State Standards (CCSS) for English Language Arts and Literacy in History/Social Studies, Science and Technical Subjects and Mathematics (CDE, 2010/2013); (2) Next Generation Science Standards (CDE, 2013); (3) History Social Science Content Standards (CDE, 1998/2000); and (4) English Language Development (ELD) Standards (CDE, 2012). Nationally, each state determines the standards that are taught in schools. A number of states across the nation have adopted the same or similar Common Core standards for English and math while others have revised, edited or created other versions to respond to their state context. As such, we expect that readers will (1) recognize similarities in the content and language standards connections presented for each vignette and (2) engage in the proposed 'reading and scoring' steps to examine practices for English Learners using the OPAL indicators.

Content focus and factors

> **Content Area:** History Social Science, Integrated ELD[1]
> **Grade:** K
> **Language Proficiency Level(s):** Emerging[2] (Beginning) to Expanding[3] (Intermediate)

Standards Connection
History and Social Science Framework Connection – Grade K[4]
Kindergarten Focus: Learning and working now and long ago

Kindergarten History Social Science Standards[5] – Grade K:

K.3 Students match simple descriptions of work that people do and the names of related jobs at the school, in the local community and from historical accounts.
K.4 Students compare and contrast the locations of people, places and environments and describe their characteristics.

California English Language Development Standards[6] – Grade K:

I.A1 **Exchanging information and ideas.** Contribute to conversations and express ideas by asking and answering yes–no and wh- questions and responding using gestures, words and simple phrases
I.B5 **Listening actively.** Demonstrate active listening to read-alouds and oral presentations by asking and answering yes–no and wh- questions with oral sentence frames and substantial prompting and support.
I.C9 **Presenting.** Plan and deliver very brief oral presentations (e.g., show and tell, describing a picture.)

School context

The vignettes in this chapter take place in a PK–five school that is part of a mid-size urban school district. The school began offering a Spanish dual language program three years ago. Dual language programs teach English Learner and English only students literacy and content in two languages (e.g. English and Spanish) to foster bilingualism/biliteracy, sociocultural competence and high levels of academic achievement. The principal has been at this school for one year. Teachers at this site have between two and 20 years' experience and most have worked at this same site for more than 10 years. The school is beginning the second semester of instruction on a traditional year calendar. Parent participation at this school has increased since the new site administrator began.

Lesson context

Two kindergarten teachers present their lessons on community workers. Mrs Garcia's class is a 50/50 dual language class in Spanish and English. Reading and math are taught in Spanish while social science and science are taught in English. Half of the students are English-only and the other half are Spanish speakers identified as English Learners. Mrs Sousa's class is a mix of English Learners whose home language is Korean or Spanish, and English-only students, all of whom have attended the state-sponsored preschool on this campus. The proficiency level of English Learners in both classes ranges from Emerging to Expanding.

Classroom vignette 1: Mrs Garcia – Room 11 (Grade K)

Room 11 has four regular activity-based centers available to students in the four corners of the classroom. A sign-in sheet is posted at each center so that when children visit a center, they write their name on the list. Based on these sign-in sheets, the dress up area is one of the most popular activity centers in the classroom. The dress up area in Mrs Garcia's classroom has a clothes rack with various work uniforms, hats and tools. The bulletin board has photos of actual workers in the students' community. The photos are labeled in English and Spanish. Some are pictures of students' parents or older siblings at work. Others are familiar people from the community including Mrs Garcia, their teacher; Mr Lara the school nurse; Mrs Penny the cafeteria lady; and Father Caray, the priest from the local parish. Other photos include a road-repair flagman, a landscape maintenance worker, a tortilla maker, a nurse, a caregiver for a child, a cook in a lunch truck, a doctor, a teacher, a priest and a firefighter.

The children are seated on the rug and Mrs Garcia begins by reminding the students of the meaning of community and that in every community there is much work to do. In their community, children help recycle. Other children work with their parents selling at the swap meet. Some grown-ups work in their own home taking care of children and some work in other people's homes. Other adults provide services in a workplace such as the doctor, the firefighter, the mechanic, the teacher, the priest. Some grown-ups make things to sell such as the tortilla maker and the cook in the lunch truck.

Mrs Garcia has the class stand up and leads the students in a song about community workers which uses hand motions to imitate the work they do. They have already learned the song in Spanish.

> *An auto technician*
> *is like a magician.*
> *When your car is broken*
> *a mechanic repairs it for you.*
> *An auto technician makes it run as good as new.*
>
> *A firefighter works hard each day*
> *to put out fires night and day.*
> *When you call 9-1-1*
> *the fire truck will quickly run*
> *so the firefighter can save your house*
> *with a water hose the flames to douse.*

Mrs Garcia calls students' names to form triads and numbers off each trio by threes. From the class roster provided before the observation it is clear that Mrs Garcia has intentionally clustered the students into mixed language ability groupings.

She gives each triad a small set of the photos. The cards are distributed to each member of the triad. Mrs Garcia demonstrates that one student begins and the others listen. Student number 1 shows the photo to the members of the triad. They say,

> This person is a _____. A _____ helps our community by _____.

The other members of the group repeat.

When students are done, Mrs Garcia pulls out the clothes box from the play dress-up area. She holds up different hats and students associate them with the community worker who would wear that hat. After each one, she asks the class, 'Do you think a _____ wears this hat?'

> Student oral response scaffold: Yes, a _____ wears this hat. This is the hat of a _____.

After going through all the hats, she reminds students that they have learned to count and to work with numbers and asks, 'How do you think numbers are helpful to a _____?' 'How do you think reading is important to a _____?'

> Student oral response scaffold: Numbers are helpful to a _____ because _____. Reading is important to a _____ because _____.

Anecdotal notes:

Students are given free time and Mrs Garcia has set up the clothes dress-up center. In the art center she tells students to draw a picture of the work they would like to do when they grow up. She has placed some non-fiction picture books about community workers in the reading corner and puzzles with pictures of workers with different jobs on the puzzle table.

After free play time, Mrs Garcia takes students on a walking tour of the school to visit the workers in the office, the library, the cafeteria and the busses. She reminds them that at the beginning of the school year they took this tour to meet the adults in their school and learn their names, but now Mrs Garcia will emphasize the work each person does. Before the class begins their walking tour, Mrs Garcia rehearses with them two questions they can use to interview the school workers. Mrs Garcia shows a photo of each person, models introducing each worker to the class and asks the worker in the photo to tell the class,

> 'Mr(s) _____, what do you do at our school?' or
> 'Mr(s) _____, what kind of work do you do at our school?'

Anecdotal notes:

Classroom vignette 2: Ms Sousa – Room 12 (Grade K)

Upon entering room 12 one sees a large blank bulletin board with a capital *D* and lowercase *d* in the center. There are work tables and chairs and in each corner of the room there is an activity center. One has paint easels and smocks, another has a library shelf with children's books arranged neatly by size from smallest to tallest. Another center has large wooden building blocks and another center has a play kitchen and a table with wooden frame puzzles.

Students in Ms Sousa's class begin by sitting at their table groups and tracing a pattern to make a picture of a community worker. When they are finished they bring their picture up to the front of the room and Ms Sousa asks them what community worker they have drawn. Many students are silent, looking down at the floor which she tells them she finds puzzling since they are always so noisy and wild at play time. Ms Sousa tells them they made a doctor and staples their pictures to the bulletin board. 'Do you know what a doctor does?' Once again, most of the children look down at the floor. 'A doctor helps you stay healthy'. One student, Yoon, tells Ms Sousa, 'Teacher, my mother doctor' to which Ms Sousa replies, 'No, Yoon, my mother IS a doctor.' Yoon replies, 'You mother doctor?' Ms Sousa closes her eyes and sighs aloud.

Next, she gives them all a worksheet with a capital D and a lowercase *d* at the top. Ms Sousa reminds them that they learned how to form the letter *d* in preschool. She tells them that the letter *d* makes the sound of /d/ and asked students to name some community workers that begin with the sound of /d/. After a silence, she models, dentist, doctor, domestic, dry cleaner, donut baker, driver, drummer. She tells the students to practice writing the letter *d* and to remember that *d* makes the /d/ sound. While students are writing, she circulates through the tables to check on their work.

When they finish, she tells them to put their papers in their cubbies and then to go play in one of the centers.

Anecdotal notes:

Reading and Scoring STEP 2: Examine Evidence and Assign an OPAL Rating

Now that you've had an opportunity to read the classroom vignettes and note anecdotal evidence, review the sources of evidence and OPAL ratings. Review the overall definition of this domain to determine how each of the indicators contributes to providing a comprehensive view of how the classroom context contributes to promoting connections for English Learners. Review each of the descriptors on the scoring rubric (Table 6.2). Use your anecdotal notes to determine a rating for each of the OPAL indicators included in OPAL Domain 2: Connections (Indicators 2.1–2.3).

Table 6.2 Descriptor rubric for OPAL Domain 2: Connections

OPAL Domain: Connections

Teachers are mindful about providing opportunities for students to link content to their lives, histories and realities to create change.

Opal indicators	1 Novice [rarely or never]	2 Apprentice [basic attempts]	3 Developing [sometimes]	4 Capable [often]	5 Accomplished [consistent]	6 Expert [exceptional]	n/o Not observable
2.1 Relates instructional concepts to social conditions in the students' community	Teacher *rarely or never* helps students connect classroom learning to students' community, history or social reality	Teacher *makes basic attempts* to help students connect classroom learning to students' community, history or social reality	Teacher *sometimes* helps students connect classroom learning to students' community, history or social reality	Teacher *often* helps students connect classroom learning to students' community, history or social reality	Teacher *consistently* helps students connect classroom learning to students' community, history or social reality	Teacher shows *exceptional ability* to *consistently* help students connect classroom learning to students' community, history or social reality	The skill or concept is not applicable in the context of this lesson/activity. It may be evident during another observation, but it was *not observable* during this classroom visit
2.2 Helps students make connections between subject matter concepts and previous learning	Teacher *rarely or never exhibits sufficient knowledge* of how subjects relate to one another and helps students see relationships and connections between school work and subject matter.	Teacher exhibits a *basic working knowledge* of how subjects relate to one another and *makes basic attempts* to help students see relationships and connections between school work and subject matter.	Teacher exhibits a *developing working knowledge* of how subjects relate to one another and *sometimes* helps students see relationships and connections between school work and subject matter.	Teacher exhibits a *good working knowledge* of how subjects relate to one another and *often* helps students see relationships and connections between school work and subject matter.	Teacher *consistently* exhibits *in-depth knowledge* of how subjects relate to one another and helps students see relationships and connections between school work and subject matter.	Teacher *consistently* exhibits extensive knowledge of how subjects relate to one another and shows *exceptional ability* in helping students see relationships and connections between school work and subject matter	The skill or concept is not applicable in the context of this lesson/activity. It may be evident during another observation, but it was *not observable* during this classroom visit
2.3 Builds on students' life experiences and interests and prior knowledge to make the content relevant and meaningful to them	Teacher *rarely or never* builds on students' life experiences and prior knowledge to make connections Classroom context or teacher behaviors *rarely or never* reflect an acceptance of students' culture and language	Teacher *makes basic attempts* to build on students' life experiences and prior knowledge to make connections Classroom context or teacher behaviors *reflect basic attempts* to accept students' culture and language	Teacher *sometimes* builds on students' life experiences and prior knowledge to make connections Classroom context or teacher behaviors *sometimes* reflect an acceptance of students' culture and language	Teacher *often* builds on students' life experiences and prior knowledge to make connections Classroom context or teacher behaviors *often* reflect an acceptance of students' culture and language	Teacher *consistently* builds on students' life experiences and prior knowledge to make connections Classroom context or teacher behaviors *consistently* reflect an acceptance of students' culture and language	Teacher shows *exceptional ability* to *consistently* build on students' life experiences and prior knowledge to make connections Classroom context or teacher behaviors *consistently* reflect an *exceptional ability* to accept students' culture and language	The skill or concept is not applicable in the context of this lesson/activity. It may be evident during another observation, but it was *not observable* during this classroom visit

After Scoring

Review your OPAL ratings for Domain 2: Connections. Reflect on what you recorded as you analyzed the written vignettes. Compare your scores to those proposed in Table 6.3 below. Note anecdotal evidence and rationale for each rating. Discuss observations about sources of evidence and ratings with a colleague.

Table 6.3 Anecdotal evidence and scores for written vignettes

OPAL Domain 2: Connections	Vignette 1 Mrs Garcia (Grade K)	Vignette 2 Ms Sousa (Grade K)
Indicator 2.1	Anecdotal evidence: Mrs Garcia connects the study of community workers directly to the students' community and their lives by including pictures of family members at work. She includes a variety of jobs and professions that are familiar to students in her class but that do not appear in the nationally prepared curriculum adopted by her school, which helps students connect the lesson content to their lives. She takes students on a tour of their school to connect the people they see every day with the notion of working and helping their community. Score: 4	Anecdotal evidence: During the phonics exercise, Ms Sousa makes basic attempts to provide some examples of workers that students might know in their community, such as the dry cleaner, donut baker and doctor, but does not explicitly draw the student's attention to how these are important in their community. Score: 1
Indicator 2.2	Anecdotal evidence: Mrs Garcia connects counting and reading to the community workers during dress-up time by asking them how they think reading and numbers are helpful to each community worker. Mrs Garcia helps students see the connection between what they are learning in her lesson as well as in the independent work activities. Score: 5	Anecdotal evidence: The History-Social Science standard calls for students to tie the names of jobs to be matched with a simple description of what the worker does. This lesson focused instead on the sound of /d/ and which jobs begin with that sound rather than on the concept of the work these workers do. There are basic attempts to understand and integrate subject matter learning, but with the focus on phonics, it is unclear that students see relationships and connections between school work, subject matter and daily life. Score: 2
Indicator 2.3	Anecdotal evidence: During the dress-up time, Mrs Garcia makes the lesson explicitly meaningful to students by tying the work she talks about to the work their parents do and the jobs they hold. By visiting adults they know in their daily lives and connecting them with the work they do at the school, Mrs Garcia helps students connect to their life experiences and interests. Score: 5	Anecdotal evidence: When a student tries to connect to the lesson and relates that his mother is a doctor, Ms Sousa focuses on his grammar and the correction provided creates some confusion for the student. There is little evidence of knowledge and incorporation of students' context or acceptance of the students' language. The follow up work is for students to color in a prepared coloring page rather than to draw or color a picture of a self-selected worker to add meaning to their work. When asked what they had colored, students could not answer. The students' practice work is a missed opportunity to help students connect learning to their life experience. Score: 1

Summary

Making connections for English Learners allows educators to create and maximize opportunities to link content to students' lives, histories and realities. To fully enact this, educators must become aware of students' backgrounds, academic experiences, linguistic journeys, cultural knowledge and norms, as well as the political and social dimensions of their communities. In this way, teachers can leverage students' assets and affirm, honor and value their families, culture and language.

Reflection

Think about the content of this chapter and the focus questions posed to frame the content of this chapter. Reflect on the following: How has my knowledge in identifying and supporting *connections* for English Learners increased? What can I do to continue to explore this construct to refine my work with English Learners?

Notes

(1) The California English Language Arts/English Language Development Framework uses the term Integrated ELD to describe instruction for English Learners in content areas guided by the ELD and ELA standards. This new term encompasses previously used terms such as sheltered instruction or Specially Designed Academic Instruction in English (SDAIE).

(2) *Emerging Proficiency Level*: Students at this level typically progress very quickly, learning to use English for immediate needs as well as beginning to understand and use academic vocabulary and other features of academic language. California Department of Education (CDE) English Language Proficiency Level Definition in English Language Development Standards Publication (2012) www.cde.ca.gov/sp/el/er/documents/eldstndspublication14.pdf.

(3) *Expanding Proficiency Level*: Students at this level are challenged to increase their English skills in more contexts and learn a greater variety of vocabulary and linguistic structures, applying their growing language skills in more sophisticated ways that are appropriate to their age and grade level. California Department of Education (CDE) English Language Proficiency Level Definition in English Language Development Standards Publication (2012) www.cde.ca.gov/sp/el/er/documents/eldstndspublication14.pdf.

(4) California Department of Education (2017) *History social science framework for California public schools: Kindergarten through grade 12*. www.cde.ca.gov/ci/hs/cf/documents/hssframeworkwhole.pdf.

(5) California Department of Education (1998, 2000) *History social science content standards for California public schools: Kindergarten through grade 12*. www.cde.ca.gov/be/st/ss/documents/histsocscistnd.pdf.

(6) California Department of Education (2012) *English language development standards kindergarten through grade 12*. www.cde.ca.gov/sp/el/er/documents/eldstndspublication14.pdf.

7 Using the OPAL for Professional Learning, Research and Evaluation Purposes

> *The OPAL allows me to observe teachers across my school to get a school-wide sense of where we need to focus to improve learning and teaching of EL students. The domains are super relevant to teacher practice so looking for them is easy.*
> – OPAL Institute Participant (School Administrator)

The OPAL is intended to be used to support teachers of English Learners in a variety of ways. In this chapter we describe various ways the OPAL and its results can be used to inform school- and district-level professional development priorities, as well as how it can inform a variety of research and evaluation efforts. This chapter focuses on the following questions:

FOCUS QUESTIONS:
1. How can we use the OPAL in professional learning contexts with teachers of English Learners?
2. How can we use the OPAL for research and evaluation purposes?

This chapter provides several examples of ways our past OPAL participants have adapted the instrument and extended its use. For example, one group of participants 'scaffolded' the original three-day OPAL Institute over time to maximize delivery and minimize disruption to the instructional day; this allowed them to avoid the costs related to releasing teachers from instruction to attend professional development. This sample OPAL dissemination plan spreads out the time required for learning about the instrument itself (Appendix F). Additionally, we provide examples of how the OPAL levels of implementation results are currently being used in schools to (1) prioritize the types of professional development; (2) assess changes in teachers' practices over time; and (3) align OPAL indicators and domains with other professional development initiatives, such as lesson study, so that the needs of English Learners are adequately addressed.

We use the results from survey data and interviews collected from OPAL Institute graduates between 2010 and 2016 to provide examples of how the OPAL tool has been used to create and refine professional learning contexts at school sites through peer coaching, as well as to describe how past OPAL-certified trainers have taught others how to use the tool. We created an OPAL implementation planning tool (Appendix E) so that at the end of each of our institutes, participants have an opportunity to meet in their school teams to discuss and plan for possible dissemination and uses of the OPAL for their schools and districts. Many of the participants wanted to stay connected with us to ask our advice and to share what they had learned because of the adoption of the OPAL.

Professional Learning Uses of the OPAL

One of the most important considerations about the uses of the OPAL is to establish clarity of purpose for its use. Over the years, many of the OPAL Institute participants have shared with us the ways that they have implemented the OPAL training at their school and/or district sites. In some cases, they invited us to replicate the three-day training at their sites; in others they asked us to create a 'springboard' that would allow them to break the training down into more manageable chunks, to eliminate the need for substitute teachers or to avoid disrupting the school day. Based on the information we collected from our participants, along with our collaboration with schools and districts, we highlight the following professional learning uses of the OPAL:

1. Training on the use the OPAL as a future focus of professional development.
2. Peer coaching with the OPAL.
3. Using OPAL in district-wide inquiry.
4. The OPAL as a pre/post-measure to assess the impact of professional development.
5. Research and evaluation purposes of the OPAL.

In the next section, we highlight the cases of three school sites[1] in the southern California area: Garnet Elementary School and two elementary charter schools[2] that form part of a charter organization, Diamond and Emerald.

Garnet Elementary School

Garnet is a traditional public elementary school that shares a campus with a Fine and Performing Arts Magnet (or specialized) School. Principal Ruby completed the three-day OPAL Institute along with one of her teacher leaders. They were excited about the OPAL's possibilities for teachers of English Learners at their site and saw the OPAL protocol as means to bring together the staffs from two schools on their site. Ms Ruby invited us to do a series of brief OPAL training sessions as part of the regularly scheduled after-school staff meetings. After these trainings, the principal created the 'Peer Buddies Project', pairing up teachers with one another. The Peer Buddies Project was a form of peer coaching that facilitated the observation cycle and resulting support within grade levels. Figure 7.1 includes the memo that Ms Ruby created for the two schools' staffs, inviting pairs or triads of teachers from the same grade level to work together as 'buddies'. Buddies would observe each other and then debrief on their observations to identify their own professional learning goals based on the evidence they gleaned from their OPAL observations.

Figure 7.1 OPAL dissemination at Garnet Elementary School ('Peer Buddies Project')

The two rounds of observations took place over the spring semester. To avoid the cost of hiring substitute teachers for the observation or debriefing times, currently credentialed/licensed staff covered for released teachers. These staff members included the physical education teacher, a teaching assistant who was fully licensed, the principal or the teacher leader. Indeed, Ms Ruby called this project the 'Prius model' for professional development: it offered 'high yield and low cost!' At the end of the semester, the entire staff came together to plan for the type of professional learning support they would need the following year, based on the OPAL results. For example, the OPAL interactions domain consistently received the most attention in observations across the grade levels and generated important questions from staff and peers on how to best refine practices in this area. Accordingly, one major recommendation for the following year was to prioritize professional development that would support greater student collaboration. This school-wide decision to prioritize *interactions* also prompted the allocation of additional instructional resources for professional books that would support teachers in learning about other cooperative learning practices.

Topaz Charter School Organization

Topaz is a non-profit organization that supports low-income women in the greater Los Angeles area and sponsors two elementary (K–five) charter schools. The two schools, Diamond and Emerald, adopted the OPAL as a school-wide professional development model to support teachers of English Learners. The schools created an annual professional development plan that identified ten monthly sessions that 'chunked' the OPAL domains, along with observation and debriefing cycles, over the course of a school year. (Appendix F, the OPAL dissemination plan) provides a detailed scope and sequence of the prioritized planning broken down by OPAL domain, along with suggestions for how to structure the 30-minute release time for teachers to plan, to observe and to debrief. Noteworthy, is the last column that identifies for the presenters what materials and handouts are needed. As mentioned in Chapter 2, once the inter-rater reliability and calibration processes have been completed, we encourage OPAL users to hone their note-taking skill set so that they can learn how to note observational evidence without needing to score the level of implementation. The OPAL coaching form included in Appendix G is another tool to help develop the skill of anecdotal note-taking. It can be practiced by teachers within each of the domains as well as holistically for all the domains. The type of dissemination plan adopted by the Topaz Charter Schools can also be modified based on a school's specific context and needs. We have recommended introducing the OPAL tool by beginning with the *comprehensibility* domain as this domain and its indicators are most familiar to teachers of English Learners, and most OPAL-adopting schools have stayed with this pattern.

Coaching and the OPAL

Teaching, like many other careers, offers professional development to continuously hone the science and art of teaching (Hollins, 2011). Key to this is establishing safe climates for continuous and shared learning. As teachers develop their expertise, and in particular their expertise with English Learners, they are recognized by their peers as having expertise in the field and many become the 'go to' professional. Since most teachers' work has been traditionally conducted in isolation from other adults, many teachers may find the idea of having a colleague come into the classroom to observe a lesson very unsettling. However, the teacher/peer coaching literature affirms that instructional coaching as a model of professional development benefits K–12 teachers by helping them translate research into practice through reflection and evidence-based support (Kohler et al., 1995; Neuman & Cunningham, 2009; Skiffington et al., 2011; Teemant, 2014; Teemant et al., 2022). Using the OPAL to collect evidence from classrooms of teachers of English Learners for the purposes of developing 'collaborative conversations' and peer coaching practices has been one of the many uses of the OPAL that we encourage.

Hattie (2012) conducted a statistical meta-analysis of the research around effective practices to explore the impact of strategies/practices on student achievement. He measured this with a statistical method called 'effect size': an effect size of 0.5 equals one year of academic achievement growth. Table 7.1 describes the relative impact of different types of professional development experiences on actual classroom practices. As highlighted in this table, coaching between teachers and/or between teachers and designated coaching staff was found to have the greatest impact, and therefore the greatest likelihood that the training received was adopted into teachers' practices.

We point out the research on the impact of coaching on implementation of professional development to stress that the OPAL represents an opportunity for educators to discuss, observe, reflect on and address specific aspects of content area instruction with the types of interactions/tasks (processes) that can yield maximum results for English Learners across language proficiency levels.

Table 7.1 Impacts of professional development

Component of training	Knowledge level	Skill attainment	Transfer to practice
Theory	10%	5%	0%
Demonstration	30%	20%	0%
Practice	60%	60%	5%
Coaching	95%	95%	99%

Source: Joyce, B. & Showers, B. (2002) *Student Achievement through Staff Development* (3rd edn). Association for Supervision & Curriculum Development.

Engaging with colleagues in non-evaluative and non-judgmental conversations can create school-wide climates of trust, mutual respect and individual and collective professional growth; however, this takes time and strategic planning. To begin the trust-building process, we recommend developing norms and ground rules for the observed teacher and the observer. In the cases of Garnet and Topaz, the first step was to offer teachers low-stress invitations to learn about the OPAL as a tool for professional development. As school staffs gain familiarity with the OPAL domains and indicators, they then can mutually agree on processes for collecting evidence (with or without scores). It also must be made clear from the outset that OPAL is a peer coaching instrument, not an evaluative one. Participation in the coaching process must be voluntary. We strongly advise *against* using the OPAL as a part of any teacher evaluation decision-making process. Instead, we encourage using evidence gathered with the OPAL to generate conversations about effective practices for English Learners. Figure 7.2 contrasts the purposes of coaching and evaluation and highlights the key differences and intent of each. This information should be shared with teachers to clarify any misconceptions, concerns or anxiety related to having peers observing in each other's classrooms.

Effective coaching and collaborating begin with ensuring that participants have clarity around the purposes, processes and outcomes for using the OPAL as part of a coaching model. Figure 7.3 offers guidelines that should be mutually agreed upon, shared and enacted as part of the

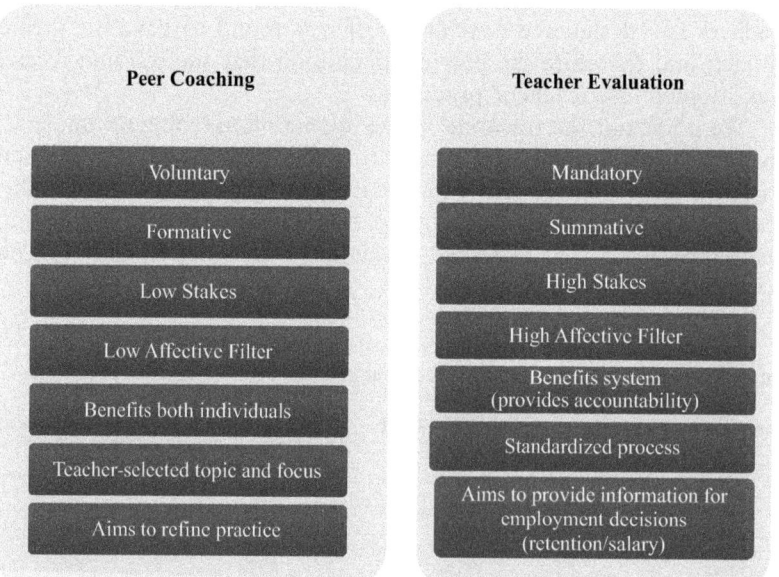

Figure 7.2 Purposes of classroom observation: Peer coaching versus evaluation

> 1. Participation is voluntary.
> 2. Build mutual trust. Keep confidentiality. Do not permit students to see what is being written. Do not share anything without permission from the teacher observed.
> 3. The learning should be reciprocal and mutually beneficial. Peer Coaching is not the same as mentoring and it is not evaluation.
> 4. Plan on staying through the agreed upon time frame/lesson/instructional period.
> 5. Focus on evidence observed and practices, not on judging or criticism.
> 6. Stay focused on the OPAL domains/indicators chosen by the teacher being observed.
> 7. Feedback should be interactive rather than just written comments. Any written documents should be turned over to the teacher after the debriefing meeting.
> 8. The coach should not interrupt the lesson.
> 9. Be specific with feedback, especially when responding to the focus identified by the teacher being observed.
> 10. Approach recommendations through asking reflection questions to elicit missed opportunities, not things done 'wrong'.

Figure 7.3 Guidelines for peer coaching with the OPAL

observation cycles. These guidelines can also include other mutually agreed upon considerations, as needed to build a climate of trust, confidentiality and collaboration. Once these ground rules have been decided, the coaching cycle can begin!

Coaching cycles with the OPAL

Establishing coaching cycles with the OPAL presumes that the OPAL has been part of a professional development program/sessions such as those shared in previous sections describing Garnet, Diamond and Emerald's sample schedules. Effective coaching with the OPAL begins long before the classroom visits with a pre-observation meeting between the observers and/or coach and the teacher participant. It is an opportunity to discuss the process and set the focus, as well as to discuss and plan the lesson together. By co-planning the lesson, peers once again review the OPAL instrument, discuss priority domains and/or indicators, share lesson ideas/topics and challenges that they are planning and brainstorm activities and strategies. We recommend a three-part cycle for coaching: (1) a pre-visit; (2) the actual OPAL observation(s); and (3) the post-observation debrief. The next sections delineate each part of the OPAL coaching cycle and provide examples of conversation starters for peer-observers/teacher-coaches.

Step 1: The pre-visit conversation

The purpose of the pre-visit meeting is to help the coach focus on the teacher's priorities and to co-plan the lesson and strategies. It is far more powerful to share ideas and strategies in the planning stage, and then teach by including those ideas. The teacher being observed is then enriched in the planning stage, not just by seeing the final product of instruction.

> **Before – Explore:**
> - Meet with the teacher to review the OPAL and together select a focus area for the visit.
> - As coach, explain that you will be noting various sections of the lesson on the OPAL form but that you will concentrate on the areas you have agreed upon.
> - Also, reach agreement with the teacher as to whether you will use the Likert numeric rating scale on the OPAL instrument form (Appendix D) or whether you will use the form without the scale.
> - You may choose to design the lesson together, using the opportunity to share strategies for each of the areas on the protocol.
> - Explain that you will watch the lesson and record evidence-based statements about what the teacher says and does and how students respond. Ask whether the teacher will want recommendations or questions for next steps to be included on the OPAL instrument or coaching form.
> - Sample pre-visit questions:
>   - *How can I be of help to you?*
>   - *What would you like me to focus on? Are there OPAL domains or indicators that you have considered in planning your lesson?*
>   - *What would be helpful for me to know about your class?*
>   - *What standards are you working on? What are your objectives for the lesson?*
>   - *Where would you like me to sit during the visit? When can we get together after the visit to debrief?*

Step 2: The OPAL observation – Focus on evidence

The observer uses the OPAL form *or* the OPAL coaching form to record evidence that corresponds to the area of focus and the OPAL indicators highlighted during the pre-visit conversation. Evidence statements should be brief and non-judgmental and may include notes from the lesson as well as evidence from artifacts and/or materials in the room.

> - Focus on recording quality examples in bullet points or brief notes rather than trying to capture everything (review Chapter 2 if necessary).

- Write out a factual statement about what you saw the teacher do or say. Then add a statement about what the students did. Finally (and *only* if the teacher has asked for recommendations during the pre-visit meeting), include 'One thing to consider ... ' or make notes in the 'Next Steps' part of the OPAL form.
- Remain a detached observer so that you don't interrupt the lesson progress or interact with students in the classroom; your role as a trained OPAL observer requires you to focus on the facts, not to intervene in the situation.

Step 3: After the observation – Reflections and next steps

A post-observation conference should be scheduled as soon as possible after the observation. The focus of the conversation should be guided by the agreements made during the pre-visit meeting, and the observer should use evidence from the OPAL form to provide examples and pose questions to the teacher who was observed.

- Meet to debrief immediately after the lesson observed.
- Thank the teacher for the experience and for allowing the visit. It is not helpful to give false praise but every person can be thanked and there is always something positive that can be found in the experience. Begin by saying, 'Thank you. I appreciated the opportunity to visit your classroom today'.
- Structure the feedback so it is a conversation rather than a one-way report or summary of the observation. The purpose is for the teacher to better understand his/her own practice.
- Support teacher reflections on effective practices for English Learners; observers may use any of the OPAL indicators or domains previously agreed upon as 'frames' for the conversation;
- Ask questions that serve as prompts for the conversation; this is not an inquisition. Strive for a natural and collaborative conversation, and be sure to include what you learned from the experience of being invited in to observe, gather data and support effective practices for English Learners. Some sample post-observation questions:
  - *How did the lesson compare to what you had expected?*
  - *I remember that you planned to do_____, but during the lesson, I noticed you did _____ instead. What led you to change your mind?*
  - *As I watched you and your students do _____, I thought about how I could use that idea with my class. What would you think if I added _____ or changed _____ for my students?*

- Would you like me to share the notes from my observation? [If yes] During the opening of the lesson you said _____

- During our pre-observation meeting, you mentioned that you would like specific feedback on promoting more oral language from your English Learners. During the lesson I observed, I noticed that you responded to students' questions and referred them to classroom resources. How do you elicit additional oral language and encourage students to restate answers using academic language?
- Looking at the OPAL form, which indicators would you like to continue to work on?

Beginning OPAL observers and peer coaches have found it helpful to role-play this process as part of a professional development meeting. For example, in our trainings we may use one of the vignettes in this book to role-play the teacher and the observer, and then use the steps outlined in this section to 'model' a scenario whereby teachers can listen, see and ask questions about setting up the observation/coaching cycles. The follow-up questions above are helpful to initiate the post-observation peer coaching conversation.

District-Level Inquiry Uses of the OPAL

Throughout this book, we have focused on the OPAL as a valuable process for observing classrooms with English Learners. The OPAL has led to powerful teacher learning experiences through peer coaching and support. Next, we turn to how OPAL observational data may be used for district-wide inquiry related to English Learner instructional practices. During the 2012–2013 school year, we partnered with the Mountain Union High School District (MUHSD-a pseudonym) in Southern California to use the OPAL to determine teaching practices for the district's Long-Term English Learners (LTELs). The LTEL designation had been recently codified into the state's education code,[3] and the district asked a sample of 30% of classrooms in their high schools to respond to the following questions:

- What are MUHSD teachers' current practices in instruction for English Learners in English Language Arts, English Language Development and Academic Language Development courses?
- How do these practices reflect current research on effective instruction of culturally and linguistically diverse students as measured by the OPAL (Observation Protocol for Academic Literacies)?

These two questions were framed in order to help inform the district on current levels of research-based practices for English Learners using

Collecting Anecdotal Evidence from Professional Development Inquiry

Rigorous and Relevant Curriculum

Overall Observation: Across classrooms, students have few opportunities for problem solving, critical thinking and transference of skills from L1 to L2. Instructional pacing plans are evident in ELA classrooms, given that similar units were being taught. ELD classrooms utilized core and supplemental materials. ALD classrooms lacked a defined curriculum and focus.

Examples:
- *Teacher talk:* Tell us about the book you read? Would you recommend it?
- Materials—LCD projector-1 computer—not being used
- Document reader in use by teacher
- Reading corner-books, cushions

Connections

Overall Observation: Opportunities for connections to content are driven by core curriculum with some opportunity to relate concepts to students' realities

Examples:
- Quotes from Walden posters students created
- Newspaper articles
- Discussion of community businesses and connection to terms
- Teacher gives examples from own life—relates to students
- Students encouraged to select topics and examples from school or home life

Comprehensibility

Overall observation: Instructional delivery often includes visuals, graphic organizers, and other supports to make content comprehensible. Some opportunities exist for student output (oral and written).

Examples:
- Use of hand gestures, internet pictures
- Storyboards for planning writing
- Vocabulary work → root words to create new words
- Organizer: Theme/Narrative/Explanation
- Vocabulary Knowledge Rating Chart
- Storyboards for expository writing by students displayed.
- Color-coded sentences with embedded quotes. Students also color code in their notes.
- Vocabulary sheet. Sheet segmented into KWL graph.

Interactions

Overall observation: Classroom interaction was primarily teacher directed with some opportunities for working with partners and few opportunities for small group work.

Examples:
- Chairs/desks arranged in rows
- Students working independently—reading, completing posters, or doing homework
- Whole class Q & A
- Independent "reading" of story selection

Figure 7.4 Mountain Union High School District: Reporting on overall anecdotal evidence by OPAL domain

the OPAL, and then to use that information to help guide the district's decision-making about professional development priorities for the subsequent school years (Figure 7.4).

In a later section of this chapter, we suggest how quantitative OPAL results can be shared as part of research and evaluation processes; however, MUHSD's approach provides an example of how *qualitative* OPAL results can be synthesized using the anecdotal evidence from the OPAL tool. District and school site level decisions on whether to use a quantitative or qualitative approach will depend on the local context, relationships between administration and teaching staffs and above all, the overall purpose for the use of the OPAL.

Using the OPAL for Research and Evaluation Purposes

Over the last ten years, we have used the OPAL process of collecting, analyzing and reporting on current practices across a variety of school or district contexts to drive programmatic improvement and to inform and prioritize professional development for teachers of English Learners.

As with any research endeavor, we begin with good research questions to guide the collection of classroom observation data on teachers' practices with English Learners. Sample research/evaluation questions might include the following:

- *What are SAMPLE SCHOOL DISTRICT'S teachers' current practices in instruction for English Learners in English Language Arts, English Language Development and Academic Language Development courses?*
- *How do these practices reflect current research on effective instruction of culturally and linguistically diverse students as measured by the OPAL (Observation Protocol for Academic Literacies)?*

Such questions have been used to measure the impact of professional development programs on teachers' practices in pre/post evaluation studies, as in grant programs like Project STELLAR: Teaching for Critical Transitions (Science Teaching for English Learners – Leveraging Academic Rigor) and California State University, Chico's Collaborative Professional Development (CPD) Project, described below (U.S. Department of Education, 2014). The questions are also used in district-level reform efforts such as the PROMISE –Pursuing Regional Opportunities for Mentoring, Innovation and Success for English Learners – Initiative (PROMISE Design Center, 2005–2015). We have used the OPAL instrument to collect data on the changes in teachers' practices as a result of specific types of professional development used with teachers of English Learners in the early grades – for example with training in Dialogic Reading – and examined the impact of that professional development with and without the benefit of coaching (Matera *et al.*, 2016). This study and others are described in the next section, along with examples from doctoral students conducting observational studies in classrooms focused on teachers of English Learners.

Planning a research/evaluation project using the OPAL

Earlier in this chapter we noted that good research and evaluation projects begin with a set of questions that guide research design and data collection approaches. While this book serves as an introduction to the OPAL and its uses, we will not go into detail about criteria for observational research designs (Hilberg *et al.*, 2004). Instead, we will share examples of processes and support tools, gleaned from a selection of projects and studies, that we have used and experienced successfully. Figure 7.5 is a brief description of the OPAL that we have used as part of a variety of studies and grant proposals. We have found this synopsis to be useful not only for research and evaluation purposes, but also as a frame for planning for professional development with schools and classrooms with the OPAL itself.

> **Observation Instrument – Observation Protocol for Academic Literacies (OPAL)**
>
> *The OPAL is a research-based classroom observation tool that captures classroom practices and interactions from sociocultural and language acquisition perspectives. This observation protocol utilizes a six-point Likert scale (1-6, Low to High) to describe instruction for academic literacies, defined as a set of 21st - century skills, abilities, and dispositions developed through the affirmation of and in response to students' identities, experiences, and backgrounds. It is aligned with the National and California Standards for the Teaching Profession and encapsulates the four domains of research on teacher expertise for English Learners: Rigorous and Relevant Curriculum, Connections, Comprehensibility, and Interactions.*

Figure 7.5 Brief OPAL description

Table 7.2 Sample OPAL reporting chart

OPAL domain results		Results by content area		
	All N = 52	English Language Arts (n = 20)	English Language Development (n = 5)	Sheltered Biology (n = 5)
Rigorous and relevant Curriculum	M = 2.63; SD = 0.68	M = 2.55; SD = 0.87	M = 3.13; SD = 0.66	M = 2.37; SD = 0.95
Connections	M = 2.97; SD = 1.04	M = 2.88; SD = 1.21	M = 3.07; SD = 0.97	M = 2.93; SD = 1.15
Comprehensibility	M = 3.01; SD = 0.93	M = 2.90; SD = 1.41	M = 3.30; SD = 0.85	M = 3.00; SD = 1.04
Interactions	M = 3.10; SD = 0.95	M = 3.10; SD = 0.76	M = 3.30; SD = 1.08	M = 3.00; SD = 0.93

Scores represented are in aggregate form; no individual teacher scores are reported to ensure confidentiality.[4]

The sample OPAL reporting chart illustrated in Table 7.2 has been used in a variety of evaluation and research projects to provide simple descriptive statistics (means and standard deviations). The next section highlights two doctoral studies that used the OPAL to gather and report on levels of implementation of teacher practices.

Doctoral research and using the OPAL to observe teacher practices

Doctoral students and other researchers who are interested in exploring questions that address the practices of teachers of English Learners often must create new instruments to capture these practices, and subsequently, to establish the validity of such instruments. Because the OPAL is a validated instrument (see Appendix A), several of Loyola Marymount University's doctoral students have used it to gather evidence for their doctoral studies. One such student, Dr Ricardo Pedroarias, was interested in the way teachers at an elite Catholic all-boy high school in Los

Angeles were responding pedagogically to the academic and language needs of their increasingly culturally and linguistically diverse students (Pedroarias, 2011). Two of his three research questions are listed here:

- *To what extent do heritage language speakers become bilingual and bicultural in an honors level bilingual Spanish program through classroom lessons in the target language?*
- *To what extent is the native speaker Spanish program at this school attaining the goal of bilingualism and biculturalism in terms of student interaction in the heritage language through travel immersion programs and service project interaction?*

His dissertation study, entitled 'Heritage Language Spanish Study: Reconciling the Tension Between the Organizational Focus on Assimilation and the Goal of Bilingualism and Biculturalism', used both anecdotal evidence from the OPAL as well as numeric evidence from the Likert scale scores along with other sources of data such as interviews, surveys and document analyses to answer the research questions.

In a study on the practices of teachers of LTELs at a large public high school in a large metropolitan school district in southern California, another doctoral student used the OPAL along with interview data to understand teachers' perspectives and professional development needs related to this population. OPAL observation results for the six teachers of LTEL students yielded low-mid-range score ($X = 2.67$) across the taught content areas observed, such as math, biology and history/social studies (Alamo, 2018). Quantitative scores, along with the anecdotal notes and interview results, led to increased attention that content area teachers desire about professional development regarding the academic language and literacy needs in their content areas for LTELs.

Using the OPAL in a university context: Aligning with lesson study and pre-service teacher education at California State University, Chico

In 2011, Drs Esther L. Delgado-Larocco and Charles G. Zartman, Jr, both of the School of Education at California State University, Chico, received a major United States Department of Education National Professional Development grant for the Collaborative Professional Development (CPD) Project, administered by the Center for Bilingual/Multicultural Studies at the university. A major part of the grant was several one-week summer institutes featuring Science Inquiry and English Language Development (ELD) strategies for in-service and pre-service teachers and paraprofessionals in the CSU Chico service area. In addition to the summer institute, participants engaged in a one- or two-year follow-up 'lesson study' process to develop, present and reflect on lessons implementing an inquiry approach to teaching science and ELD strategies. Originating in Japan, lesson study is a model of professional development in which teachers systematically and collaboratively examine and refine their practice. After the group of teachers agrees on an overarching goal, they then engage in a selected number of 'study cycles' of planning, teaching, observing and critiquing lessons. When California State University Chico adopted the lesson study approach, they agreed to focus on the teaching of science and integrated ELD at the elementary level. To ensure that the lessons enabled beginning level English Learners to access the science content, participants were trained in using the OPAL instrument to guide lesson development and reflections. During the summer institute, participants were trained in the four OPAL domains and their indicators. They learned to identify the various indicators by gathering evidence in sample lessons and discussing in small groups how each domain was met. They also determined how Institute activities reflected the OPAL domains and indicators.

Following the summer institute, participants attended a planning day at which they formed their lesson study teams, comprised of pre-service, in-service and paraprofessionals and an assigned lesson study facilitator from the university. The groups also decided on the first lesson's topic and grade level and discussed the logistics for their lesson study planning, delivery and reflection meetings. Using the OPAL domains and indicators, they rated their overall existing practice, identified one or two indicators of an OPAL domain that they wished to focus on individually, as well as identifying the domain and indicators that would be the focus for the lesson they were going to develop as a team. Team members implemented the lessons in their classrooms, documented and shared their work using notes and/or videotapes, and discussed their observations of the lesson. Each team met several times during the semester to plan a lesson guided by the four OPAL domains and indicators and choose the teachers who would present that lesson. Although there were focus indicators chosen, every effort was made to address all the OPAL indicators. Every team member observed the lesson presentation and met afterwards to reflect on the lesson components and outcomes. The OPAL also guided these post-delivery reflections. Each participant rated the lesson on all indicators before discussing their individual scores with team members. As a team, they not only shared their score, but also what evidence they found to support it. As they discussed their evidence they came up with a team score for each OPAL domain. The lesson was revised based on what they had observed and discussed. A second team member taught the lesson to a new group of students and the post-lesson discussion process was followed again – individual OPAL scoring followed by discussion of evidence and a team score. After two such planning/teaching/reflection cycles were completed the lesson study facilitator separately scored the team lesson cycle using the OPAL instrument. This process was followed each semester the participants were in CPD. At the end of year, participants completed a summative self-reflection on their overall practice using the OPAL instrument.

In a two-semester span, there were two overall-practice self-reflection scores for each participant, four team reflection scores (two per semester lesson) and two facilitator reflections. There was a positive trend in all the scores and for each constituent group – pre-service and in-service teachers, and paraprofessionals. Participants felt that the OPAL instrument was very useful in helping them ensure English Learners' access to academic content. Lesson study facilitators found OPAL so powerful that they incorporated it in their university teacher training coursework and/or supervision repertoire. The success experienced by the participants in using OPAL prompted the project co-directors to implement OPAL training in a second US Department of Education National Professional Development project, titled Community and Instruction for Expanding English Learners' Opportunities (CIELO), which was funded in 2017 for five years (California State University Chico, 2023).

Using the OPAL in program evaluations: Assessing the impact of professional development

The preceding example describes how faculty at CSU Chico used the OPAL instrument in two federal grant programs that provided professional development for teachers of English Learners. Another similarly funded grant program is Project STELLAR (Science Teaching for English Learners: Leveraging Academic Rigor). Through a partnership with urban ecologists at the Center for Urban Resilience at Loyola Marymount University and four local school districts, STELLAR aimed to improve educational outcomes for English Learners in grades four to eight during 'critical transition' periods by increasing the capacity of teachers and administrators to provide high quality, content-based language and literacy development in the field of urban ecology while addressing the social-emotional needs of long-term English Learners. Project STELLAR used the OPAL as the measure to determine the degree to which teaching practices changed over time because of the professional development. We reported the overall results on changes in teacher practices using the OPAL results/reporting chart illustrated in Table 7.2 (above), both annually as a required part of our reporting process and cumulatively at the end of the five-year period that ended in April 2018.

Conclusion

As we discussed in Chapter 1, there is a scarcity of technically research-based classroom observation measures that are valid and reliable for teachers of English Learners. This chapter has highlighted a variety of ways that the OPAL instrument can be used as a tool for professional development: through peer coaching; by aggregating scores and anecdotal notes to illuminate school-or-district-wide patterns of practice and inform professional development needs; and as an instrument for data collection in evaluation and research projects. These examples of collaboration and expanded uses of the OPAL have enriched our understanding of the instrument and brought the OPAL to life in meaningful, constructive and productive ways. Our experiences over the last decade of developing, validating and using the OPAL tool have been valuable not only for the projects described herein, but also to elevate the professional dialogue in schools about research-based practice for English Learners.

Notes

(1) Pseudonyms have been assigned for all districts, schools and educators named in this book, with the exception of research studies.
(2) In California and other states, charter schools are a form of publicly funded public schools that are approved by the state, school district or local educational agency and managed independently by another organization. Charters have greater independence from districts and can be managed by teachers, parents or other organizations.
(3) The California Education Code – EDC § 313.1 defines an LTEL as:

> an English Learner who is enrolled in any of grades 6 to 12, inclusive, has been enrolled in schools in the United States for six years or more, has remained at the same English language proficiency level for two or more consecutive prior years, or has regressed to a lower English language proficiency level as determined by the English language development test identified or developed pursuant to Section 60810, or a score developed by the Superintendent on any successor test. 'English Learner at risk of becoming a long-term English Learner' means an English learner who is enrolled in any grades 3 to 12, has been enrolled in schools in the United States for four to five years, scores at the intermediate level or below on the English language development test, and has scored in the fourth or fifth year at the below basic or far below basic level on the prior year's English language arts standards-based achievement test. (Senate Bill 750, 2015)

(4) When the OPAL is used as an instrument/tool in a research project, we make sure to protect the confidentiality of teachers and in some cases, schools and districts. We use this language when submitting to the Institutional Review Board (IRB) policies for the protection of human subjects.

Appendix A

Technical Report for the Observation Protocol for Academic Literacies (OPAL)

The Observation Protocol for Academic Literacies (OPAL) was developed in tandem with a large educational reform movement in California that focused on implementing a principles-based reform through a co-design process involving county, district and schools with large percentages of English Learners. Observational data for the validation sample were collected from 15 sites involved in this reform effort and eight non-participating reform sites with proportionate numbers of English Learners.

Design

This validity study employed a descriptive/observational research design. Descriptive/observational research is used to gain an understanding of, or to give an explanation of a situation or event, an individual or a group of individuals. In descriptive/observational research, the researcher observes and records 'real life' settings as opposed to contrived, artificial research situations (McMillan & Schumacher, 2006). This design allowed the researchers to collect structured observational data using the OPAL instrument to examine variables in classroom contexts that affect teaching and learning for English Learners. Validation analysis consisted of the use of Exploratory Factor Analysis (EFA) and Confirmatory Factor Analysis (CFA) using AMOS 16.0 to determine the fit between the hypothesized model and the data observed. CFA examines the unidimensionality and reliability of the OPAL domains and indicators. Latent factor structures of the OPAL constructs/subscales based on individual indicators/items were examined.

> A descriptive/observational research design allowed researchers to collect structured observational data using the OPAL.

OPAL's Phases of Development

In response to the need for observation instruments to measure the effectiveness of English Learner teacher practices, the OPAL was developed in 2006 using a three-phase process to define and test the model: phase one – content validity; phase two – construct validity; and phase three – predictive validity (pending study). The OPAL is a research-based behavioral observation tool that measures teacher practices and classroom interactions from sociocultural and language acquisition perspectives. This observation protocol utilizes a six-point Likert-type scale (one to six, low to high) to rate instruction for academic literacies, defined as a set of 21st-century skills, abilities and dispositions developed through the affirmation of, and in response to students' identities, experiences and backgrounds.

Phase one: Establishing content validity for the OPAL

The first phase, item development, was established based on key elements from the literature and from the authors' previous work (Chamot & O'Malley, 1994; Cummins, 1981, 2000; Echevarria & Short, 2004; Gibbons, 2002; Krashen, 1982, 2003; Lavadenz & Armas, 2008; Schleppegrell & Colombi, 2002). Development of the OPAL included a comprehensive analysis of descriptors from the California Standards for the Teaching Profession (California Department of Education, 2009) and the National Board for Professional Teaching Standards: English as a New Language Focus (National Board for Professional Teaching Standards, 2010). This correlation is available in the OPAL Training Manual. Selected teaching standards and essential elements outlined in the theoretical underpinnings of effective instruction for meeting the needs of linguistically diverse learners were also considered during the development phase.

> Development of the OPAL included a comprehensive analysis of the California Standards for the Teaching Profession and the National Board for Professional Teaching Standards.

The team of content experts recognized that language and literacy development for English Learners require monitoring of learning and assurances that support daily lessons for maximum understanding of every content and language lesson. Thus, avenues for effective instruction were conceptualized around four constructs derived from the literature: (1) rigorous and relevant curriculum; (2) connections; (3) comprehensibility and; (4) interactions. Each of the constructs was defined and indicators were developed for each of the four areas. Content expert panel members composed of classroom teachers, teacher coaches and facilitators, professors in colleges of education, educational research consultants and an assistant district superintendent were then asked to

Table A1 Cronbach's Alpha internal consistency reliability estimate

Construct	α
Rigorous and relevant curriculum	0.80
Connections	0.80
Comprehensibility	0.90
Interactions	0.77

Note. α = Cronbach's Alpha.

> Measures of internal consistency yielded acceptable reliabilities. Results indicate that each OPAL construct includes indicators that are closely related.

review the indicators to eliminate redundancy or lack of clarity for various indicators.

During this first phase, 74 classrooms were utilized to field test the instrument and complete the content validity process. Reliability testing was conducted to ascertain a measure of internal consistency. The OPAL reliability analysis resulted in acceptable reliabilities as determined by the Cronbach's Alpha estimate presented in Table A1.

Phase two: Establishing construct validity of the OPAL

Phase two in the validation process was conducted to establish construct validity for the OPAL. The following outlines the procedures taken to collect data for the construct validation process.

Inter-rater reliability

Once the OPAL's content validity was established, two lead raters identified classroom videos at the elementary and the secondary level to use as a model for training other raters on the use of the observation protocol. The lead raters worked with an expert panel to view the videos and establish anchor OPAL scores for each of the indicators. Scores ranged from one (low level of implementation) to six (high level of implementation) and were corroborated by noting and cross-checking evidence through anecdotal notes taken during the observation session. These classroom videos exemplified a medium to high level of implementation, with ratings ranging from 3–6 for each of the OPAL's 18 indicators.

Training sessions for each subsequent rater were conducted using the process described here. First, raters attended a session where an overview of the observation instrument (the OPAL) was provided, including its conceptual framework and alignment to the California Professional Standards to the Teaching Profession (California Department of Education, 2009) and the National Board for Professional Teaching Standards: English as a New Language (National Board for Professional Teaching Standards, 2010). During this same session, each of the OPAL's constructs (rigorous and relevant curriculum, connections, comprehensibility and interactions) was introduced, and the rating scale for each indicator was discussed. Sample ratings were presented using written exemplars for each indicator. Particular attention

> Each rater was trained on how to interpret and apply the rating scale to the point where each of the scores given by different raters could be treated as equivalent

was given to the wording for each indicator; the alignment of each indicator to the standards for the teaching profession; the significance of each indicator for classroom contexts with culturally and linguistically diverse students; and the qualitative difference between ratings (e.g. the difference between a rating of two and a three or a five and a six). The selected classroom videos were presented, and raters scored the observation using the OPAL. Each rater's score was recorded, compared and discussed. Given that all of the raters were experienced educators, the examination of scores for consensus-building provided an opportunity for each rater to discuss his/her score based on specific, observable evidence recorded in the anecdotal section of the OPAL. Practice with two video lessons afforded raters multiple instances to clarify rating procedures.

Prior to independent scoring, each rater practiced applying the rating scale with one of the lead raters in a common classroom. This set of observations was used to establish inter-rater reliability and certify the rater as an independent scorer. Inter-rater reliability was examined using a consensus approach (Stemler, 2004). This study warranted the use of consensus estimates of inter-rater reliability because the OPAL is a nominal rating scale that represents a linear continuum of a construct, based on a Likert-type scale. Each rater was trained on how to interpret and apply the rating scale to the point where each of the scores given by different raters could be treated as equivalent. Inter-rater reliability evidence was calculated for 10% of classroom observation ratings of the OPAL instrument using Cohen's kappa statistic as an estimate of inter-rater reliability (Cohen, 1960, 1968). An exact rater percent agreement was attained between OPAL raters, resulting in a minimally acceptable Kappa index of .72.

Participants

The OPAL validation study was conducted with a sample size of 303 classrooms selected from 22 schools in the southern California region, wherein reside over 65% of the 1.6 million English Learners in the state.

Table A2 presents school site demographics. The 22 schools service students in pre-K through grade 12, and represent the full spectrum of educational situations for English Learners, from schools where as few as 14.7% of the students are socioeconomically disadvantaged (SED), to schools where as many as 86.5% of the students are SED.

A two-tiered, cluster-random sampling procedure (Keppel, 1991) was utilized to select teachers instructing students in grades pre-K–12. Careful attention was given to the identification of an equal number of classrooms at each grade level in the elementary, middle and high school grade spans. Additionally, proportional representation of program

Table A2 School demographics

School	Student enrollment	Percent of ELs	Total RFEP	Total teachers
Pre-school				
Early education Learning program	80	62.3%	Not Applicable	5
Elementary schools				
Elementary school A	833	54.1%	32	40
Elementary school B	526	49.8%	18	23
Elementary school C	773	62.4%	45	32
Elementary school D	650	81.4%	2	34
Elementary school E	853	51.9%	27	41
Elementary school F	730	49.0%	95	30
Elementary school G	996	66.8%	91	46
Elementary school H	431	72.6%	26	23
Elementary school I	592	56.6%	21	27
Middle schools				
Middle school A	1,633	28.4%	62	65
Middle school B	663	25.5%	53	29
Middle school C	1,274	40.2%	75	9
Middle school D	1,963	46.8%	297	78
Middle school E	905	29.6%	19	46
Middle school F	730	49.0%	95	30
Middle school G	1086	18.4%	29	35
High schools				
High school A	2,418	20.0%	78	72
High school B	2,328	25.5%	5	75
High school C	2,839	19.1%	103	103
High school D	1,842	9.9%	17	78
High school E	411	33.8%	35	12

Note. ELs = English Learners, RFEP = Reclassified Fluent English Proficient.

types for English Learners (i.e. Structured English Immersion, dual language, transitional bilingual program and mainstream English program) was selected for observational data collection. Demographic data gathered for the targeted teacher group reveal that the average teaching experience was 8.99 years with a range of 1 month to 34 years. The average length of time teaching at the respective school sites ranged from one month to 32 years, with a mean of 5.85 years. Of the teachers observed, 19% were male while 81% were female.

> Demographic data gathered for the targeted teacher group reveal that the average teaching experience was 8.99 years with a range of 1 month to 34 years.

Raters

Observations were conducted by five raters, all with ample experience in the area of second language acquisition and effective teaching practices for linguistically and ethnically diverse learners. Three raters hold doctorates in education, and two are second- and third-year doctoral candidates. In addition, four of the five raters hold a California Clear Multiple Subject or Single Subject Teaching Credential with Spanish Bilingual Certification – Bilingual, Crosscultural, Language and Academic Development (BCLAD) or Bilingual Competence Certificate (BCC). One of the raters holds a Preliminary Single Subject Teaching Credential with Spanish Bilingual Certification (BCLAD). Two of the raters hold a California Administrative Services Credential and have served in school and district leadership positions. All raters have taught, mentored and coached in the K–12 context for an average experience level of over 25 years. Furthermore, each of the raters has taught university undergraduate and graduate level courses, with experience at this level ranging from 2 to 18 years. Three of the raters serve as full-time faculty in the school of education at a private university in southern California.

Classroom observations

Classroom observations were conducted during school hours and were 20–30 minutes in length. A schedule of observations was provided to participating school sites one to two weeks prior to the visitations. Observations occurred primarily during Language Arts, English Language Development (ELD) and Mathematics instructional periods at the elementary school level. Secondary classroom observations were conducted in Language Arts, Mathematics, ELD/ESL (English as a Second Language), History-Social Science and Science classrooms.

Teachers were informed in writing of the purpose and procedures of the research study, as well as their right to refuse to participate in or withdraw from the research at any time. The anonymity of all participants was insured through the use of a numbered coding system. A single rater entered each classroom without interrupting the lesson or activity and sat in the back of the room, remaining as unobtrusive as possible. The trained observer rated classroom practices for all indicators under each of the OPAL's four constructs (rigorous and relevant curriculum, connections, comprehensibility and interactions). Classroom practices and interactions were rated on a six-point scale (one to six, low to high). Anecdotal notes were written for each OPAL construct, delineating teacher practices, student engagement and interaction and classroom environmental print and materials.

> Anecdotal notes were written for each OPAL construct.

Data analysis and results

Confirmatory Factor Analysis (CFA) was selected as the primary statistical analysis method used to extend the usefulness of exploratory methods (Daniel & Siders, 1994) and to establish construct validity of the OPAL. The researchers rearranged and revised the items on the OPAL and consequently tested a four-factor solution using CFA. It was hypothesized that the OPAL contains research-based essential practices as determined by four constructs/factors: rigorous and relevant curriculum, connections, comprehensibility and interactions.

Maximum likelihood estimation was used for the CFA using AMOS 16.0 since the latent constructs were found to be normally distributed. The data came from 18 items on a Likert-type scale classroom observation instrument. A sample size of $N = 303$ was determined to be adequately large to establish a minimum of 10 cases per latent variable (Schreiber et al., 2006). A correlation table with means, standard deviations, number of items and alpha levels for all latent constructs is provided in Table A3.

The theoretical model with standardized parameter estimates and squared multiple correlations is presented in Figure A1. It was hypothesized that a four-factor model would be confirmed in the measurement portion of the model. Normality assumptions for the

Table A3 Descriptive statistics with correlations

Construct	M	SD	Item	α	1	2	3
Rigorous and Relevant Curriculum	3.10	1.05	6	.80			
Connections	2.93	1.16	3	.80	.67**		
Comprehensibility	3.69	1.31	5	.90	.73**	.57**	
Interactions	3.32	1.03	4	.77	.48**	.42**	.48**

Note. M = Mean, SD = Standard Deviation, α = Cronbach's Alpha.
**$p < .01$

four OPAL constructs were verified using the AMOS 16.0 and SPSS 15.0 programs. A total of 303 OPAL classroom observation samples were available for analysis. Individual ratings for every indicator were recorded in all but 12 cases where the raters deemed the indicator 'not observable'. We used a mean imputation procedure to replace each missing value with plausible values using the variable mean of the complete cases. The CFA provided an excellent fit to the data ($\chi^2 = 362.68$, $df = 125$, CFI = .93; TLI = .92; RMSEA = .079).

> The confirmatory factor analysis provided an excellent fit to the data. Results indicate the OPAL is a valid and reliable instrument.

These values indicate a good fit between the hypothesized model and the observed data. Standardized parameter estimates are indicated in Figure A1 and standardized factor loadings by latent construct are given in Table A4. The squared multiple correlation values also are provided and indicate (lower limit) the reliability of the observed variable in relation to the latent construct; observed variables 2.2 and observed variables 1.4 have the highest and lowest squared multiple correlations, respectively (see Figure A1). A sample interpretation of the squared multiple

Table A4 Factor loadings for each item by latent construct

	Latent construct	Item	Factor loadings
Factor 1	Rigorous and relevant curriculum	1.1	.69
		1.2	.77
		1.3	.47
		1.4	.33
		1.5	.79
		1.6	.79
Factor 2	Connections	2.1	.49
		2.2	.95
		2.3	.68
Factor 3	Comprehensibility	3.1	.74
		3.2	.83
		3.3	.84
		3.4	.87
		3.5	.78
Factor 4	Interactions	4.1	.74
		4.2	.72
		4.3	.66
		4.4	.59

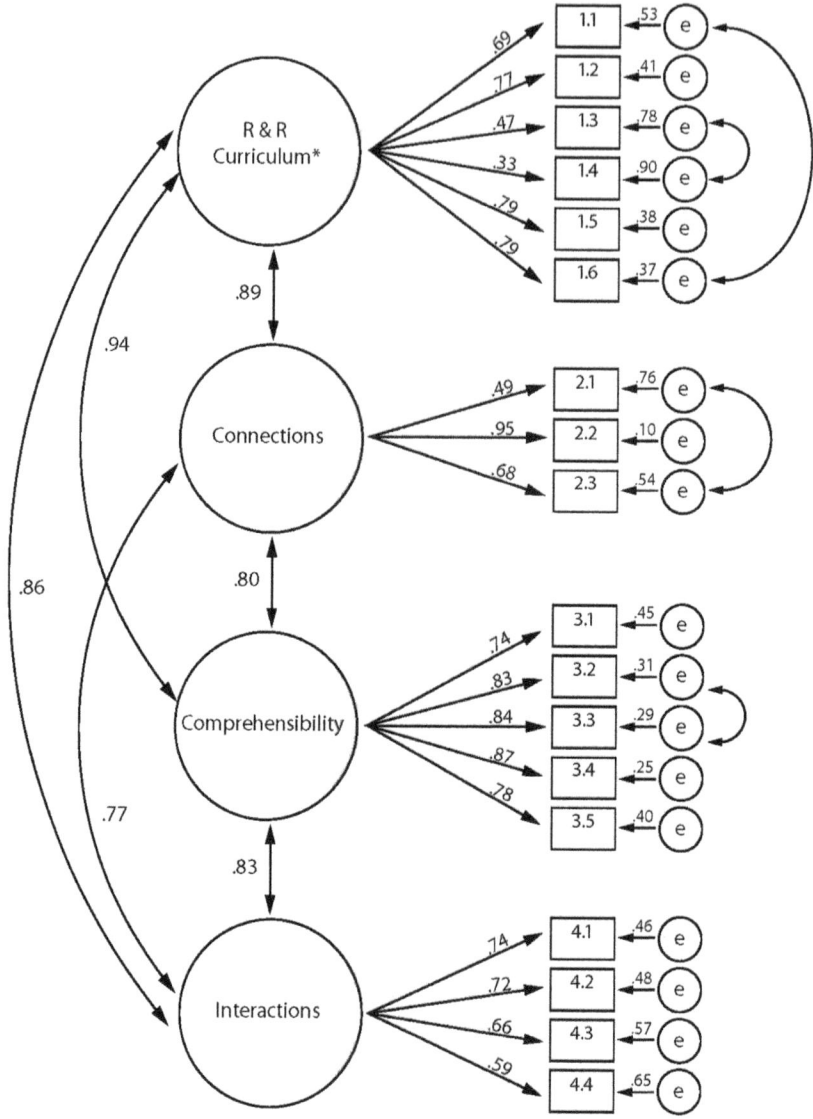

*Rigorous & Relevant Curriculum

Figure A1 OPAL model

correlations, for example, is that the construct Content accounts for 69% of the variance in observed variable 1.1 in these data. No post-hoc modifications were indicated from the analysis due to good-fit indices results, and the residual analysis did not indicate any need for further modifications of the model.

Conclusions and Significance

Our results indicate that the OPAL has good potential for use in classrooms with ethnically and linguistically diverse students, including ELs. The contributions of the instrument in K–12 classrooms are immense. Given the national achievement gap between ELs and their native English-speaking peers, the OPAL, when used appropriately in supportive and guided professional development settings, can serve as a vehicle for examining dynamic teaching and learning in schools. The OPAL can be used in teacher education programs in the preparation of teachers of ELs as a coaching tool to focus teacher practices in each of the domains.

A condition for the use of the OPAL will be the adequate training of the observers (Roberson, 1998). Key studies on classroom observations indicate that the skill, bias and preparation of the observers are essential factors that affect the accuracy of results. Additional research with the OPAL will include correlational research designs, such as predictive validity identified in phase three of this study. This will serve to investigate the relationship between classroom observation results and student achievement measures. Predictive validity for the OPAL, as well as concurrent validation of the OPAL and other classroom observation measures (as they become available), would be valuable in the national discussion on multiple measures.

> The OPAL, when used appropriately in supportive and guided professional development settings, can serve as a vehicle for examining dynamic teaching and learning in schools.

More explicitly, the dramatic growth in teacher evaluation in American public schools (Lovison & Taylor, 2018) has brought greater pressures on the educational community to accurately use observational research to guide and inform instructional practices for ELs. As one of the most underserved groups among the school-age population in this nation, using theoretically and empirically grounded measures to examine classroom practices for ELs is direly needed.

Appendix A references

California Department of Education, California Commission on Teacher Credentialing (2009) *California Standards for the Teaching Profession.* www.ctc.ca.gov/educator-prep/standards/CSTP-2009.pdf

Chamot, A.U. and O'Malley, J.M. (1994) *The CALLA Handbook: Implementing the Cognitive Academic Language Learning Approach.* Reading, MA: Addison-Wesley Publishing Company.

Cohen, J. (1960) A coefficient for agreement for nominal scale. *Educational and Psychological Measurement* 20, 37–46.

Cohen, J. (1968) Weighten kappa: Nominal scale agreement with provision for scale disagreement or partial credit. *Psychological Bulletin* 70, 213–220.

Cummins, J. (1981) The role of primary language development in promoting educational success for language minority students. In California State Department of Education (ed) *Schooling and Language Minority Students: A Theoretical Framework* (pp. 3–49). Los Angeles, CA: National Dissemination and Assessment Center.

Cummins, J. (2000) *Language, Power and Pedagogy: Bilingual Children in Crossfire*. Clevedon: Multilingual Matters.

Daniel, L. and Siders, J. (1994) Validation of teacher assessment instruments: A confirmatory factor analytic approach. *Journal of Personnel Evaluation in Education* 1, 29–40.

Echevarria, J. and Short, D. (2004) Using multiple perspectives in observations of diverse classrooms: The Sheltered instruction observation protocol (SIOP). In H. Waxman, R. Tharp and S. Hilberg (eds) *Observational Research in U.S. Classrooms: New Approaches for Understanding Cultural and Linguistic Diversity* (pp. 21–47). Boston: Cambridge University Press.

Gibbons, P. (2002) *Scaffolding Language, Scaffolding Learning: Teaching Second Language Learners in the Mainstream Classroom*. Westport, CT: Heinemann.

Keppel, G. (1991) *Design and Analysis: A Researcher's Handbook* (3rd edn). Englewood Cliffs, NJ: Prentice Hall.

Krashen, S. (1982) *Principles and Practice in Second Language Acquisition*. New York: McGraw-Hill.

Krashen, S. (2003) *Explorations in Language Acquisition and Use: The Taipei Lectures*. Porstmouth, NH: Heinemann.

Lavadenz, M. and Armas, E. (2008) Differentiated instruction for English learners. *California English* 13 (4), 16–20.

Lovison, V. and Taylor, Er. (2018). *Can Teacher Evaluation Programs Improve Teaching? Getting Down to Facts II Technical Report*. Stanford University and Policy Analysis for California Education (PACE). http://gettingdowntofacts.com/publications/can-teacher-evaluation-programs-improve-teaching.

McMillan, J.H. and Schumacher, S. (2006) *Research in Education: Evidence-Based Inquiry*. Boston, MA: Ally and Bacon.

National Board for Professional Teaching Standards (2010) *English as a New Language Standards* (2nd edn). www.nbpts.org/wp-content/uploads/ECYA-ENL.pdf.

Roberson, T.J. (1998) *Classroom Observation: Issues Regarding Validity and Reliability*. Paper presented at the Annual Meeting of the Mid-South Educational Research Association.

Schleppegrell, M.J. and Colombi, M.C. (eds) (2002) *Developing Advanced Literacy in First and Second Languages: Meaning with Power*. Mahwah, NJ: Lawrence Erlbaum Associates.

Schreiber, J.B., Stage, F.K., King, J., Nora, A. and Barlow, E.A. (2006) Reporting structural equation modeling and confirmatory factor analysis results: A review. *The Journal of Educational Research* 99 (6), 323–338.

Stemler, S.E. (2004) A comparison of consensus, consistency and measurement approaches to estimating interrater reliability [electronic version]. *Practical Assessment, Research & Evaluation* 9 (4). http://PAREonline.net/getvn.asp?v=9&n=4.

Appendix B

Observation Protocol for Academic Literacies (OPAL©) Observation Guidelines

Observation element	Description	Key points
Observation timeframe	20–30 minutes per classroom.	• It is ideal to develop an observation schedule prior to the visitation. This will eliminate conflicts in scheduling with the teacher and will allow teachers to tell students about the purpose of the visitation; • The OPAL is intended to capture elements of instruction, classroom environment and student to teacher, teacher to student and student-to-student interactions. This is regardless of where the teacher is in the lesson delivery. The OPAL does not require the observer to remain in the classroom for the duration of the lesson; • Prior to visiting the classroom, observer should have information about: the grade level(s), English Language Development Level (ELD) level(s) and type of program (Structured English Immersion, Transitional Bilingual Program, Dual Language Program, Mainstream English Program)
Observer etiquette	Detached observation technique.	• The observer enters the room and finds a place to sit so that the observation is unobtrusive in nature; • The observer is silent during the observation period. Time is dedicated to rating items on the OPAL and taking anecdotal notes as evidence of implementation; • Limited interaction occurs between the observer and the students or the teacher and the students; • The intent is to not interrupt the activity in the classroom.
Room environment	'Reading the room'.	• The observer should 'read the room' as soon as he/she enters. • Specific comments should be written in the anecdotal note section of the OPAL under the appropriate domain. *Questions to guide 'reading the room':* • How are tables and chairs arranged (sign of group interactions)? • What materials are available – books (core and supplemental), classroom library, technology (computers, teaching aids)? Are materials available in students' primary language? • What student work is visible – on bulletin boards/walls, in cubbies, on desk, in student notebooks?

Observation element	Description	Key points
		• What teacher-generated text is displayed – on bulletin boards/walls? • What evidence is there of standards, goals and objectives communicated to students? • What evidence is visible denoting long-term planning? What evidence is visible to inform the observer of the teaching and learning that have taken place in the classroom?
Rigorous and relevant curriculum	The curriculum is cognitively complex, relevant, challenging and appropriate for linguistically diverse populations.	The observer captures evidence of teaching and learning practices and scores implementation on rating scale, ranging from low to high (see OPAL indicator descriptors and sample rating sheet). *Questions to guide the observation:* • What evidence indicates that the instructional practice is appropriate for students' grade level and/or language development level? • How are goals and objectives communicated to students? • How does the teacher communicate expectations to students? • What is the teacher's demeanor when approaching the class? • Does he/she communicate respect and value for diversity? • What instructional program is offered in this classroom (Structured English Immersion – Mainstream English – Transitional Bilingual Program – Dual Language? • What materials and resources are evident in the classroom? • Are they in use? How is this determined? • How is language allocated in this classroom – are there opportunities for students to use primary language? If a BCLAD teacher, how does she/he use knowledge of the students' primary language to enhance and support delivery of the lesson? Observer writes anecdotal notes stating what was seen, heard and said by either the teacher or the students.
Connections	Teachers are mindful about providing opportunities for students to link content to their lives, histories and realities to create change.	The observer captures evidence of teaching and learning practices and scores implementation on rating scale, ranging from low to high (see OPAL indicator descriptors and sample rating sheet). *Questions to guide the observation:* • What evidence exists in the classroom that shows students have had the opportunity to relate concepts to their social conditions and realities of their community (bulletin boards, posters, journals, teacher/student comments, etc.)? • What techniques elicit students' prior knowledge and/or learning and invite this to be part of the current lesson and/or activity? • How is students' previous learning acknowledged and utilized as a resource for the lesson? • What connections are made to capitalize on students' interests and experiences? • How are lessons/activities structured to increase student motivation?

Appendix B 155

Observation element	Description	Key points
Comprehensibility	Instruction allows for maximum student understanding and teachers utilize effective strategies to help students access content.	The observer captures evidence of teaching and learning practices and scores implementation on rating scale, ranging from low to high (see OPAL indicator descriptors and sample rating sheet). *Questions to guide the observation:* • How does the teacher scaffold instruction so that all students can access the material? • How does the teacher 'recast' student language to validate response and extend student language ('i + 1' concept)? • How are graphic organizers or other visuals used so that students are part of the process and use these devices to practice language and skills in oral and written contexts? • What evidence exists in the classroom that shows how key terms and concepts are illustrated for students? • What type of questions and comments are provided to students as on-going feedback during the lesson/activity? How do these questions help elicit student thinking and give the classroom teacher an understanding of whether students have grasped concepts? • What assessments are used during the lesson/activity? • What evidence exists that shows the teacher has made adjustments to the lesson/activity to accommodate for students' linguistic, cognitive, and developmental needs?
Interactions	Varied participation structures allow for interactions that maximize engagement, leadership opportunities and access to the curriculum.	The observer captures evidence of teaching and learning practices and scores implementation on rating scale, ranging from low to high (see OPAL indicator descriptors and sample rating sheet). • The observer makes note of table and chair configuration, including independent and small group centers available in the classroom; • The observer looks for evidence of cooperative grouping (charts with roles and tasks for group work, group projects, group folders, baskets or bins to store on-going group projects, etc.); • The observer looks for evidence of differentiated, small group instruction (list of small groups – list of group tasks – list of students working on planned, targeted mini-lessons, etc.). *Questions to guide the determination of grouping practices?* • What evidence exists that students are engaged in varied groupings? • How is lesson delivery sequenced to allow for student participation and interaction? • How are students given an opportunity to take leadership roles in the classroom?
Overall observations: student engagement	Student on-task behavior.	• The observer watches for student engagement in the lesson, activity or task. *Questions to guide the observation of student engagement:* • How are students encouraged to be active listeners? • How do students practice and interact with content in all four language domains: listening, speaking, reading and writing?

Observation element	Description	Key points
		• How do students record and monitor their learning? • How is the teacher monitoring student engagement? • If an independent activity, what is the level of participation? • How is the teacher monitoring the activity?
Options for next steps for building teacher capacity	Refining teacher practices through: • Reflection protocol; • Coaching; • School and/or district professional development based on theme analysis.	Reflection protocol: peer observations through lesson study or video taping. Coaching: Observer selects one recommendation, or next step, for each OPAL domain. *Questions to prompt 'next steps':* • How can the teacher improve student access to rigorous and relevant curriculum? • What techniques can be employed to assist students in making connections to prior learning and/or knowledge in the targeted lesson? • What strategies can increase student understanding? • How can the teacher refine grouping practices to allow for varied participation structures? School/district P.D. based on theme analysis: • Data collection through OPAL observations; • Score analysis to determine themes; • Action research; • Inquiry cycles.

Note. Use this chart along with the OPAL tool to plan for your observations, as a key reminder to 'see what's there' during the observation, and as a post-observation resource.

Appendix C

Observation Protocol for Academic Literacies (OPAL©) DESCRIPTOR RUBRIC

158 The Observation Protocol for Academic Literacies

The OPAL is a research-based tool for observing teacher practices and classroom interactions from sociocultural and language acquisition perspectives. The OPAL uses a six-point scale to rate instruction for academic literacies, defined as a set of 21st century skills, abilities, and dispositions developed through the affirmation of and in response to students' identities, experiences and backgrounds. This descriptor rubric is intended to be a companion to the OPAL. It defines the rubric competencies for each of the OPAL indicators in four domains: *Rigorous & Relevant Curriculum, Connections, Comprehensibility, and Interactions*. An overview of the numeric rating, the label for level of implementation, and a description for each point on the OPAL rubric is provided here.

Rating	Label	Description
6	Expert	The observed teacher behaviors, classroom context, and interactions reflect an <u>exceptional level of understanding</u> of students' academic, developmental, and linguistic needs. An <u>extensive knowledge</u> of the content area(s) is evidenced by thoughtful, integrated instructional planning, resulting in the consistent use of <u>highly effective instructional practices</u> that allow all students to access rigorous and relevant curriculum, culturally-responsive methods and materials, and equitable classroom interactions.
5	Accomplished	The observed teacher behaviors, classroom context, and interactions reflect a <u>consistent level of understanding</u> of students' academic, developmental, and linguistic needs. An <u>in-depth knowledge</u> of the content area(s) is evidenced by thoughtful, integrated instructional planning, resulting in the consistent use of <u>effective instructional practices</u> that allow all students to access rigorous and relevant curriculum, culturally-responsive methods and materials, and equitable classroom interactions.
4	Capable	The observed teacher behaviors, classroom context, and interactions <u>often reflect a sufficient level of understanding</u> of students' academic, developmental, and linguistic needs. A <u>good working knowledge</u> of the content area(s) is evidenced by thoughtful, integrated instructional planning, often resulting in the use of <u>effective instructional practices</u> that allow all students to access rigorous and relevant curriculum, culturally-responsive methods and materials, and equitable classroom interactions.
3	Developing	The observed teacher behaviors, classroom context, and interactions <u>sometimes reflect a sufficient level of understanding</u> of students' academic, developmental, and linguistic needs. A <u>developing working knowledge</u> of the content area(s) is evidenced by thoughtful, integrated instructional planning, sometimes resulting in the use of <u>effective instructional practices</u> that allow all students to access rigorous and relevant curriculum, culturally-responsive methods and materials, and equitable classroom interactions.
2	Apprentice	The observed teacher behaviors, classroom context, and interactions reflect <u>basic attempts towards understanding</u> of students' academic, developmental, and linguistic needs. A <u>basic working knowledge</u> of the content area(s) is evidenced by disjointed instructional planning, often resulting in the limited use of <u>effective instructional practices</u> that allow all students to access rigorous and relevant curriculum, culturally-responsive methods and materials, and equitable classroom interactions.
1	Novice	The observed teacher behaviors, classroom context, and interactions <u>rarely or never reflect sufficient understanding</u> of students' academic, developmental, and linguistic needs. A <u>minimal level of knowledge</u> of the content area(s) is evidenced by disjointed instructional planning, consistently resulting in the limited use of <u>effective instructional practices</u> that allow all students to access rigorous and relevant curriculum, culturally-responsive methods and materials, and equitable classroom interactions.
N/O	Not Observable	The skill or concept is not applicable in the context of this lesson/activity. It may be evident during another observation, but it was <u>not observable or not applicable</u> during this classroom visit.

Appendix C 159

OPAL DOMAIN: RIGOROUS AND RELEVANT CURRICULUM

The curriculum is cognitively complex, relevant, challenging and appropriate for linguistically diverse populations.

OPAL INDICATORS	1 Novice [RARELY OR NEVER]	2 Apprentice [BASIC ATTEMPTS]	3 Developing [SOMETIMES]	4 Capable [OFTEN]	5 Accomplished [CONSISTENT]	6 Expert [EXCEPTIONAL]	N/O Not Observable
1.1. Engages students in problem solving, critical thinking and other activities that make subject matter meaningful	Teacher **rarely or never** engages students in problem solving activities and supports students in critically investigating subject matter through multiple approaches that make subject matter meaningful	Teacher **makes basic attempts** to engage students in problem solving activities and supports students in critically investigating subject matter through multiple approaches that make subject matter meaningful	Teacher **sometimes** engages students in problem solving activities and supports students in critically investigating subject matter through multiple approaches that make subject matter meaningful	Teacher **often** engages students in problem solving activities and supports students in critically investigating subject matter through multiple approaches that make subject matter meaningful	Teacher **consistently** engages students in problem solving activities and supports students in critically investigating subject matter through multiple approaches that make subject matter meaningful	Teacher shows **exceptional ability to consistently** engage students in problem solving activities and support students in critically investigating subject matter through multiple approaches that make subject matter meaningful	The skill or concept is not applicable in the context of this lesson/activity. It may be evident during another observation, but it was not observable during this classroom visit
1.2 Facilitates student and teacher access to materials, technology, and resources to promote learning	Teacher **rarely or never** allows access to and incorporates the use of a variety of instructional materials, technology, and supplemental resources that reflect diversity and support and enhance student learning	Teacher **makes basic attempts** to allow access to and incorporate the use of a variety of instructional materials, technology, and supplemental resources that reflect diversity and support and enhance student learning	Teacher **sometimes** allows access to and incorporates the use of a variety of instructional materials, technology, and supplemental resources that reflect diversity and support and enhance student learning	Teacher **often** allows access to and incorporates the use of a variety of instructional materials, technology, and supplemental resources that reflect diversity and support and enhance student learning	Teacher **consistently** allows access to and incorporates the use of a variety of instructional materials, technology, and supplemental resources that reflect diversity and support and enhance student learning	Teacher shows **exceptional ability to consistently** allow access to and incorporate the use of a variety of instructional materials, technology, and supplemental resources that reflect diversity and support and enhance student learning	The skill or concept is not applicable in the context of this lesson/activity. It may be evident during another observation, but it was not observable during this classroom visit
1.3 Organizes curriculum and teaching to support students' understanding of instructional themes or topics	Teacher **rarely or never** selects and sequences units of study and lessons that promote student understanding of themes and topics and show relationships to other subject areas	Teacher **makes basic attempts** to select and sequence units of study and lessons that promote student understanding of themes and topics and show relationships to other subject areas	Teacher **sometimes** selects and sequences units of study and lessons that promote student understanding of themes and topics and show relationships to other subject areas	Teacher **often** selects and sequences units of study and lessons that promote student understanding of themes and topics and show relationships to other subject areas	Teacher **consistently** selects and sequences units of study and lessons that promote student understanding of themes and topics and show relationships to other subject areas	Teacher shows **exceptional ability to consistently** select and sequence units of study and lessons that promote student understanding of themes and topics to other subject areas	The skill or concept is not applicable in the context of this lesson/activity. It may be evident during another observation, but it was not observable during this classroom visit
1.4 Establishes high expectations for learning that build on students' linguistic and academic strengths and needs	Teacher **rarely or never** establishes high expectations and clearly explains learning goals that are academically, linguistically, and developmentally appropriate	Teacher **makes basic attempts** to establish high expectations and clearly explain learning goals that are academically, linguistically, and developmentally appropriate	Teacher **sometimes** establishes high expectations and clearly explains learning goals that are academically, linguistically, and developmentally appropriate	Teacher **often** establishes high expectations and clearly explains learning goals that are academically, linguistically, and developmentally appropriate	Teacher **consistently** establishes high expectations and clearly explains learning goals that are academically, linguistically, and developmentally appropriate	Teacher shows **exceptional ability to consistently** establish high expectations and clearly explain learning goals that are academically, linguistically, and developmentally appropriate	The skill or concept is not applicable in the context of this lesson/activity. It may be evident during another observation, but it was not observable during this classroom visit

160　The Observation Protocol for Academic Literacies

OPAL DOMAIN: RIGOROUS AND RELEVANT CURRICULUM (continued)

The curriculum is cognitively complex, relevant, challenging and appropriate for linguistically diverse populations.

OPAL INDICATORS	1 Novice [RARELY OR NEVER]	2 Apprentice [BASIC ATTEMPTS]	3 Developing [SOMETIMES]	4 Capable [OFTEN]	5 Accomplished [CONSISTENT]	6 Expert [EXCEPTIONAL]	N/O Not Observable
1.5 *Provides access to content and materials in students' primary language*	Teacher **rarely or never uses** the students' primary language (L1) as a teaching and learning tool to support all students in achieving learning goals	Teacher **makes basic attempts to use** the students' primary language (L1) as a teaching and learning tool to support all students in achieving learning goals	Teacher **sometimes uses** the students' primary language (L1) as a teaching and learning tool to support all students in achieving learning goals	Teacher **often uses** the students' primary language (L1) as a teaching and learning tool to support all students in achieving learning goals	Teacher **consistently uses** the students' primary language (L1) as a teaching and learning tool to support all students in achieving learning goals	Teacher shows **exceptional ability to consistently use** the students' primary language (L1) as a teaching and learning tool to support all students in achieving learning goals	The skill or concept is not applicable in the context of this lesson/activity. It may be evident during another observation, but it was not observable during this classroom visit.
1.6 *Provides opportunities for students to transfer skills between primary language and target language*	Teacher **rarely or never capitalizes** on primary language (L1) skills that transfer to second language (L2) and uses student knowledge of L1 and L2 as learning tools, appropriate to instructional goals	Teacher **makes basic attempts to capitalize** on primary language (L1) skills that transfer to second language (L2) and uses student knowledge of L1 and L2 as learning tools, appropriate to instructional goals	Teacher **sometimes capitalizes** on primary language (L1) skills that transfer to second language (L2) and uses student knowledge of L1 and L2 as learning tools, appropriate to instructional goals	Teacher **often capitalizes** on primary language (L1) skills that transfer to second language (L2) and uses student knowledge of L1 and L2 as learning tools, appropriate to instructional goals	Teacher **consistently capitalizes** on primary language (L1) skills that transfer to second language (L2) and uses student knowledge of L1 and L2 as learning tools, appropriate to instructional goals	Teacher shows **exceptional ability to consistently capitalize** on primary language (L1) skills that transfer to second language (L2) and use student knowledge of L1 and L2 as learning tools, appropriate to instructional goals	The skill or concept is not applicable in the context of this lesson/activity. It may be evident during another observation, but it was not observable during this classroom visit.

Appendix C 161

OPAL DOMAIN: CONNECTIONS

Teachers are mindful about providing opportunities for students to link content to their lives, histories, and realities to create change.

OPAL INDICATORS	1 Novice [RARELY OR NEVER]	2 Apprentice [BASIC ATTEMPTS]	3 Developing [SOMETIMES]	4 Capable [OFTEN]	5 Accomplished [CONSISTENT]	6 Expert [EXCEPTIONAL]	N/O Not Observable
2.1 Relates instructional concepts to social conditions in the students' community	Teacher **rarely or never** helps students connect classroom learning to students' community, history, or social reality	Teacher **makes basic attempts to** help students connect classroom learning to students' community, history, or social reality	Teacher **sometimes** helps students connect classroom learning to students' community, history, or social reality	Teacher **often** helps students connect classroom learning to students' community, history, or social reality	Teacher **consistently** helps students connect classroom learning to students' community, history, or social reality	Teacher shows **exceptional ability to consistently** help students connect classroom learning to students' community, history, or social reality	The skill or concept is not applicable in the context of this lesson/activity. It may be evident during another observation, but it was not observable during this classroom visit
2.2 Helps students make connections between subject matter concepts and previous learning	Teacher **rarely or never** exhibits sufficient knowledge of how subjects relate to one another and helps students see relationships and connections between school work, subject matter and daily life	Teacher exhibits a **basic working knowledge** of how subjects relate to one another and **makes basic attempts to** help students see relationships and connections between school work, subject matter and daily life	Teacher exhibits a **developing working knowledge** of how subjects relate to one another and **sometimes** helps students see relationships and connections between school work, subject matter and daily life	Teacher exhibits a **good working knowledge** of how subjects relate to one another and **often** helps students see relationships and connections between school work, subject matter and daily life	Teacher **consistently exhibits in-depth knowledge** of how subjects relate to one another and helps students see relationships and connections between school work, subject matter and daily life	Teacher **consistently exhibits extensive knowledge** of how subjects relate to one another and shows **exceptional ability** in helping students see relationships and connections between school work, subject matter and daily life	The skill or concept is not applicable in the context of this lesson/activity. It may be evident during another observation, but it was not observable during this classroom visit
2.3 Builds on students' life experiences and interests to make the content relevant and meaningful to them	Teacher **rarely or never** builds on students' life experiences and prior knowledge to make connections	Teacher **makes basic attempts to** build on students' life experiences and prior knowledge to make connections	Teacher **sometimes** builds on students' life experiences and prior knowledge to make connections	Teacher **often** builds on students' life experiences and prior knowledge to make connections	Teacher **consistently** builds on students' life experiences and prior knowledge to make connections	Teacher shows **exceptional ability to consistently** build on students' life experiences and prior knowledge to make connections	The skill or concept is not applicable in the context of this lesson/activity. It may be evident during another observation, but it was not observable during this classroom visit
	Classroom context or teacher behaviors **rarely or never** reflect an acceptance of students' culture and language	Classroom context or teacher behaviors **reflect basic attempts to** accept students' culture and language	Classroom context or teacher behaviors **sometimes reflect an** acceptance of students' culture and language	Classroom context or teacher behaviors **often reflect an** acceptance of students' culture and language	Classroom context or teacher behaviors **consistently reflect an** acceptance of students' culture and language	Classroom context or teacher behaviors **consistently reflect an exceptional ability to** accept students' culture and language	

162 The Observation Protocol for Academic Literacies

OPAL DOMAIN: COMPREHENSIBILITY

Instruction allows for maximum student understanding and teachers utilize effective strategies to help students access content.

OPAL INDICATORS	1 Novice [RARELY OR NEVER]	2 Apprentice [BASIC ATTEMPTS]	3 Developing [SOMETIMES]	4 Capable [OFTEN]	5 Accomplished [CONSISTENT]	6 Expert [EXCEPTIONAL]	N/O Not Observable
3.1 Uses scaffolding strategies and devices (i.e. outlines, webs, compare/contrast charts, KWL) to make subject matter understandable	Teacher rarely or never uses a variety of learning experiences and strategies that make complexity and depth of subject matter understandable	Teacher makes basic attempts to use a variety of learning experiences and strategies that make complexity and depth of subject matter understandable	Teacher sometimes uses a variety of learning experiences and strategies that make complexity and depth of subject matter understandable	Teacher often uses a variety of learning experiences and strategies that make complexity and depth of subject matter understandable	Teacher consistently uses a variety of learning experiences and strategies that make complexity and depth of subject matter understandable	Teacher shows exceptional ability to consistently use a variety of learning experiences and strategies that make complexity and depth of subject matter understandable	The skill or concept is not applicable in the context of this lesson/activity. It may be evident during another observation, but it was not observable during this classroom visit
3.2 Amplifies student input by: questioning/restating/ rephrasing/ contextualizing	Teacher rarely or never asks questions and/or facilitates discussions to clarify and extend student oral or written output	Teacher makes basic attempts to ask questions and/or facilitates discussions to clarify and extend student oral or written output	Teacher sometimes asks questions and/or facilitates discussions to clarify and extend student oral or written output	Teacher often asks questions and/or facilitates discussions to clarify and extend student oral or written output	Teacher consistently asks questions and/or facilitates discussions to clarify and extend student oral or written output	Teacher shows exceptional ability to consistently ask questions and/or facilitate discussions to clarify and extend student oral or written output	The skill or concept is not applicable in the context of this lesson/activity. It may be evident during another observation, but it was not observable during this classroom visit
3.3 Explains key terms, clarifies idiomatic expressions, uses gestures and/or visuals to illustrate concepts	Teacher rarely or never makes concepts comprehensible and provides a context for students to understand key terms through the use of demonstrations, concrete objects, or visuals	Teacher makes basic attempts to make concepts comprehensible and provides a context for students to understand key terms through the use of demonstrations, concrete objects, or visuals	Teacher sometimes makes concepts comprehensible and provides a context for students to understand key terms through the use of demonstrations, concrete objects, or visuals	Teacher often makes concepts comprehensible and provides a context for students to understand key terms through the use of demonstrations, concrete objects, or visuals	Teacher consistently makes concepts comprehensible and provides a context for students to understand key terms through the use of demonstrations, concrete objects, or visuals	Teacher shows exceptional ability to consistently make concepts comprehensible and provides a context for students to understand key terms through the use of demonstrations, concrete objects, or visuals	The skill or concept is not applicable in the context of this lesson/activity. It may be evident during another observation, but it was not observable during this classroom visit
3.4 Provides frequent feedback and checks for comprehension	Teacher rarely or never asks incisive questions during instruction to determine how well every student understands central ideas and concepts	Teacher makes basic attempts to ask incisive questions during instruction to determine how well every student understands central ideas and concepts	Teacher sometimes asks incisive questions during instruction to determine how well every student understands central ideas and concepts	Teacher often asks incisive questions during instruction to determine how well every student understands central ideas and concepts	Teacher consistently asks incisive questions during instruction to determine how well every student understands central ideas and concepts	Teacher shows exceptional ability to consistently ask incisive questions during instruction to determine how well every student understands central ideas and concepts	The skill or concept is not applicable in the context of this lesson/activity. It may be evident during another observation, but it was not observable during this classroom visit
	Teacher rarely or never provides positive, constructive feedback to students guide next steps	Teacher makes basic attempts to provide positive, constructive feedback to students guide next steps	Teacher sometimes provides positive, constructive feedback to students guide next steps	Teacher often provides positive, constructive feedback to students guide next steps	Teacher consistently provides positive, constructive feedback to students guide next steps	Teacher shows exceptional ability to consistently provide positive, constructive feedback to students guide next steps	

OPAL DOMAIN: COMPREHENSIBILITY (continued)

Instruction allows for maximum student understanding and teachers utilize effective strategies to help students access content.

OPAL INDICATORS	1 Novice [RARELY OR NEVER]	2 Apprentice [BASIC ATTEMPTS]	3 Developing [SOMETIMES]	4 Capable [OFTEN]	5 Accomplished [CONSISTENT]	6 Expert [EXCEPTIONAL]	N/O Not Observable
3.5 Uses informal assessments of student learning to adjust instruction while teaching	Teacher **rarely or never** makes formative assessment an integral part of the learning process to provide all students information about their progress as they engage in activities	Teacher **makes basic attempts to** make formative assessment an integral part of the learning process to provide all students information about their progress as they engage in activities	Teacher **sometimes** makes formative assessment an integral part of the learning process to provide all students information about their progress as they engage in activities	Teacher **often** makes formative assessment an integral part of the learning process to provide all students information about their progress as they engage in activities	Teacher **consistently** makes formative assessment an integral part of the learning process to provide all students information about their progress as they engage in activities	Teacher shows **exceptional ability to consistently** make formative assessment an integral part of the learning process to provide all students information about their progress as they engage in activities	The skill or concept is not applicable in the context of this lesson/activity. It may be evident during another observation, but it was not observable during this classroom visit

OPAL DOMAIN: INTERACTIONS

Varied participation structures allow for interactions that maximize engagement, leadership opportunities, and access to the curriculum.

OPAL INDICATORS	1 Novice [RARELY OR NEVER]	2 Apprentice [BASIC ATTEMPTS]	3 Developing [SOMETIMES]	4 Capable [OFTEN]	5 Accomplished [CONSISTENT]	6 Expert [EXCEPTIONAL]	N/O Not Observable
4.1 Facilitates student autonomy and choice by promoting active listening, questioning, and/or advocating	Teacher **rarely or never employs** classroom structures that involve student choice and opportunities for students to critically interact with and examine content through diverse perspectives	Teacher **makes basic attempts** to employ classroom structures that involve student choice and opportunities for students to critically interact with and examine content through diverse perspectives	Teacher **sometimes** employs classroom structures that involve student choice and opportunities for students to critically interact with and examine content through diverse perspectives	Teacher **often** employs classroom structures that involve student choice and opportunities for students to critically interact with and examine content through diverse perspectives	Teacher **consistently** employs classroom structures that involve student choice and opportunities for students to critically interact with and examine content through diverse perspectives	Teacher shows **exceptional ability to consistently employ** classroom structures that involve student choice and opportunities for students to critically interact with and examine content through diverse perspectives	The skill or concept is not applicable in the context of this lesson/activity. It may be evident during another observation, but it was not observable during this classroom visit
4.2 Modifies procedures and rules to support student learning	Teacher **rarely or never** redirects students in a positive manner, with a focus on learning and modifying lesson sequence to accommodate student needs	Teacher **makes basic attempts** to redirect students in a positive manner, with a focus on learning and modifying lesson sequence to accommodate student needs	Teacher **sometimes** redirects students in a positive manner, with a focus on learning and modifying lesson sequence to accommodate student needs	Teacher **often** redirects students in a positive manner, with a focus on learning and modifying lesson sequence to accommodate student needs	Teacher **consistently** redirects students in a positive manner, with a focus on learning and modifying lesson sequence to accommodate student needs	Teacher shows **exceptional ability to consistently redirect** students in a positive manner, with a focus on learning and modifying lesson sequence to accommodate student needs	The skill or concept is not applicable in the context of this lesson/activity. It may be evident during another observation, but it was not observable during this classroom visit
4.3 Effectively communicates subject matter knowledge in the target language	Teacher **shows little or no use of** appropriate target language, including pronunciation, articulation, tone, and age-appropriate/level-appropriate language	Teacher **makes basic attempts to use** appropriate target language, including pronunciation, articulation, tone, and age-appropriate/level-appropriate language	Teacher **sometimes** uses appropriate target language, including pronunciation, articulation, tone, and age-appropriate/level-appropriate language	Teacher **often** models appropriate use of the target language, including pronunciation, articulation, tone, and age-appropriate/level-appropriate language	Teacher **consistently** models appropriate use of the target language, including pronunciation, articulation, tone, and age-appropriate/level-appropriate language	Teacher shows **exceptional ability to consistently model** appropriate use of the target language, including pronunciation, articulation, tone, and age-appropriate/level-appropriate language	The skill or concept is not applicable in the context of this lesson/activity. It may be evident during another observation, but it was not observable during this classroom visit
4.4 Uses flexible groupings to promote positive interactions and accommodations for individual and group learning needs	Teacher **rarely or never establishes** classroom routines and structures that provide opportunities for varied collaborative work	Teacher **makes basic attempts to establish** classroom routines and structures that provide opportunities for varied collaborative work	Teacher **sometimes** establishes classroom routines and structures that provide opportunities for varied collaborative work	Teacher **often** establishes classroom routines and structures that provide opportunities for varied collaborative work	Teacher **consistently** establishes classroom routines and structures that provide opportunities for varied collaborative work	Teacher shows **exceptional ability to consistently establish** classroom routines and structures that provide opportunities for varied collaborative work	The skill or concept is not applicable in the context of this lesson/activity. It may be evident during another observation, but it was not observable during this classroom visit
	Teacher **rarely or never** supports and monitors equity-based student collaboration	Teacher **makes basic attempts** to support and monitor equity-based student collaboration	Teacher **sometimes** supports and monitors equity-based student collaboration	Teacher **often** supports and monitors equity-based student collaboration	Teacher **consistently** supports and monitors equity-based student collaboration	Teacher shows **exceptional ability to consistently support** and monitor equity-based student collaboration	

Appendix D

The OPAL Instrument

OBSERVATION PROTOCOL FOR ACADEMIC LITERACIES | OPAL©

Teacher Name: Grade: Subject/Lesson Focus: ELD Level(s):

The OPAL is a research-based tool for observing teacher practices and classroom interactions from sociocultural and language acquisition perspectives. Academic literacies are defined as a set of 21st century skills, abilities, and dispositions developed through the affirmation of and in response to students' identities, experiences and backgrounds.

Components of Empowering Pedagogy	Implementation Scale				Evidence and Next Steps
	Low 1-2	Med 3-4	High 5-6	Not Observable n/o	

RIGOROUS & RELEVANT CURRICULUM
The curriculum is cognitively complex, relevant, challenging and appropriate for linguistically diverse populations.

1.1 Engages students in problem solving, critical thinking and other activities that make subject matter meaningful.
1 | 2 | 3 | 4 | 5 | 6 | n/o

1.2 Facilitates student and teacher access to materials, technology, and resources to promote learning.
1 | 2 | 3 | 4 | 5 | 6 | n/o

1.3 Organizes curriculum and teaching to support students' understanding of instructional themes or topics.
1 | 2 | 3 | 4 | 5 | 6 | n/o

1.4 Establishes high expectations for learning that build on students' linguistic and academic strengths and needs.
1 | 2 | 3 | 4 | 5 | 6 | n/o

1.5 Provides access to content and materials in students' primary language.
1 | 2 | 3 | 4 | 5 | 6 | n/o

1.6 Provides opportunities for students to transfer skills between their primary language and target language.
1 | 2 | 3 | 4 | 5 | 6 | n/o

Evidence   Next Steps

CONNECTIONS
Teachers are mindful about providing opportunities for students to link content to their lives, histories, and realities to create change.

2.1 Relates instructional concepts to social conditions in the students' community.
1 | 2 | 3 | 4 | 5 | 6 | n/o

2.2 Helps students make connections between subject matter concepts and previous learning.
1 | 2 | 3 | 4 | 5 | 6 | n/o

2.3 Builds on students' life experiences and interests to make the content relevant and meaningful to them.
1 | 2 | 3 | 4 | 5 | 6 | n/o

Evidence   Next Steps

… The Observation Protocol for Academic Literacies

OBSERVATION PROTOCOL FOR ACADEMIC LITERACIES | OPAL©

Teacher Name: _____ Grade: _____ Subject/Lesson Focus: _____ ELD Level(s): _____

Components of Empowering Pedagogy	Implementation Scale Low 1-2 | Med 3-4 | High 5-6 | Not Observable n/o	Evidence and Next Steps
COMPREHENSIBILITY	Instruction allows for maximum student understanding and teachers utilize effective strategies to help students access content.	
3.1 Uses scaffolding strategies and devices (i.e. outlines, webs, semantic maps, compare/contrast charts, KWL) to make subject matter understandable. 1 | 2 | 3 | 4 | 5 | 6 | n/o	Evidence	Next Steps
3.2 Amplifies student input by: questioning / restating / rephrasing / expanding / contextualizing. 1 | 2 | 3 | 4 | 5 | 6 | n/o		
3.3 Explains key terms, clarifies idiomatic expressions, uses gestures and/or visuals to illustrate concepts. 1 | 2 | 3 | 4 | 5 | 6 | n/o		
3.4 Provides frequent feedback and checks for comprehension. 1 | 2 | 3 | 4 | 5 | 6 | n/o		
3.5 Uses informal assessments of student learning to adjust instruction while teaching. 1 | 2 | 3 | 4 | 5 | 6 | n/o		
INTERACTIONS	Varied participation structures allow for interactions that maximize engagement, leadership opportunities, and access to the curriculum.	
4.1 Facilitates student autonomy and choice by promoting active listening, questioning, and/or advocating. 1 | 2 | 3 | 4 | 5 | 6 | n/o	Evidence	Next Steps
4.2 Modifies procedures and rules to support student learning. 1 | 2 | 3 | 4 | 5 | 6 | n/o		
4.3 Effectively communicates subject matter knowledge in the target language. 1 | 2 | 3 | 4 | 5 | 6 | n/o		
4.4 Uses flexible groupings to promote positive interactions and accommodations for individual and group learning needs. 1 | 2 | 3 | 4 | 5 | 6 | n/o		

Appendix E

Observation Protocol for Academic Literacies (OPAL) Planning for Dissemination and Implementation

		Phase I Introductory/pilot implementation	Phase II Larger-scale dissemination and implementation
Why?	Purpose		
Who?	Participants facilitators/leadership		
What?	Opal domain(s)		
When?	Implementation timeline		
	Resources		

Appendix F
Diamond Academy

Observation Protocol for Academy Literacies (OPAL) Dissemination Plan

Please note that for this sample Dissemination Plan, the school focused on only one domain as they began their dissemination, thus other domains are not mentioned.

Appendix F 169

DATE	OUTCOMES	ACTIVITIES	MATERIALS/RESOURCES
Oct. 2	• Become familiar with the OPAL instrument and the four domains		• OPAL • Fact v. Opinion
Nov. 6	• Review OPAL Observation Guidelines for Reading the Room and recording evidence		• OPAL Observation Guidelines
Dec. 4	• Become familiar with the OPAL **Comprehensibility Domain** • Practice recording anecdotal evidence through a video observation • Review 'Reading the Room' and recording objective evidence • Come to consensus on Peer Coaching/ Observation Norms and Guidelines	• Introduce OPAL **Comprehensibility Domain: Research and Indicators** • Focused Viewing: Ms G, 2nd grade Mathematics • Recording Factual Evidence • Introduce Peer Coaching Norms & Guidelines – Seek staff input	• OPAL Dissemination Manual • OPAL Coaching Form (**Comprehensibility**) • OPAL Fact vs. Opinion statements • OPAL Peer Coaching Norms & Guidelines • **Other:** • Peer coaching List of Partners • Peer observation release schedule/sign up for observations in January
Jan. 22	• Conduct an OPAL pre-conference session with peer partner • Identify observation focus within the **Comprehensibility Domain**	• Pre-conference – Planning our first Peer Observation (20 minutes during PD period to have a peer coaching pre-conference) • Teachers partner with peer partners and identify an area of focus from the **Comprehensibility Domain**	• OPAL Coaching Form (**Comprehensibility**) • **Other:** • Peer coaching List of Partners • Peer observation release schedule/sign up for observations in January
Jan. 23 to Feb. 12		Plan OPAL observations and conduct pre-conferences	
Feb. 19	• Review Peer Coaching/Observation Norms and Guidelines • Develop deeper understanding of the OPAL **Comprehensibility Domain** • Practice recording anecdotal evidence through a video observation • Review 'Reading the Room' and recording objective evidence • Participate in or extend pre-OPAL observation peer conversation	• Review revised OPAL implementation plan and highlight connection to NASA's ongoing PD: CCSS ELA and Math, 21st-century skills, etc. • Provide overview of evaluation vs. coaching • Review Peer Coaching/Observation Norms and Guidelines • Review OPAL **Comprehensibility Domain: Research and Indicators** • Focused Viewing: Ms Mack, 2nd grade ELD (Idiomatic Expressions + Writing) • Recording Factual Evidence • Meet with OPAL peer partner to discuss observation	• OPAL Dissemination Manual • OPAL Coaching Form (Connections) • OPAL Peer Coaching Norms & Guidelines • **Other:** • Peer Coaching List of Partners • Peer Observation release schedule/sign up for observations in Feb/March 2014

Feb. 20 to Mar. 26	**Conduct OPAL observations #1**	
Mar. 26	• Debrief OPAL observation experience and protocol process • Participate in a post-OPAL observation peer conversation • Establish focus with partners for a 2nd OPAL observation (pre-conference)	• Conduct focus group feedback session for staff input • Meet with OPAL peer partner to discuss observation and plan 2nd observation	• Notes from OPAL Peer Observation • OPAL Dissemination Manual
Mar. 27 to Apr. 30	**Conduct OPAL observations #2**	
Apr. 30	• Participate in a post-OPAL observation peer conversation • End-of-year survey and input for Year 2	• Seek staff input for OPAL peer partner observations and next steps	• Notes from OPAL Peer Observation • OPAL Dissemination Manual

Appendix G

Opal Coaching: Note-Taking Form

Focus: Rigorous and relevant curriculum

Indicator	Lesson notes and things to consider
1.1 Engages students in problem solving, critical thinking and other activities that make subject matter meaningful OPAL self-rating	
1.2 Facilitates student and teacher access to materials, technology and resources to promote learning OPAL self-rating	
1.3 Organizes curriculum and teaching to support students' understanding of instructional themes or topics OPAL self-rating	
1.4 Establishes high expectations for learning that build on students' linguistic and academic strengths and needs OPAL self-rating	
1.5 Provides access to content and materials in students' primary language OPAL self-rating	
1.6 Provides opportunities for students to transfer skills between their primary language and target language OPAL self-rating	

Next steps:

Focus: Connections

Indicator	Lesson notes and things to consider
2.1 Relates instructional concepts to social conditions in the students' community OPAL self-rating	
2.2 Helps students make connections between subject matter concepts and previous learning OPAL self-rating	
2.3 Builds on students' life experiences and interests to make the content relevant and meaningful to them OPAL self-rating	

Next steps:

Focus: Comprehensibility

Indicator	Lesson notes and things to consider
3.1 Uses scaffolding strategies and devices (i.e. outlines, webs, semantic maps, compare/contrast charts, KWL) to make subject matter understandable OPAL self-rating	
3.2 Amplifies student input by: questioning/restating/rephrasing/ expanding/contextualizing OPAL self-rating	
3.3 Explains key terms, clarifies idiomatic expressions, uses gestures and/or visuals to illustrate concepts OPAL self-rating	
3.4 Provides frequent feedback and checks for comprehension OPAL self-rating	
3.5 Uses informal assessments of student learning to adjust instruction while teaching OPAL self-rating	

Next steps:

Focus: Interactions

Indicator	Lesson notes and things to consider
4.1 Facilitates student autonomy and choice by promoting active listening, questioning and/or advocating OPAL self-rating	
4.2 Modifies procedures and rules to support student learning OPAL self-rating	
4.3 Effectively communicates subject matter knowledge in the target language OPAL self-rating	
4.4 Uses flexible groupings to promote positive interactions and accommodations for individual and group learning needs OPAL self-rating	

Next steps:

References

Abedi, J. (2008) Measuring students' level of English proficiency: Educational significance and assessment requirements. *Educational Assessment* 13 (2–3), 193–214. https://doi.org/10.1080/10627190802394404.

Achugar, M., Shleppegrell, M. and Orteiza, T. (2007) Engaging teachers in language analysis: A functional linguistics approach to reflective literacy. *English Teaching: Practice and Critique* 6 (2), 8–24.

Alamo, D.W. (2018) Teachers' Knowledge, Perceptions and Practices Regarding Academic Literacy Development of Long-Term English Learners. Doctoral dissertation, Loyola Marymount University. Digital Commons @ Loyola Marymount University and Loyola Law School. https://digitalcommons.lmu.edu/etd/536.

Alvarez, L., Ananda, S., Walqui, A., Sato, E. and Rabinowitz, S. (2014) *Focusing Formative Assessment on the Needs of English Language Learners*. San Francisco, CA: WestEd.

August, D. and Shanahan, T. (eds) (2006) *Developing Literacy in Second-Language Learners: Report of the National Literacy Panel on Language-Minority Children and Youth*. Mahwah, NJ: Lawrence Erlbaum. https://doi.org/10.1080%2F10862960903340165.

August, D. and Blackburn, T. (2019) *Promoting Success for Teachers of English Learners Through Structured Observations*. Washington, DC: Council of Chief State School Officers.

Benson, P. (2011) *Teaching and Researching: Autonomy in Language Learning* (2nd edn). London: Longman. https://doi.org/10.4324/9781315833767.

Bransford, J.D., Brown, A.L. and Cocking, R.R. (2000) *How People Learn: Brain, Mind, Experience, and School*. Washington, DC: National Academies Press. https://doi.org/10.17226/6160.

Brinton, D.M., Snow, M.A. and Wesche, M.B. (1989) *Content-Based Second Language Instruction*. Boston, MA: Heinle & Heinle.

Bruner, J.S. (1978) Appendix: The role of dialogue in language acquisition. In A. Sinclair, R.J. Jarvella and W.J.M. Levelt (eds) *The Child's Conception of Language* (pp. 241–256). New York, NY: Springer-Verlag.

Bruner, J.S. (1983) *Child's Talk: Learning to Use Language*. New York, NY: Norton.

Bunch, G.C. and Martin, D. (2021) From 'academic language' to the 'language of ideas' A disciplinary perspective on using language in K-12 settings. *Language and Education* 35 (6), 539–556.

Byrne, B. and Schneider, B.H. (1986) Student-teacher concordance of dimensions of student social competence: A multitrait-multimethod analysis. *Journal of Psychopathology and Behavioral Assessment* 8 (3), 263–279. https://doi.org/10.1007/BF00959837.

California Department of Education (2000) *History Social Science Content Standards for California Public Schools: Kindergarten Through Grade Twelve*. www.cde.ca.gov/be/st/ss/documents/histsocscistnd.pdf (Original work published 1998).

California Department of Education (2009) *California Standards for the Teaching Profession*. www.ctc.ca.gov/docs/default-source/educator-prep/standards/cstp-2009.pdf (Original work published 1997).

California Department of Education (2012) *English Language Development Standards: Kindergarten Through Grade 12*. www.cde.ca.gov/sp/el/er/documents/eldstndspublication14.pdf.

California Department of Education (2013a) *California Common Core State Standards: English Language Arts & Literacy in History/Social Studies, Science, and Technical Subjects*. www.cde.ca.gov/be/st/ss/documents/finalelaccssstandards.pdf (Original work published 2010).

California Department of Education (2013b) *California Common Core State Standards: Mathematics*. www.cde.ca.gov/be/st/ss/documents/ccssmathstandardaug2013.pdf (Original work published 2010).

California Department of Education (2013c) *Next Generation Science Standards for California Public Schools: Kindergarten Through Grade Twelve*https://www.cde.ca.gov/pd/ca/sc/ngssstandards.asp. https://www.cde.ca.gov/pd/ca/sc/ngssstandards.asp.

California Department of Education (2014) *English Language Arts/English Language Development Framework*. www.cde.ca.gov/ci/rl/cf/elaeldfrmwrksbeadopted.asp.

California Department of Education (2017) *History Social Science Framework for California Public Schools: Kindergarten Through Grade Twelve*. www.cde.ca.gov/ci/hs/cf/documents/hssframeworkwhole.pdf.

California Education Code - EDC § 313.1. ARTICLE 3.5. English Language Proficiency Assessment [313 -313.5] https://leginfo.legislature.ca.gov/faces/codes_displayText.xhtml?lawCode=EDC&division=1.&title=1.&part=1.&chapter=3.&article=3.5.

California State University Chico (2023) *The CIELO Project: Community and Instruction for Expanding English Learners' Opportunities*. Center for Bilingual Multicultural Studies. www.csuchico.edu/cbms/cielo.shtml.

Carlo, M.S., August, D., McLaughlin, B., Snow, C.E., Dressler, C., Lippman, D.N. and White, C.E. (2004) Closing the gap: Addressing the vocabulary needs of English-language learners in bilingual and mainstream classrooms. *Reading Research Quarterly* 39 (2), 188–215. https://doi.org/10.1598/RRQ.39.2.3.

Cazden, C.B. (1986) Classroom discourse. In M.C. Wittrock (ed) *Handbook of Research on Teaching* (pp. 432–463, 3rd edn). New York, NY: Macmillan.

Cazden, C.B. (2001) *Classroom Discourse: The Language of Teaching and Learning* (2nd edn). Portsmouth, NH: Heinemann.

Celce-Murcia, M., Dörnyei, Z. and Thurrell, S. (1993) A pedagogical framework for communicative competence: Content specifications and guidelines for communicative language teaching. *Deseret Language and Linguistic Society Symposium* 19 (1), 3.

Center on Education Policy (2005) *States Try Harder, but Gaps Persist: High School Exit Exams 2005*. www.cep-dc.org/displayDocument.cfm?DocumentID=253.

Chamot, A.U. and O'Malley, J.M. (1994) *The CALLA Handbook: Implementing the Cognitive Academic Language Learning Approach*. White Plains, MA: Addison-Wesley.

Coady, M., Miller, M.D., Jing, Z., Heffington, D., Lopez, M., Olszewska, A., De Jong, E., Yilmaz, T. and Ankeny, R. (2019) Can English learner teacher effectiveness be observed? Validation of an el-modified framework for teaching. *TESOL Quarterly* 54, 1. https://doi.org/10.1002/tesq.544.

Cohen, J. (1960) A coefficient for agreement for nominal scales. *Educational and Psychological Measurement* 20, 37–46. https://doi.org/10.1177%2F001316446002000104.

Cohen, A.D. (1998) *Strategies in Learning and Using a Second Language*. London: Longman. https://doi.org/10.4324/9781315833200.

Collier, V. and Thomas, W. (2002) *A National Study of School Effectiveness for Language Minority Students' Long-Term Academic Achievement*. Center for Research on Education, Diversity and Excellence, UC Berkeley.

Cummins, J. (2000) *Language, Power, and Pedagogy: Bilingual Children in the Crossfire*. Clevedon: Multilingual Matters.

Cummins, J. (2001) *Negotiating Identities: Education for Empowerment in a Diverse Society*. Covina, CA: California Association for Bilingual Education.

de Charms, R. (2013) *Personal Causation: The Internal Affective Determinants of Behavior*. New York: Routledge. https://doi.org/10.4324/9781315825632.

de Jong, E.J. (2013) Policy discourses and U.S. language in education policies. *Peabody Journal of Education* 88 (1), 98–111. https://doi.org/10.1080/0161956X.2013.752310.

de Jong, E.J. (2022) Multilingualism as norm: Advocating for equity for multilingual learners. In G. Prasad, N. Auger and E. Le Puichon-Vortsmann (eds) *Multilingualism in Education: Researchers' Perspectives and Trajectories*. Cambridge: Cambridge University Press.

de Oliveira, L.C., Obenchain, K.M., Kenny, R.H. and Oliveira, A.W. (eds) (2018) *Teaching the Content Areas to English Language Learners in Secondary Schools: English Language Arts, Mathematics, Science, and Social Studies* (pp. 327–340). Cham: Springer. https://doi.org/10.1007/978-3-030-02245-7.

Dolson, D.P. and Burnham-Massey, L. (eds) (2011) *Redesigning English-Medium Classrooms: Using Research to Enhance English Learner Achievement*. Covina, CL: California Association for Bilingual Education (CABE).

Dong, Y.R. (2017) Tapping into English language learners' (ELLs') prior knowledge in social studies instruction. *The Social Studies* 108 (4), 143–151. https://doi.org/10.1080/00377996.2017.1342161.

Douglas, K. (2009) Sharpening our focus in measuring classroom instruction. *Educational Researcher* 38 (7), 518–521. https://doi.org/10.3102/0013189X0935088.

Dwordin, J.E. (2006) The family stories project: Using funds of knowledge for writing. *The Reading Teacher* 59 (6), 510–520. https://doi.org/10.1598/RT.59.6.1.

Echevarria, J. and Short, D. (2004) Using multiple perspectives in observations of diverse classrooms: The Sheltered instruction observation protocol (SIOP). In H. Waxman, R. Tharp and S. Hilberg (eds) *Observational Research in U.S. Classrooms: New Approaches for Understanding Cultural and Linguistic Diversity* (pp. 21–47). Cambridge: Cambridge University Press.

Echevarria, J., Vogt, M.E. and Short, D. (2010) *The SIOP Model for Teaching Mathematics to English Learners*. Allyn & Bacon. https://doi.org/10.11114/jets.v1i2.173.

Emerson, R.M., Fretz, R.I. and Shaw, L.L. (1995) *Writing Ethnographic Fieldnotes*. University of Chicago Press. http://dx.doi.org/10.7208/chicago/9780226206851.001.0001.

Enright, K.A. (2013) Adolescent writers and academic trajectories: Situating L2 writing in the content areas. In L.C. de Oliveira and T. Silva (eds) *L2 Writing in the Secondary Classroom: Experiences, Academic Issues, Student Experiences and Teacher Education* (pp. 27–43). New York, NY: Routledge.

Fang, Z. and Schleppegrell, M. (2010) Disciplinary literacies across content areas: Supporting secondary reading through functional language analysis. *Journal of Adolescent & Adult Literacy* 53 (7), 587–597. https://doi.org/10.1598/JAAL.53.7.6.

Fillmore, L.W. and Snow, C. (2018) What teachers need to know about language. In C. Adger, C. Snow and D. Christian (eds) *What Teachers Need to Know About Language* (2nd edn, pp. 8–51). Bristol: Multilingual Matters/Center for Applied Linguistics.

Francis, D.J., Lesaux, N.K. and August, D. (2006) Language of instruction. In D. August and T. Shanahan (eds) *Developing Literacy in Second-Language Learners: Report of the National Literacy Panel on Language–Minority Children and Youth* (pp. 365–413). Mahwah, NJ: Lawrence Erlbaum Associates Publishers.

Freeman, D. and Freeman, Y. (2007) *English Language Learners: The Essential Guide.* New York, NY: Scholastic Teaching Resources.

García, O. (2009) Emergent bilinguals and TESOL: What's in a name? *TESOL Quarterly* 43, 322–326. https://doi.org/10.1002/j.1545-7249.2009.tb00172.x.

Genesee, F., Lindholm-Leary, K., Saunders, W. and Christian, D. (2006) *Educating English Language Learners.* Cambridge: Cambridge University Press. https://psycnet.apa.org/doi/10.1017/CBO9780511499913.

Gersten, R. and Baker, S. (2000) What we know about effective instructional practices for English learners. *Exceptional Children* 66, 454–470. https://doi.org/10.1177%2F001440290006600402.

Gibbons, P. (2006) *Bridging Discourses in the ESL Classroom: Students, Teachers and Researchers.* London: Continuum.

Gibbons, P. (2009) *English Learners, Academic Literacy, and Thinking: Learning in the Challenge Zone.* Portsmouth, NH: Heinemann.

Gibbons, P. (2015) *Scaffolding Language, Scaffolding Learning: Teaching English Language Learners in the Mainstream Classroom* (2nd edn). Portsmouth, NH: Heinemann.

Gibbons, P. (2018) *Bridging Discourses in the ESL Classroom: Students, Teachers and Researchers.* New York, NY: Bloomsbury Academic.

Ginsberg, D., Honda, M. and O'Neil, W. (2011) Looking beyond English: Linguistic inquiry for English language learners. *Language and Linguistics Compass* 5 (5), 249–264. https://doi.org/10.1111/j.1749-818X.2011.00271.x.

Goldenberg, C. (2012) Research on English learner instruction. In M. Calderón (ed.) *Breaking Through: Effective Instruction & Assessment for Reaching English Learners* (pp. 39–61). Bloomington, IN: Solution Tree Press.

Goldenberg, C., Haertel, E., Coleman, R., Reese, L. and Rodriguez-Mojica, C. (2013) *Classroom Qualities for English Language Learners in Language Arts Instruction: Technical Report.* https://claudeg.people.stanford.edu/cqell.

Gonzalez, N., Moll, L.C. and Amanti, C. (eds) (2005) *Funds of Knowledge: Theorizing Practices in Households and Classrooms.* Mahwah, NJ: Lawrence Erlbaum Associates.

Hammond, J. and Gibbons, P. (2005) Putting scaffolding to work: The contribution of scaffolding in articulating ESL education. *Prospect: An Australian Journal of TESOL* 20 (1), 6–30.

Hartshorn, K. and McMurry, B. (2020) Effects of the COVID-19 pandemic on ESL learners and TESOL practitioners in the United States. *International Journal of TESOL Studies* 2, 140–157.

Hattie, J. (2012) *Visible Learning for Teachers: Maximizing Impact on Learning.* New York: Routledge. https://doi.org/10.1111/j.1467-8535.2012.01347_7.x.

Hattie, J. and Clarke, S. (2018) *Visible Learning Feedback.* New York: Routledge. https://doi.org/10.4324/9780429485480.

Hensley, M. (2005) Empowering parents of multicultural backgrounds. In N. Gonzalez, L. Moll and C. Amanti (eds) *Funds of Knowledge: Theorizing Practices in Households and Classrooms* (pp. 143–151). Mahwah, NJ: Lawrence Erlbaum Associates.

Heritage, M. (2010) *Formative Assessment: Making It Happen in the Classroom.* Thousand Oaks, CA: Corwin Press. http://dx.doi.org/10.4135/9781452219493.

Heritage, M., Walqui, A. and Linquanti, R. (2015) *English Language Learners and the New Standards: Developing Language, Content Knowledge, and Analytical Practices in the Classroom.* Cambridge, MA: Harvard Education Press.

Hilberg, R.S., Waxman, H.C. and Tharp, R.G. (2004) Introduction: Purposes and perspectives on classroom observation research. In H.C. Waxman, R.G. Tharp and R.S. Hilberg (eds) *Observational Research in the U.S. Classrooms: New Approaches for Understanding Cultural and Linguistic Diversity* (pp. 1–20). Cambridge: Cambridge University Press. https://psycnet.apa.org/doi/10.1017/CBO9780511616419.001.

Hoge, R.D. (1985) The validity of direct observation measures of pupil classroom behavior. *Review of Educational Research* 55, 469–483. https://doi.org/10.3102%2F00346543055004469.

Hollins, E.R. (2011) Teacher preparation for quality teaching. *Journal of Teacher Education* 62 (4), 395–407. https://doi.org/10.1177%2F0022487111409415.

Holt, D. (ed.) (1993) *Cooperative Learning: A Response to Linguistic and Cultural Diversity*. Cupertino, CA: Delta Systems.

Hopkins, D. (2017) *Re-Envisioning English Language Arts and English Language Development for English Language Learners* (2nd edn). Washington, DC: Council of the Great City Schools.

Hopkins, M., Lowenhaupt, R. and Sweet, T.M. (2015) Organizing English learner instruction in new immigrant destinations: District infrastructure and subject-specific school practice. *American Educational Research Journal* 52 (3), 408–439. https://doi.org/10.3102/0002831215584780.

Hurley, S.R. and Tinajero, J.V. (2001) *Literacy Assessment of Second Language Learners*. Boston, MA: Allyn and Bacon.

Hyson, M.C., Hirsh-Pasek, K. and Rescorla, L. (1990) The classroom practices inventory: An observational instrument based on NAEYC's guidelines for developmentally appropriate practices for 4- and 5-year-old children. *Early Childhood Research Quarterly* 5, 475–494. https://doi.org/10.1016/0885-2006(90)90015-S.

Joyce, B. and Showers, B. (2002) *Student Achievement Through Staff Development*. Alexandria, VA: Association for Supervision & Curriculum Development.

Kibler, A., Valdés, G. and Walqui, A. (eds) (2020) *Reconceptualizing the Role of Critical Dialogue in American Classrooms: Promoting Equity Through Dialogic Education* (1st edn). Routledge. https://doi.org/10.4324/9780429330667.

Kibler, A.K., Walqui, A. and Bunch, G.C. (2015) Transformational opportunities: Language and literacy instruction for English language learners in the common core era in the United States. *TESOL Journal* 6 (1), 9–35. https://doi.org/10.1002/tesj.133.

King, K. and Lanza, E. (2019) Ideology, agency, and imagination in multilingual families: An introduction. *International Journal of Bilingualism* 23 (3), 717–723. https://doi.org/10.1177/1367006916684907.

Kohler, F.W., McCullough, K.M. and Buchan, K.A. (1995) Using peer coaching to enhance preschool teachers' development and refinement of classroom activities. *Early Education & Development* 6, 215–239. https://doi.org/10.1207/s15566935eed0603_2.

Krashen, S. (1982) *Principles and Practice in Second Language*. New York, NY: Pergamon.

Krashen, S.D. (1985) *The Input Hypothesis: Issues and Implications*. London: Addison-Wesley Longman Ltd.

Lavadenz, M. (2003) *Think Aloud Protocols: Teaching Reading Processes to Young Bilingual Students*. ERIC Digest EDO-FL-03-14. Washington, DC: Center for Applied Linguistics.

Lavadenz, M., Kaminski, L.R.G., Armas, E.G. and López, G.V. (2021) Equity leadership for English learners during COVID-19: Early lessons. *Frontiers in Education*. https://doi.org/10.3389/feduc.2021.636281.

Lave, J. and Wenger, E. (1991) *Situated Learning: Legitimate Peripheral Participation*. Cambridge: Cambridge University Press. https://doi.org/10.2307/2804509.

Learning Forward (2022) *National Standards for Professional Learning*. https://standards.learningforward.org/standards-for-professional-learning/ (Original work published 2011).

Lee, O. (2019) Aligning English language proficiency standards with content standards: Shared opportunity and responsibility across English learner education and content areas. *Educational Researcher* 48 (8), 534–542. https://doi.org/10.3102/0013189X19872497.

Leseaux, N.K. and Harris, J.R. (2015) *Cultivating Knowledge, Building Language: Literacy Instruction for English Learners in Elementary School*. Portsmouth, NH: Heinemann.

Lightbown, P. and Spada, N. (2013) *How Languages are Learned* (4th edn). Oxford: Oxford University Press.

Llopart, M. and Esteban-Guitart, M. (2018) Funds of knowledge in 21st century societies: Inclusive educational practices for under-represented students: A literature review. *Journal of Curriculum Studies* 50 (2), 145–161. https://doi.org/10.1080/00220272.2016.1247913.

Lopez, C.G. and Musanti, S.I. (2019) Fostering identity negotiation in sixth-grade ELLs: Examining an instructional unit on identity in English language arts. *NABE Journal of Research and Practice* 9 (2), 61–77. https://doi.org/10.1080/26390043.2019.1589290.

Lucas, S.R. and Beresford, L. (2010) Naming and classifying: Theory, evidence, and equity in education. *Review of Research in Education* 34 (1), 24–84. https://doi.org/10.3102%2F0091732X09353578.

MacSwan, J. (2020) Academic English as standard language ideology: A renewed research agenda for asset-based language education. *Language Teaching Research* 24 (1), 28–36. https://doi.org/10.1177/136216881877754.

Mansilla, V.B. and Jackson, A. (2011) *Educating for Global Competence: Preparing Our Youth to Engage the World*. Asia Society. https://asiasociety.org/files/book-global-competence.pdf.

Martínez, R.A. (2018) *Beyond the 'English Learner' Label: Recognizing the Richness of Bi/Multilingual Students' Linguistic Repertoires*. Newark, DE: The Reading Teacher.

Matera, C., Armas, E. and Lavadenz, M. (2016) Using scaffolded dialogic reading to foster the language and literacy development of dual language learners in transitional kindergarten. *National Head Start Association Dialog* 18 (4), 80–104.

Matsumura, L.C., Patthey-Chavez, G.G., Valdes, R. and Garnier, H. (2002) Teacher feedback, writing assignment quality, and third-grade students' revision in higher and lower achieving schools. *The Elementary School Journal* 103 (1), 3–25. https://doi.org/10.1086/499713.

Mercuri, S. (2015) Teachers' understanding of practice: Planning and implementing preview/view/review in the dual language classroom. *Advances in Research on Teaching* 24, 81–106.

Merriam, S.B. (1998) *Qualitative Research and Case Study Applications in Education*. San Francisco, CA: Jossey-Bass.

Micceri, T., Peterson, D. and Borg, J.M. (1990, April 16–20) Consistent Patterns in Observed Teacher Performance: Results from a Large-Sample Multi-Year Study. Paper presentation. The Annual Meeting of the American Educational Research Association, Boston, MA.

Moje, E.B., McIntosh-Ciechanowski, K., Kramer, K., Ellis, L., Carrillo, R. and Collazo, T. (2004) Working toward third space in content area literacy: An examination of everyday funds of knowledge and discourse. *Reading Research Quarterly* 39 (1), 38–70. https://doi.org/10.1598/RRQ.39.1.4.

Morita-Mullaney, T. (2018) The intersection of language and race among English learner (EL) leaders in desegregated urban midwest schools: A LangCrit narrative study. *Journal of Language, Identity & Education*, 1–17. https://doi.org/10.1080/15348458.2018.1494598.

National Academies of Sciences, Engineering, and Medicine (2017) *Promoting the Educational Success of Children and Youth Learning English: Promising Futures*. The National Academies Press. https://doi.org/10.17226/24677.

National Center for Education Statistics (2015) http://nces.ed.gov/nationsreportcard.

National Research Council (2012) *Education for Life and Work: Developing Transferable Knowledge and Skills in the 21st Century*. Washington, DC: The National Academies Press. https://doi.org/10.17226/13398.

Neuman, S. and Cunningham, L. (2009) *The Impact of Professional Development and Coaching on Early Language and Literacy Instructional Practices*. London: Sage. https://doi.org/10.3102%2F0002831208328088.

Ovando, C., Collier, V. and Combs, M. (2003) *Bilingual and ESL Classrooms: Teaching Multicultural Contexts* (3rd edn). New York, NY: McGraw-Hill.

Ovando, C.J. and Combs, M.C. (2018) *Bilingual and ESL Classrooms: Teaching in Multicultural Contexts* (6th edn). Lanham, MD: Rowman & Littlefield.

Paris, D. and Alim, H.S. (2014) What are we seeking to sustain through culturally sustaining pedagogy? A loving critique forward. *Harvard Educational Review* 84 (1), 85–100. https://doi.org/10.17763/haer.84.1.982l873k2ht16m77.

Partnership for 21st Century Learning, a Network of Battelle for Kids. (2019a) *P21 Network*. www.battelleforkids.org/networks/p21.

Partnership for 21st Century Learning, a Network of Battelle for Kids. (2019b) *P21 Framework Definitions*. https://static.battelleforkids.org/documents/p21/P21_Framework_DefinitionsBFK.pdf.

Patall, E.A., Dent, A.L., Oyer, M. and Wynn, S.R. (2013) Student autonomy and course value: The unique and cumulative roles of various teacher practices. *Motivation and Emotions* 37 (1), 14–32. https://doi.org/10.1007/s11031-012-9305-6.

Pedroarias, R.J. (2011) Organizational Assimilation Through Heritage Language Programming: Reconciling Justice and Bilingualism. Doctoral dissertation, Loyola Marymount University. Digital Commons @ Loyola Marymount University and Loyola Law School. https://digitalcommons.lmu.edu/etd/252.

Pianta, R.C. and Hamre, B.K. (2009) Conceptualization, measurement, and improvement of classroom processes: Standardized observation can leverage capacity. *Education Researcher* 38 (2), 109–119. https://doi.org/10.3102%2F0013189X09332374.

PROMISE Design Center (2005–2015) *PROMISE Initiative (Pursuing Regional Opportunities for Mentoring Innovation, and Success for English Learners*. San Bernardino County Superintendent of Schools in cooperation with RIMS CTAP (California Technology Assistance Project), Region 10.

Roberson, T.J. (1998, November 4–6) *Classroom Observation: Issues Regarding Validity & Reliability*. Paper presentation. Mid-South Education Research Association 27th Annual Meeting, New Orleans, LA.

Rogoff, B. (2003) *The Cultural Nature of Human Development*. New York, NY: Oxford University Press.

Rosa, J. (2019) *Looking Like a Language, Sounding Like a Race*. New York, NY: Oxford University Press.

Rosenthal, R. and Jacobson, L. (2000) Teacher expectations for the disadvantaged. In P.K. Smith and A.D. Pellegrini (eds) *Psychology of Education: Major Themes* (pp. 286–291). London: Routledge Falmer.

Rubie-Davies, C., Hattie, J. and Hamilton, R. (2006) Expecting the best for students: Teacher expectations and academic outcomes. *British Journal of Educational Psychology* 76 (3), 429–444. https://doi.org/10.1348/000709905X53589.

Ruiz Soto, A.G., Hooker, S. and Batalova, J. (2015) *Top Languages Spoken by English Language Learners Nationally and by State*. Migration Policy Institute. www.migrationpolicy.org/sites/default/files/publications/ELLFact%20Sheet-No4.pdf.

Saunders, W. and Goldenberg, C. (2010) Research to guide English language development instruction. In *Improving Education for English Learners: Research-Based Approaches* (pp. 21–82). Sacramento, CA: California Department of Education.

Schleppegrell, M.J. (2012) Academic language in teaching and learning: Introduction to the special issue. *The Elementary School Journal* 112 (3), 409–418. https://doi.org/10.1086/663297.

Schreiber, J.B., Nora, A., Stage, F.K., Barlow, E.A. and King, J. (2006) Reporting structural equation modeling and confirmatory factor analysis results: A review. *The*

Journal of Educational Research 99 (6), 323–337. https://doi.org/10.3200/JOER.99.6.323-338.

Shulman, L.S. (1987) Knowledge and teaching: Foundations of the new reform. *Harvard Educational Review* 57 (1), 1–23. https://doi.org/10.17763/haer.57.1.j463w79r56455411.

Singleton, G.E. (2021) *Courageous Conversations About Race: A Field Guide for Achieving Equity in Schools and Beyond*. Thousand Oaks, CA: Corwin Press.

Skiffington, S., Washburn, S. and Elliott, K. (2011) Instructional coaching: Helping preschool teachers reach their full potential. *Young Children* 66 (3), 12–19. www.jstor.org/stable/42730938.

Skutnabb-Kangas, T. (2000) *Linguistic Genocide in Education – Or Worldwide Diversity and Human Rights?* Mahwah, NJ: Lawrence Erlbaum Associates. https://doi.org/10.4324/9781410605191.

Sleeter, C.E. and Grant, C.A. (2009) *Making Choices for Multicultural Education: Five Approaches to Race, Class and Gender* (6th edn). Hoboken, NJ: Wiley.

Solano-Flores, G. and Trumbull, E. (2003) Examining language in context: The need for new research and practice paradigms in the testing of English-language learners. *Educational Researcher* 32 (2), 3–13. https://doi.org/10.3102%2F0013189X032002003.

Star, D., Prunty, E., Herrera, J. and Ugo, I. (2022, December 14) Test scores show six-year setback for California students. www.ppic.org/blog/test-scores-show-six-year-setback-for-california-students/.

Strauss, A. and Corbin, J.M. (1990) *Basics of Qualitative Research: Grounded Theory Procedures and Techniques*. Newbury Park, CA: Sage.

Sugarman, J. and Lazarin, M. (2020) *Educating English Learners During the COVID-19 Pandemic: Policy Ideas for States and School District*. Washington, DC: Migration Policy Institute. www.migrationpolicy.org/research/english-learners-covid-19-pandemic-policy-ideas.

Swaffield, S. (2011) Getting to the heart of authentic assessment for learning. *Assessment in Education: Principles, Policy & Practice* 18 (4), 443–449. https://doi.org/10.1080/0969594X.2011.582838.

Swain, M. (1986) Communicative competence: Some roles of comprehensible input and comprehensible output in its development. In J. Cummins and M. Swain (eds) *Bilingualism in Education* (pp. 116–137). London: Longman.

Swain, M. and Watanabe, Y. (2012) Languaging: Collaborative dialogue as a source of second language learning. In *The Encyclopedia of Applied Linguistics*. Blackwell Publishing. https://doi.org/10.1002/9781405198431.wbeal0664.pub2.

Tang, G. (2007) Cross-linguistic analysis of Vietnamese and English with implications for Vietnamese language acquisition and maintenance in the United States. *Journal of Southeast Asian American Education and Advancement* 2 (1), Article 3. https://doi.org/10.7771/2153-8999.1085.

Teemant, A. (2014) A mixed-methods investigation of instructional coaching for teachers of diverse learners. *Urban Education* 49 (5), 574–604. https://doi.org/10.1177%2F0042085913481362.

Teemant, A., Sherman, B. and Tyra, S.K. (2022) *Enduring Principles of Learning Research Brief: Theory and Evidence for Pedagogy, Learning, and Coaching*. Cambridge: Teemant & Associates, LLC.

Tenenbaum, H.R. and Ruck, M.D. (2007) Are teachers' expectations different for racial minority than for European American students? A meta-analysis. *Journal of Educational Psychology* 99 (2), 253–273. https://psycnet.apa.org/doi/10.1037/0022-0663.99.2.253.

Tharp, R. (2018) *Teaching Transformed: Achieving Excellence, Fairness, Inclusion, and Harmony*. New York, NY: Routledge.

Tharp, R. and Gallimore, R. (1988) *Rousing Minds to Life: Teaching, Learning and Schooling in Social Context*. Cambridge: Cambridge University Press.

Thomas, W.P. and Collier, V.P. (2003) Reforming education policies for English learners: Research evidence from U.S. schools. *The Multilingual Educator* 4 (1), 16–19.
Tomlinson, C.A. (2001) *How to Differentiate Instruction in Mixed-Ability Classrooms* (2nd edn). Alexandria, VA: Association for Supervision and Curriculum Development (ASCD).
Tomlinson, C.A. and McTighe, J. (2006) *Integrating Differentiated Instruction and Understanding by Design: Connecting Content and Kids*. Alexandria, VA: Association for Supervision and Curriculum Development (ASCD).
U.S. Department of Education, National Clearinghouse for English Language Acquisition (2014) *National Professional Development (NPD) Program 2011 and 2012 Grantee Profiles*. https://ncela.ed.gov/files/uploads/51/NPD%20Grantee%20Profiles%20Booklet.pdf.
U.S. Department of Education, Office of English Language Acquisition (2017) *English Learner Toolkit for State and Local Education Agencies (SEAs and LEAs)*. www2.ed.gov/about/offices/list/oela/english-learner-toolkit/index.html.
U.S. Department of Education, Office of English Language Acquisition (2022) *English Learners Demographic Trends: Fact Sheet*. https://ncela.ed.gov/resources/fact-sheet-english-learners-demographic-trends-august-2022-.
Van den Bergh, L., Denessen, E., Hornstra, L., Voeten, M. and Holland, R.W. (2010) The implicit prejudiced attitudes of teachers: Relations to teacher expectations and the ethnic achievement gap. *American Educational Research Journal* 47 (2), 497–527. https://doi.org/10.3102%2F0002831209353594.
Van Lier, L. (1996) *Interaction in the Language Curriculum: Awareness, Autonomy and Authenticity*. Pearson Education Limited. https://doi.org/10.4324/9781315843223.
Van Lier, L. (2004) *The Ecology and Semiotics of Language Learning: A Sociocultural Perspective*. Dordrecht, NL: Kluwer Academic Publishers.
Van Lier, L. and Walqui, A. (2012) *Language and the Common Core State Standards*. Paper presentation. Understanding Language Conference, Stanford, CA.
Villegas, A.M. and Lucas, T. (2002) Preparing culturally responsive teachers: Rethinking the curriculum. *Journal of Teacher Education* 53 (1), 20–32. https://doi.org/10.1177%2F0022487102053001003.
Vygotsky, L.S. (1962) *Thought and Language*. Cambridge, MA: MIT Press.
Vygotsky, L.S. (1978) *Mind in Society: The Development of Higher Psychological Processes* (M. Cole, V. John-Steiner, S. Scribner and E. Souberman, eds). Cambridge, MA: Harvard University Press.
Wagner, T. (2008) Rigor redefined. *Educational Leadership* 66 (2), 20–25.
Walqui, A. (2001) Accomplished teaching with English learners: A conceptualization of teacher expertise. *Multilingual Educator* 1 (4), 51–55.
Walqui, A. (2010) Rigor, Expectations, and Interactions—Joint Construction through Language [Video file]. Talk presented at Loyola Marymount University Center for Equity for English Learners, Los Angeles, CA. www.youtube.com/watch?v=R7IHk7jzc18.
Walqui, A. and van Lier, L. (2010) *Scaffolding the Academic Success of Adolescent English Language Learners: A Pedagogy of Promise*. San Francisco, CA: WestEd.
Walqui, A. and Heritage, M. (2012) Instruction for Diverse Groups of English Language Learners. Paper presentation. Understanding Language Conference, Stanford, CA.
Waxman, H.C., Padron, Y.N., Franco-Fuenmayor, S.E. and Huang, S.-Y.L. (2009) Observing classroom instruction for ELLs from student, teacher, and classroom perspectives. *National Association for Bilingual Education Journal* 11 (1), 63–95.
Wenger, E. (1998) *Communities of Practice: Learning, Meaning, and Identity*. Cambridge: Cambridge University Press. https://doi.org/10.1017/CBO9780511803932.
Wenger-Trayner, E. and Wenger-Trayner, B. (2020) *Learning to Make a Difference: Value-Creation in Social Learning Spaces*. Cambridge: Cambridge University Press. https://doi.org/10.1017/9781108677431.

Wright, W.E. (2019) *Foundations for Teaching English Language Learners: Research, Theory, Policy, and Practice* (3rd edn). Caslon Publishing.

Zipke, M. (2007) The role of metalinguistic awareness in the reading comprehension of sixth and seventh graders. *Reading Psychology* 28 (4), 375–396. https://psycnet.apa.org/doi/10.1080/02702710701260615.

Zipke, M., Ehri, L.C. and Cairns, H.S. (2009) Using semantic ambiguity instruction to improve third graders' metalinguistic awareness and reading comprehension: An experimental study. *Reading Research Quarterly* 44 (3), 300–321. https://doi.org/10.1598/RRQ.44.3.4.

Zwiers, J. and Crawford, M. (2011) *Academic Conversation: Classroom Talk That Fosters Critical Thinking and Content Knowledge*. Portland, ME: Stenhouse Publishers.

Zwiers, J., O'Hara, S.P. and Pritchard, R.H. (2014) *Common Core Standards in Diverse Classrooms: Essential Practices for Developing Academic Language and Disciplinary Literacy*. Portland, ME: Stenhouse Publishers.

Index

academic discourse 67
academic language 9, 43
academic literacies 14
accommodations 62, 67–9, 76
accountability 67, 68
achievement gaps in ELs 3
acrostic poems 82, 83–4
active listening 63–4
active participation in learning 7, 63
adapted texts 88
additive approaches to learning content and language 11, 40
additive bilingualism 6
adjusting instruction while teaching 46–7
advocating 63–4
agents of socialization, teachers as 112
Alvarez, L. 48
anecdotal notetaking 18, 19, 31, 37–8, 128, 135
anticipatory sets 64
assessment
 –cooperative group work 69
 –formative assessment 47–8, 55, 65
 –formative versus summative 47–8
 –high expectations 90
 –informal assessments 46–8
assets-based approaches to learning 4 *see also* strengths-based approaches
authentic materials 87
autonomy 12, 62, 63–4, 68, 75–6

bias 89
'bilingual buddies' 12, 69
bilingual dictionaries 88
bilingual programs 8, 83, 90, 92
biliteracy development 8, 83, 90, 93, 119
bridging connections 10
Bruner, J.S. 12, 63

California context 32
California English Language Development Standard (CDE) 32, 33, 35–7, 69
California State Board of Education standards 7, 32
capacity building 140, 156
Center on Education Policy 3
checking for comprehension 45–6
chunking 45
class surveys 64
classroom environment
 –language-rich environments 87–8
 –reading the room 31–2, 153
 –structuring for interactions 64–5
classroom observations
 –instruments/protocols 23
 –practicalities 2
 –previous research in 4, 14, 22–3
Classroom Qualities for English Language Learners (CQELL) 14
coaching 2, 4, 129–34
Coady, M. 14
cognates 9, 92, 93
Cohen's kappa coefficient 15, 145
cohesive devices 45
collaborative conversations 20, 129
collaborative inquiry 21
collaborative interactions 69
collaborative opportunities, providing 43
collaborative practices 67–8

collaborative professional development 2–3, 18, 21
collaborative routines 12, 68
collaborative skills 86
Common Core State Standards (CCSS) 7, 8, 32, 33, 35–6, 48, 80
communicative competence 13, 66
communities of practice 4, 18, 21
Community and Instruction for Expanding English Learners' Opportunities (CIELO) 140
comprehensibility 11–12, 38–59
 –checking for comprehension 45–6
 –definition 39–40
 –descriptor rubric 25, 56, 162–3
 –key indicators 40
 –key terms 25
 –note-taking form 174
 –observation guide 29, 155
conceptual organizers 42
Confirmatory Factor Analysis (CFA) 13, 148
connections 10, 110–24
 –descriptor rubric 25, 122–3, 161
 –intentional planning of 112
 –key indicators 113
 –key terms 25
 –note-taking form 173
 –observation guide 29, 154
constructivism 5
content area instruction 9–10
Content Validation 13
context, meaningful 44, 45 *see also* culture, connections to
contextualizing strategies 42
cooperative learning 12, 68
corrective feedback 45
courageous conversations 3
COVID-19 1
creativity and innovation skills 86
critical text selection 87
critical thinking 9, 83, 84, 85–6, 104
cross-age tutoring 92
cross-disciplinary connections 86
cross-domain interrelatedness 85
cross-linguistic transfer 9, 84, 90–1, 93, 106
culture, connections to 10, 87–8, 109, 116

Cummins, J. 6
curriculum *see* rigorous and relevant curriculum

de Jong, E.J. 3
debrief conversations 24, 133–4
deficit-based approaches 9, 116
Delgado-Larocco, E.L. 138–9
descriptor rubric 25–6
 –comprehensibility 25, 56, 162–3
 –connections 25, 122–3, 161
 –interactions 25, 75–6, 164
 –Likert scales 26, 158
 –rigorous and relevant curriculum 25, 104–6, 159–60
'detatched' observer technique 31
Diamond Academy 126–8, 168–70
differentiated instruction
 –additive approaches to learning content and language 11, 40
 –classroom environment 65
 –comprehensibility 45–6
 –cross-linguistic transfer 9
 –culturally-relevant materials 10
 –'Four Cs' 86
 –text selection 88
 –value of OPAL for 21
digital texts 88
directed instruction 44
discipline-specific language 45
discourse behaviors, awareness of 45
discovery, learning through 13, 63
dissemination and implementation planning 125–8, 167, 168–70
district-wide professional development 2–3, 134–5
doctoral research 137–8
domains of teacher knowledge 5, 6
dual language programs 8, 51, 83, 90, 119
duration of observations 31, 37

educated human beings, teachers as 112
'Emergent Bilingual Learners' 17n(1)
Emerson, R.M. 22–3
English Learners
 –context 3–5
 –statistics 3
English-medium instruction 8

equitable instruction for English Learners 11, 40, 67, 86
ethnographic notetaking 18, 22–3, 27
ethnography 20, 22–3, 27
etiquette, observation 30–1, 153
expanding strategies 42, 43
expertise, building teachers' 20–1
explicit teaching of cross-lingual differences 9
explicit teaching of key terms 44
Exploratory Factor Analysis (EFA) 13, 142

feedback
 –comprehensibility 45–6 *see also* assessment; responsive teaching
 –debrief conversations 133–4
 –formative assessment 47–8
Fillmore, L.W. 5, 6, 112
five domains of teacher knowledge 5, 6
flexible groupings 6, 12, 25, 62, 67–9, 76
form, OPAL 24–32
formative assessment 47–8, 55, 65
'Four Cs' 86
Framework for 21st-Century Learning 86
funds of knowledge 116

Garnet Elementary School 126–7
generalizability 13
genres 13, 66, 92
gestures 44–5
Goldenberg, C. 14
graphic organizers 42, 44
Group Framework for Teaching 14
group work 12, 62, 64, 68 *see also* flexible groupings

Hartshorn, K. 1
Hattie, J. 20, 129
Heritage, M. 80
high expectations 83, 84, 86, 88–9, 105
higher-order thinking skills 83
Hurley, S.R. 69

idiomatic expressions 33, 44–5
independent reading 11
indicators, OPAL, familiarization with 25–7

informal assessments 46–8
informal interactions 61–3, 67
in-service training 20–1, 138–9
instructional cycles 40
instructional support gap 3–4
instrument form 14, 24–32, 164–6
integrated roles/functions of teachers 112
intended meanings, listening for 43
interactions 60–79
 –definition 61–3
 –descriptor rubric 25, 164
 –informal interactions 61–3, 67
 –interaction opportunities 12–13, 25
 –key indicators 62
 –key terms 25
 –note-taking form 175
 –observation guide 29, 155
interactive writing strategies 11
interdisciplinarity 80, 85, 86
interpretive opportunities 43, 69
inter-rater reliability 15, 128, 144–5

judgment-neutral statements 19, 28
just-in-time scaffolding 43

key indicators
 –comprehensibility 40
 –connections 113
 –interactions 62
 –rigorous and relevant curriculum 84
key terms (OPAL Indicators) 25
key terms (subjects), teacher explanations of 44–5
knowledge
 –domains of teacher knowledge 5, 6
 –funds of knowledge 116
 –pedagogic content knowledge 66
 –prior knowledge 7, 42, 64, 112, 115–16
 –subject matter knowledge in target language 62, 65–6, 76
Krashen, S. 14

language-rich environments 87–8
Lavadenz, M. 1, 10
Lazarin, M. 2
Learning Forward 21
learning goals

–sharing with students 45, 64
–short and long-term 87, 115
lesson study (professional development) 139–40
life experiences, connecting to students' 10, 112, 113, 114–15, 116, 122
Likert scales
  –choosing not to use 132
  –descriptor rubric 25, 26
  –OPAL form 24
  –OPAL instrument 2, 14, 15, 19
  –technical report 148–9
Long-Term English Learners (LTELs) 134–5, 138

'making learning visible' 18, 20–1
manipulatives 44
maximum likelihood estimation 148
McMurry, B. 1
meaningful connections 10
meaningful content 85–6, 87–8, 104, 113, 116, 122 *see also* culture, connections to
meaningful context 44, 45
meaningful interactions 63
metacognitive processes 43, 45, 69, 115
metalinguistic processes
  –comprehensibility 43, 44, 45
  –cooperative group work 69
  –cross-linguistic transfer 93
  –informal assessments while teaching 47
  –positive benefits of 93
micro-level scaffolding 43
modeling by teachers 13, 63, 65, 66, 115
motivations for learning 63
Mountain Union High School District (MUHSD) 134–5
multimedia texts 88
multiple perspectives, teaching from 114–15
mutual accountability 67

National Assessment of Educational Progress (NAEP) 3
National Center for Education Statistics 3
National Standards for Professional Learning (Learning Forward 2011/2022) 21

neutral stance 19, 28
next steps ideas 57, 132, 133, 156
non-evaulative conversations 130
non-judgmental observation 18, 20–1, 130
note-taking 18, 19, 27–8, 128, 132–3
  –note-taking form 171–5

observation etiquette 30–1, 153
observation guide 28–9, 153–6
observation protocols generally 23
observation research 22–3
observation skills 18–37, 132–3
observer dispositions 30
observing students 30
Office of English Language Acquisition 8
OPAL Classroom Observation Validation Study 13–15, 142–52
OPAL Institutes 15, 25, 83–4, 125–6
OPAL instrument 14, 24–32, 165–6
oral discourse 45
oral traditions 93
output, maximizing student 42–3

pairing with other students of same primary language 65
parity of participation 8
Partnership for 21st-Century Learning 86, 114
pedagogic content knowledge 66
Pedroarias, R. 137–8
Peer Buddies Project 127
peer coaching 129–34
peer editing sessions 12
peer feedback 45
peer interactions 63, 68–9
peer learning 12
peer tutors 92
post-observation debriefs 133–4
pre-service training 20–1, 138–9
preview-review method 11–12, 45–6, 65, 92
primary language instruction 8, 83, 90–1, 92–3
primary language maintenance 90, 91–2
primary language, use of in classroom
  –access to content and materials in 84, 90–2, 105
  –bilingual teachers/paraprofessionals/community members 92

–connections 122
–cross-linguistic transfer 9, 84, 90–1, 93, 106
–opportunities for transfer of skills 84, 90–1, 106
–preview-review method 46, 65, 92
–teaching for maximum comprehensibility 11
prior information, gathering 30–1
prior knowledge 7, 42, 64, 112, 115–16
problem solving skills 83, 84, 85–6, 104
procedures and rules, modification of 62, 64–5, 75
processing, breaks for 45
professional coaching 129–34
professional collaboration 18
professional development *see also* teacher training
–awareness of bias 89
–instructional support gap 3–4
–lesson study 138–40
–program evaluations 140
–school-wide professional development 2–3, 128
–using OPAL 2–3, 126–8
–visible learning 20–1
program evaluations 140
Project STELLAR (Science Teaching for English Learners: Leveraging Academic Rigor) 140
PUENTE project 101
purpose of OPAL 19–23
purposeful opportunities, providing 44

qualitative results, sharing 135
Quality Teaching for English Learners (QTEL) 82
questioning strategies 42–3, 63–4

reading the room (observing) 31–2, 153
Reciprocal Teaching 11
reflection 5, 18, 21–2, 45
register 67
reliability measures 13–15, 128, 144–5
rephrasing strategies 42
research-based teaching practices 5
research/evaluation projects using OPAL 136–7
response times 43
responsive teaching 26, 42–3, 55, 65
restating strategies 42
rewording/recasting student responses 43
rigorous and relevant curriculum 8–9, 24, 80–109
–definition 82–5
–descriptor rubric 25, 104–6, 159–60
–key indicators 84
–key terms 25, 84
–note-taking form 172
–observation guide 28, 154
role-play 134
routines, consistency of 45, 64–5, 76
rubric scores 2 *see also* descriptor rubric
Ruiz Soto, A.G. 3
rules, modification of 62, 64–5, 75

safe spaces, offering 45, 65
scaffolding
–collaborative routines 12, 68
–comprehensibility 11, 41–2, 43, 44
–intentional planning of 55
Schleppegrell, M.J. 9, 67
school-wide professional development 2–3, 128
second language acquisition theory 5–7, 9, 14
selective coding 23
self-checks 45
self-monitoring skills 63
Sheltered Instruction Observation Protocol (SIOP) 14
Shulman, L.S. 66
Snow, C. 5, 6, 112
social conditions, linking instructional concepts to 113, 114–15, 122 *see also* culture, connections to
social justice 115
socialization, teachers as agents of 112
sociocultural theory 4, 5–7, 9, 12–13, 63
STAR (Substitute, Take things out, Add things and Rearrange) 12
Star, D. 1
STELLAR 140
strengths-based approaches 40, 43, 116
Structured English Immersion (SEI) 8, 83, 90, 92
student engagement observations 67–8, 155–6
students, observation of 30

subject matter knowledge in target language 62, 64–6, 76
subtractive bilingualism 6
Sugarman, J. 2
summative assessment 47–8
Swain, M. 13
synthesizing information 83, 86

teacher evaluation 4, 130, 151
teacher knowledge/expertise models 5, 6
teacher training *see also* professional development
  –pre-service training 20–1, 138–9
  –in-service training 20–1, 138–9
teamwork 67–8
Technical Report 13, 142–52
technology to enhance learning 88
text selection 87
text structure 45
themes/topics, organization of curriculum into 83, 84, 85–6, 105
theoretical frameworks 5–7
think-aloud protocols 10
Tinajero, J.V. 69
Tomlinson, C.A. 65
Topaz Charter School Organization 128
training (of teachers) *see* professional development; teacher training
training (on using OPAL) 15, 126–8, 151
transitional bilingual programs 90
translation 12, 46, 92
trust-building process 130
turn-taking 12, 68–9

universal themes 86

validation process 14
Van Lier, L. 21
visible learning 20–1
visuals 44
Vygotsky, L. 12, 63

wait times 43
Walqui, A. 5, 7, 21, 80, 82, 83
'what's there' focus versus 'what's not there' 20
words in context, studying 44
writing strategies 12
written discourse comprehensibility 45

Zartman Jr, C.G. 138–9
zone of proximal development (ZPD) 41

For Product Safety Concerns and Information please contact our EU Authorised Representative:

Easy Access System Europe

Mustamäe tee 50

10621 Tallinn

Estonia

gpsr.requests@easproject.com

www.ingramcontent.com/pod-product-compliance
Ingram Content Group UK Ltd.
Pitfield, Milton Keynes, MK11 3LW, UK
UKHW021943200326
4879IPUK00004B/71